Work Like An Egyptian

Other Wildside Press Books
by Ramona Louise Wheeler

Have Starship, Will Travel
Starship For Hire
A Chance To Remember
Walk Like An Egyptian: A Modern Guide To The Religion And Philosophy Of Ancient Egypt, Second edition.

WORK LIKE AN EGYPTIAN
A MODERN GUIDE TO ANCIENT TIME AND THE EGYPTIAN HOROSCOPE

Ramona Louise Wheeler

Horoscope translation by Diana Janeen Pierce

WILDSIDE PRESS
Holicong, Pennsylvania

*Work Like An Egyptian: A Modern Guide To Ancient Time
And The Egyptian Horoscope*

A publication of
Wildside Press
P.O. Box 301
Holicong, PA 18928-0301
www.wildsidepress.com

FIRST EDITION

Acknowledgements: The authors would like to thank friends and family for their unstinting support and kindness during the production of this volume. We also would like to thank Alan Rodgers and John Betancourt at Wildside Press for making this expanded edition possible. We also thank the tens of thousands of website readers who have encouraged us in the project.

Diana Janeen Pierce
Ramona Louise Wheeler

All quotes, unless otherwise noted, are from translations by Ramona Louise Wheeler, from the papyri transcribed in E.A. Wallis Budge's 1903–1911 editions of *The Book of The Dead, Tutankhamen, The Gods of Egypt vol.i,ii; Osiris And The Egyptian Resurrection, vol.i, ii; The Egyptian Heaven and Hell.* Dover Editions.

The calendar tranlations by Diana Janeen Pierce are from Dr. Adb EL-Mohsen Bakir's transcriptions of the *Cairo Papyrus.* 1966.

TABLE OF CONTENTS

Talk Like An Egyptian: Notes On "Egypt Speak" 10

The Ancient Egyptian Horoscope

The Nile Rising Calendar: Horoscope, Text And Festivals

The Yearly Five Days:	June 22 through June 26	13
· ***Thuthy***	June 27 to July 26	16
· ***Paopy***	July 27 to August 25	22
· ***Hathys***	August 26 to September 24	27
· ***Choiach***	September 25 to October 24	33
· ***Tyby***	October 25 to November 23	38
· ***Menchir***	November 24 to December 23	43
· ***Famenoth***	December 24 to January 22	48
· ***Parmuthy***	January 23 to February 21	52
· ***Pachons***	February 22 to March 23	57
· ***Paony***	March 24 to April 22	61
· ***Epipy***	April 23 to May 22	66
· ***Mesore***	May 23 to June 21	71

Horoscope At A Glance

· The Yearly Five Days	June 21 to June 26	77
· ***Thuthy***	June 27 to July 26	78
· ***Paopy***	July 27 to August 25	79
· ***Hathys***	August 26 to September 24	80
· ***Choiach***	September 25 to October 24	81
· ***Tyby***	October 25 to November 23	82
· ***Menchir***	November 24 to December 23	83
· ***Famenoth***	December 24 to January 22	84
· ***Parmuthy***	January 23 to February 21	85
· ***Pachons***	February 22 to March 23	86
· ***Paony***	March 24 to April 22	87
· ***Epipy***	April 23 to May 22	88
· ***Mesore***	May 23 to June 21	89

Ancient Time And The Egyptian Calendar

Eternal Skies 91

Out Of Timelessness And Into The Daylight:
The Ancient Egyptian Calendar 95

Five Days Outside Of Time: The Yearly Five Days And The Birth Of The *Naturu* 97
The Three Seasons Of The Nile 100
The Names And The Divine Guardians Of The Months 103
The Egyptian Calendar Today 104
The Ancient Egyptian Book Of Days 104
The Name And The Divine Guardian Of Each Day 106
Placing The Ancient Calendar Today 107
Modern Dates For The Nile Rising Calendar 110
"Anything You See This Day Will Be Good." The Daily Auspice 111
The Patterns Of Lucky, Unlucky And Mixed Days Of Each Month.. 112
History Of The Cairo Calendar Papyrus 114

Reality and The Soul, Basic Concepts Of The Ancient Philosophy

What If Love Goes On Forever? Ancient Egypt, Land Of Love On The Nile 116
The Power Of *Ma'at*: The Reality Of Reality 119
Ma'aty: The Dual Realities, The Land Under The Horizon, Inner And Outer Landscapes Of The Soul 120
The *Natur*: The Metaphor Of Metaphor, The "Gods" Of Egypt 122
Pot Natur, The Ennead: Organizations Of Human And Divine 124
Egyptian Divinity: "Who's In Charge Here?" 127
The Egyptian Trinity 130

Why The Cat Has Nine Lives The Essential Egyptian View Of The Self

The Nine Layers Of The Inner Landscape 133
Akh: Solid Light, Divine Substance Of The Human Soul 134
Sekhem: Energy Pattern Of The Divine Spirit, Song Of The Soul 136
Ib: Life Force, Territory Of The Heart 137
Khat: The Soul's Living Container Of Flesh, That Which Decays 138
Shuit: The Living Shadow, Link To Solid Reality 139
Ren: Divine Identity, The Magic Of Your Name 140
Ba: The Private Self, The Inside Of Your Soul's Mask 141
Ka: The Public Self, The Outside Of Your Soul's Mask 142
Sahu: Natural Boundary Of The Psychic Self, The Shape Of Eternity 145

Osiris, Mystery Of Mysteries, The Soul Within

Divine Bull Of The Goddess, Carrier Of An Ancient Message 147

Mud And Blood Of The Nile, Dark Substance Of The Soul 148
Throne Of The Eye And Seat Of The Action, Soul And Awareness ... 150
Land Under The Horizon: Inner Landscapes Of The Soul's Awakening 152
Djed: Backbone Of Osiris, Emblem Of The Mystery 155
Apep: Serpentine Symbol Of The Energy Of The Nervous System..... 156
Satan Is Not A Serpent: Sut's Sacrifice Of Osiris 158
The Seven *Chakra* Of Osiris' Backbone:
Egypt, India And The Serpent Within 159
The Seven Portals Of The Coiling Pathway
Of The Serpentine Embraced 161

Re: The Sun In Your Mind

Osiris And Re: Soul And Awareness 170
The Circle Of Perception: The Symbol Of Re 172
The Legend Of Isis And Re: Threats To Identity 173
Mendet And Siktet Boats: Morning And Evening Boats Of Re 175
The Eyes Of Horus And Re: The Soul's Memory 175
Khepry: Enlightenment, Gesture Of Maturity, The Egyptian Scarab.. 176
Atum: The Night Sun, Unfailing Time 177

Horus And Sut, Heroes Of Identity, The Original Jekyll And Hyde

Horus: The Face Of The Horizon, Hero Of Identity 179
Sut: Dark Reflection Of Horus, Divine Force Of Habit 182
The Pharaoh, Role Model Of The Inner Man 184
The Riddle Of The Sphinx: Better To Be A Child Than A Barbarian. 188

Thoth: Divine Thought, The Mind Of The Soul

Thoth, *Djehuty*: The Counter Of The Moon And Of The Days 190
Divine Thought, Human Mind, Intellect And Scribe Of The Gods .. 192
Sasheta: The Lady Of The House Of Books, Saint Of The Software .. 193
The Egyptian Book Of The Dead: *Per Em Hru*, "Emerging Awake" ... 194

Iman And Ptah, Organizing Force Of Pharaoh, God And Man

Iman: Divinely Organized, The Secret Contract
Of The Civilized Soul 198
Ptah: The Soul Of The Professional, Happy At Work In Reality 199
Ptah-Sokar: Silence Rules 200
Khnum: The Solar Ram, Handles Of The Mind 201

TABLE OF CONTENTS

Lady Isis: Divine Love, Power And Bonding Of The Soul

Lady Isis: The Throne Of Egypt 206
Lady Isis: The Soul In Love 207
Lady Isis Of The Many Names: Channels Of Divine Experience 208
Ankh: Life Force, Anchor Of The Soul 210
Lady Isis And Sirius: Sopdut, Activator Of The Inundation 211
The Legends Of Isis And Osiris: The Egyptian Family Saga 212
Osiris In The Coffin In The Pillar In The Palace 214
The Magic Of Lady Isis 219
The Lament Of Lady Isis 221

Forms Of The Lady, The Many Faces Of Love

The Many Faces Of Love: Masks Of The Goddess 225
Mut: Divine Motherhood, Mother Of Gods And Kings 225
Het Heru, Lady Hathor: Home Of Horus, Your Mother 226
Nobt Hut, Nepthys: "Lady Of The House," Archetype Of Loyalty And Marriage 229
Marriage 231
Lady Net: Divine Weaver, Threads Of Destiny 233
Selqet: The Poisons Of Passion, Eternal Heartache 235
Bast: The Soul In Love With Life Itself 236
The Cat: Mascot Of The Nile 236
Sekhmet: Hot-Blooded Lioness, A Rage To Live 237
Tasurt: Toeris, The Oldest Woman In The World, Archetype Of Female Wisdom 239

Sky And Earth, Breath, Life And Creation

Nut: The Star-Spangled Sky, Body Of The Divine Plane 242
Geb: Common Ground Of Waking Reality 243
Shu: Every Breath You Take In The Magic Moment Now 243
Tafnut: Twin Sister Of Shu, The Divine Wetness Of Life 244
Too Many Creation Myths: Which Came First, The Cackle Or The Egg? 245
Mythology And Religion 248
Slavery And The Pyramids 250
Ankhenaton, Egypt's *Titanic* 252

In Their Own Write

Table Of Contents For The Selected Translations 256
Introduction To The Translations 257
Bibliography 292

Talk Like An Egyptian: A Note On "Egypt Speak"

The exact pronunciation of ancient Egyptian is perhaps the most hotly debated subject after "Who built the Pyramids?" The statement that Egyptian had no written vowel sounds is not entirely accurate, since vowel sounds are, in fact, fully represented in the hieroglyphic writing system. The difficulty is with hieroglyphs which represent an entire syllable with one or more consonants. These shorthand ways of writing were in common use, and we can only make conjectures about their associated vowel sounds.

Spoken Egyptian is a lost art, even if it is no longer exactly a dead language. The resurrection of the Egyptian language is, however, a fitting testimony to their belief in the continuity of civilized existence. The words and the thoughts of the living minds who wrote the literature of Egypt lay dead and forgotten for millennia, yet we can now evoke them so vividly that, if we listen closely enough, we can almost hear their distant voices.

The precise pronunciation does help in tracing Latin derivatives, but it is more useful for studying the linguistics of ancient generations or for the evocation of ritual than for general discussion about Egyptian religion. If we want to talk to each other about the *meanings* of their written words, about the ideas and intentions behind them, we need only agreed-upon standardizations.

Textbooks on ancient Egypt vary in the English and phonetic spellings of hieroglyphic, hieratic and demotic, depending on the era and nation in which the book was published. These variations need to be taken into account when researching any specific name or word. They can become a hindrance when trying to talk about the philosophy in general.

I consider this an important distinction, because the ancient Egyptians *talked* to each other a lot. This is clear in the words that ornament everything from humble objects of daily life to the grandest of temple walls. It is clear in the dialogs recorded on tomb walls. It is clearest of all in the vivid and fantastical use of metaphor in their language. Such elaborate metaphor is drawn from a vast, shared database of idiom, puns and verbal imagery. In a world without television, radio or printing presses, word of mouth was the primary form of communication, and they were not constrained in using it. The Egyptians knew that they were going into the great silence, into Sokar, at the end. They filled their life, therefore, with talk, with laughter, with music, with all the sounds of life. We can still hear the echoes.

The Standards Used In This Volume

Words derived from Greek or Roman standards are shown in normal font. Words derived strictly from the native Egyptian are *italicized.* Foreign words in modern use are also *italicized.*

Natur rather than "god" or "gods". (This is pronounced like the modern word "nature." In older textbooks it is spelled as *neter* or *netjer.*) femine *Naturit*, plural *Naturu*, femine plural, *Naturitu.* House Of The *Natur* rather than temple. *Pot Natur* rather than ennead or pantheon. (In older textbooks it is spelled *paut neter.*)

Osiris. Isis. Horus. Hathor. Re rather than Ra. The Original Horus rather than Horus The Elder. Sut rather than Set, Seth or Sutekh. Thoth rather than *Djehuty. Nobt Hut* rather than Nepthys, Lady Of The House rather than either. Lady Net rather than Neith.

Iman rather than Amon or Amun. Itan rather that Aten or Aton. *Imenty* rather than *Amenti.* The initial vowel is written with the reed hieroglyph, which was represented in older texts with the phonetic symbol of the A with a dot over it. The dot was often lost in later editions, but the A spelling dominated before this was discovered. *Inpu* as well as Anubis. We have come to associate Anubis strictly with the funerary rites and with death rituals of mummification, and this association devalues his role as spirit-guide running the paths ahead through life toward eternity.

Ibtu rather than Abydos. Abydos is now associated only with the Valley Of The Kings and royal tombs, losing the value of its pun with "Heart's Centerpoint" that plays in the native. *Ibtu* was both the ultimate resting place of the soul and the still center from which you arise and to which you return.

Innu rather than Heliopolis, city of Ra. The name Heliopolis, unlike the names Osiris, Horus and Isis, is evocative only of Ptolemaic Egypt, which was more Greek and Roman than Egyptian. Thoth's main center, *Khemmnu*, "City Of The Eight," is used here rather than Hermopolis. *Sopdut* rather than Sirius.

Mouth Of The Far Horizon rather than *Rosetau* or *Ro-stau.* The Nile flows into the Mediterranean in the west through *Rosetta*, and through *Damietta* in the east. The name *Rosetau* became a pun on the next life to which the deceased has traveled after the journey through the western horizon, following the setting Sun. Re is swallowed by the mouth of Nut at sunset, and it is this dimension below the horizon which is referred to in the texts.

Star Of His Mother rather than *Duatmutef.* Day names and the names of the divine guardians of each day have been translated into English equivalents where possible.

THE ANCIENT EGYPTIAN HOROSCOPE

Translated from The Cairo Papyrus
by Diana Janeen Pierce.

The Yearly Five Days Between The End Of The Past Year And The Beginning Of The New Year

June 22 to June 26

(*Note*: *The Yearly Five Days* have, in addition to the day's auspice, the charms to be spoken on each of the *Natur's* birthdays and the incantation to be spoken on the first day, as well as the amulet charm spoken on the last day. – *DJP*)

The Yearly Five Days

An Introduction To The Beginning Of Infinity And The End Of Eternity Which The *Naturu* And *Naturitu* Of The Shrine And The Assembly Of The *Pot Natur* Have Made, And Which The Majesty Of Thoth Has Gathered Together In The Great House (*Per-Ur*) In The Presence Of The Lord Of The Universe (Re). What Has Been Found In The Library In The Rear-House (*Per-Ha*) Of The *Pot Natur.* House Of Re (*Per-Re*), House Of Osiris (*Per-Osiris*), House Of Horus (*Per-Horu.*)

Charm To Be Spoken:

Say these words at sunrise on the first day:

"The Great Ones are born. As for the Great Ones whose forms are not mysterious, beware of them. Their occasion or deeds will not come.

Birth of Osiris!
Birth of the Original Horus!
Birth of Sut! Birth of Isis!
Birth of Lady Of The House!

I, who know the names of the days, will not hunger. I will not thirst, and Bastet will not overpower me. I will not enter into the Great Law Court. I will not die through an enemy of the pharaoh, and will not die through the pestilence of the year. I will last every day until death arrives. No illness will take possession of me. I, who know them, (i.e., the names of the days,) will prosper, and my speech is important to listen to in the presence of Re."

(Repeat the above charm each day, adding the appropriate name of the *Natur* or *Naturit* born on that day.)

The Birth of Osiris. Words to be said on this day:

"Oh, Osiris, bull in his cavern whose name is hidden, child of his mother, hail to you! Hail to you! I am your son, oh, father Osiris.

The Name of this day is: The Pure One."

The Birth of the Original Horus.

Words to be said on this day:

"Oh, Horus Of The Spirit! It is repeated anew. It will provide good protection because of it, you make (lost...)

The name of this day is: Powerful Is The Heart."

The Birth of Sut. Words to be said on this day:

"Oh, Sut, son of Nut, great of strength, protection is in your hands of holiness. I am the son of your son.

The name of this day is: Powerful Of Arm."

The Birth of Isis. Words to be said on this day:

"Oh, Isis, daughter of Nut the Eldest, Mistress Of Magic, Provider Of The Book, Mistress Who Appeases The Two Lands, her face is glorious. I am the brother and the sister."

The name of this day is: He Who Makes Terror.."

The Birth of Lady Of The House.

Words to be said on this day:

"Oh, Lady Of The House, daughter of Nut, sister of Sut, she whose father sees a healthy daughter, stable of face, stable of face. I am divine power in the womb of my mother Nut.

The name of this day is: The Child Who Is In His Nest."

These words are to be spoken over a protective amulet on the last day before sunset. Draw the images of Osiris, The Original Horus, Sut, Isis and Lady Of The House on fine linen and place it around your neck. Then say four times:

"Hail to you, oh, Great Ones according to your names, children of the *Naturitu* who came forth from the sacred womb, *Naturu* because their father, *Naturitu* because of their mother, without yet knowing eternity.

Behold! May you make protection! May you happen again, and may you protect me, for I am one who is on their list.

This charm is called: Self-dedication Contract."

June 22
The Pure One — **Lord Osiris is born.**

June 23
Powerful Is The Heart — **Lord Horus The Original is born.**

June 24
Powerful Of Arm — **Lord Sut is born.**

June 25
He Who Makes Terror — **Lady Isis is born.**

June 26
The Child Who Is In His Nest — **Lady Of The House is born.**

THUTHY

June 27 to July 26

Thoth is the Natur.

First Month of *Akhet*

June 27 DAY ONE

New Month Day *Thoth is the Natur of this day.*

This is the first day of the New Year.

"At the beginning of the high Nile there is washing throughout the whole land. They say it comes in form of fresh Nun. The *Naturu* and *Naturitu* are in great festivity on this day, and all others."

The birth of Re.
First Day of Thuthy.

(*Note:* This is one of the rare references to the rituals for Re on New Year's Day. Everyone in Egypt bathed in the Nile this day. Nun is the Cosmic waters.)

June 28 DAY TWO

New Crescent Day *Horus is the Natur of this day.*

Anything you see will be good.

"It is the day the *Pot Natur* goes before Re. Their hearts are pleased at seeing his youthfulness after they destroyed Apep, who rebelled against their master, and for overcoming Re's foe, wherever he might be, so that he might fall on his back amidst the flood."

(*Note*: The last phrase refers to the drowning of Apep.)

June 29 DAY THREE

Arrival Day *Osiris is the Natur of this day.*

A crocodile will kill those born today.

"It is the day of making *ipy* (possibly dykes) in the river by the *Naturu.*"

The Birth of Aten.

June 30 DAY FOUR

Zem Priests Emerge *Isis is the Naturit of this day.*

Do not navigate in or travel by boat. Do nothing today.

"It is the day Hathor emerges, accompanied by her executioners, the *khatbu*, to the riverbank. The *Naturu* sail in an opposing wind."

(*Note*: This refers to the attempt at the destruction of humanind.)

July 1 DAY FIVE

Altar Offerings Day *Hapy is the Natur of this day.*

Anything you see will be good.

"The *Naturu* are peaceful in heaven sailing in the Day Boat Of Re."

July 2 DAY SIX

Sixth Day *Star Of His Mother is the Natur of this day.*

Anyone born on this day will die by the trampling of a bull. (Lost...)

Monthly feast of Re.

July 3 DAY SEVEN

First Quarter Day *Qebsenuf is the Natur of this day.*

Anything you see will be good.

"It is the day of welcoming the Nile and making offerings to the *Naturu.*"

July 4 DAY EIGHT

Main Emergence *Ma'ateff is the Natur of this day.*

Spend this day on the water. Do not go out this night.

"Because Re emerges (lost...) As for him who navigates Nun, and as for anyone who is shipwrecked at sea (lost...)"

July 5 DAY NINE

Hidden One *He Does The Talking is the Natur of this day.*

Anything you see will be good.

"This day the hearts of those who are in the horizon are pacifed in the presence of the majesty of Re."

July 6 DAY TEN

He Who Protects His Royal Name

He Makes A Name Himself is the Natur of this day.

Those born today will die of honorable old age.

"It is the day of the going forth to the House Of Peace, while the *Naturu* and *Naturitu* are in festivity."

The Second Monthly Feast of Re.

July 7 DAY ELEVEN

Great Lady Protector *Sekhmet is the Natur of this day.*

Kindle fire on this day. Do not look at a bull, and do not make love on this day.

"Today the Great Flame (The *Wadjet* Eye) is in a rage in the Inaccessible Shrine. (Lost...) who are in the following of his Majesty Re."

(*Note*: the Inaccessible Shrine is the Shrine of the Boat found in the back of the House Of Life.)

July 8 DAY TWELVE

Making Love *Bring The Advocate is the Natur of this day.*

Do not go out until Re sets in his horizon.

"It is the day Re exchanges his oarsmen one for another. Anyone who disobeys Re falls down at once."

(*Note*: At sunset and dawn Re's crew, the oarsmen of the Evening and the Morning Boats, exchanged duty at the oars.)

July 9 DAY THIRTEEN
Approach of Re *Re is the Natur of this day.*

Anyone born on this day will die blind.
"It is the day of the slaughter by Lady Net."

July 10 DAY FOURTEEN (Lost...)
Progress Of The Ba *Consider The Ba is the Natur of this day.*

The birth of Re.
"Make offering to your local *Naturu*."

July 11 DAY FIFTEEN
Half Month Day *Amauai is the Natur of this day.*

Avoid boats today. Do not continue traveling in a boat.
"It is a day of Sut's rage. One will have no knowledge thereof. Behold! The crew are on the river on this day."

July 12 DAY SIXTEEN
Two Houses Fight *Horus and Sut are the Naturu of this day.*

Anyone born this day will be killed by a crocodile.
"It is the day (lost...) by Lady Net."

July 13 DAY SEVENTEEN
Second Arrival Day *Re is the Natur of this day.*

Avoid *mehit*-fish today.
"It is the day of taking away Sobek's offering, namely taking the offering from his mouth."

Feast of the Dead. Offerings given in the Necropolis.

July 14 DAY EIGHTEEN
Moon Day *Ahi is the Natur of this day.*

Anything you see this day will be good.
"It is the day of increasing the majesty of Horus more than his brother, Sut, which the *Naturu* did at the portal."

July 15 DAY NINETEEN
Hear His Commands *Bring His Mother is the Natur of this day.*

Burn sweetly scented incense on the fire for his followers in the Evening Boat and the Morning Boat Of The Sun, and for the *Naturu*.
"A happy day in heaven in front of Re. Life! Prosperity! Health! The *Pot Natur* is in great festivity. It is the day of receiving (lost...) It is the day of going to (lost...) the *Heh* before *Babai*."

Festival of Nut and Lord Re.
Main Festival of Lord Thoth.

(*Note*: *Babai* is Sut is the guise of a baboon, attended by a pack of 77 black dogs who bit Horus when he was a child.)

July 16 DAY TWENTY
Offering Meat *Opener Of The Ways is the Naturit of this day.*

Do not work this day.

"It is the day when the Great Ones, the followers of both Horus and Sut, take sides in the dispute."

July 17 DAY TWENTY-ONE
Apru's Day *Inpu is the Natur of this day.*

"Make offerings to Re's followers. Avoid bulls. Kill none, nor let any cross in front of you. It is a day to be cautious of bulls."
(Lost...)

July 18 DAY TWENTY-TWO
Passing Of Sopdut *Nai is the Natur of this day.*

Eat no birds or fish today. Avoid heating or warming oil.

"Re calls every *Natur* and *Naturit* to him. They await his arrival. He takes them into his belly, and when they begin to move within him, he kills them.

After doing so, he vomits them into the water. Their bodies become fish, which are not caught, and their souls become birds which fly up to heaven. (Lost...) on this day."

Holy to Osiris.

July 19 DAY TWENTY-THREE
Last Quarter Day *Na-Ur is the Natur of this day.*

Do not burn incense on the fire of the *Naturu* on this day. Do not kill any *inhy*-reptile, or any creature among the birds.

Do not eat on this day. Avoid music and dancing. Do not listen to it or watch it. Those born today will not live.

"It is the day of causing the heart of Apep the enemy of Lord Re (Life! Prosperity! Health!) to suffer for what he has done against Re's children."

(*Note*: The *inhy*-reptile is a serpent who protects the dead, so this is a prohibition against disturbing gravesites or tombs.)

July 20 DAY TWENTY-FOUR
Darkness *Nekhbet is the Naturit of this day.*

Those born today will die in honorable old age.

"The majesty of the *Natur* Re sails peacefully in favorable winds (lost...) Behold! His heart grows calm as he appears in the Evening Boat and then rises in the Morning Boat."

July 21 DAY TWENTY-FIVE
Departing *Shem is the Natur of this day.*

Do not leave your house or travel at the time of night on any roads.

"Sekhmet goes to the eastern district and drives back the confederates of Sut. Any lion they approach passes away at once.'

Holy to Sekhmet.
Mysteries of Osiris.
Feast of Lights of Isis.

(*Note*: lions were the transformed followers of Sut, as are hippopotami, crocodiles, pigs, serpents and certain birds. Lion was also a title given to warriors, confering the lion's ferocity and strength upon them. There is evidence that this Festival is the true Festival of Intoxication, and that the myth of Sekhmet's threatened destruction of humankind is the basis for this festival. The Nile turns red with silt as in the re-enactment of this flood of beer. This feast of intoxication is the ancient Egyptian's annual October fest. The mistaken belief that it honors Thoth stems from the fact that the feast falls in the month of Thoth.)

July 22 DAY TWENTY-SIX

House Of Appearances *Ma'atef-f is the Natur of this day.*

Do nothing on this day.

"On this day Horus struggles with Sut. They grapple with each other in the form of men.

They turn into ebony and spend three days and four nights this way.

Then Isis lets down a harpoon and it fell before her son Horus. She calls upon the harpoon, saying, "Loosen! Looson from my son Horus!" Thereupon, the harpoon loosened from Horus.

Another harpoon is let down, which falls in front of Sut. He cries out to it, saying, "Behold! I am her brother Sut."

Then Isis calls out to this harpoon, "Be strong! Be strong!"

Then Sut shouts to his sister many times, "Do you prefer the foreign man to a mother's brother?"

Then she (lost...) evil (lost...) called on the harpoon, saying, "Loosen! Loosen! Behold! My brother of my mother!"

Thereupon, the harpoon turned away from Sut.

The opponents stand up as two men once more, and they turn their backs on each other.

Then the majesty of Horus becomes angry with his mother, and he turns on her like a panther.

She flees before him."

Honors the Battle between Horus and Sut.

July 23 DAY TWENTY-SEVEN

Funerary Offerings *Khnum is the Natur of this day.*

Make a holiday. Avoid killing reptiles.

"There is peace between Horus and Sut."

Honors the Peace between Horus and Sut.

July 24 DAY TWENTY-EIGHT
Jubilee Of The Sky *Nut is the Naturit of this day.*

Anything you see this day will be good.
"The *Naturu* are happy today when they see the children of Nut peaceful and content."

July 25 DAY TWENTY-NINE
Weaknes *Utettef-f is the Natur of this day.*

Light no fires in your home. Burn no ointment. Stay in this night.
(Lost...)

Sky Feast of Lord Re.

(*Note*: the ointment referred to is the fragrant oil that might be on someone's hands. The warning refers to accidentally burning any that may have rubbed off onto the day's burnt offering.)

July 26 DAY THIRTY
Awaken *Horus Advocates For Him is the Natur of this day.*

Anything you see this day will be good.
"Last Day.
House Of Re, House Of Osiris, House Of Horus."

Ritual day in the Houses Of Re, Of Osiris and Of Horus.

PAOPY

July 27 to August 25

Ptah is the Natur.

Second Month of *Akhet*

July 27 DAY ONE

New Month Day *Thoth is the Natur of this day.*

(Lost...)

"Jubilation. The Great *Pot Natur* is in celebration this day. On this day the heritage of the Great Heir is established."

First Day Of Paopy.

Holy day of Re.

(*Note*: The Great Heir is Horus, who inherits the throne of Osiris.)

July 28 DAY TWO (omission)

New Crescent Day *Horus is the Natur of this day.*

It is important that you listen on this day. Offer to all the *Naturu.*

"The majesty of *Saut* (Sais) of Lower Egypt proceeds to his mother. She sees that he was suffering from his buttocks. Repetition of birth (lost...) great festivity."

Procession of Horus to the city of Lady Net.

July 29 DAY THREE

Arrival Day *Osiris is the Natur of this day.*

Anything you see will be good.

"Thoth is in the presence of Re in the inaccessible shrine. Re gives him the written order of the reconciliation of the *Wadjet* Eye. Hu and Sia are in the midst of his followers (lost...) in his manner."

"Thoth orders the Eye of Horus healed."

(*Note*: Hu and Sia are the senses and intelligence of Re.)

July 30 DAY FOUR

Zem Priests Emerge *Isis is the Naturit of this day.*

Those born today will die of a skin rash.

"It is the day of the emergence of *Inpu* to inspect the *wabet* for the protection of the body of the *Naturu* (Osiris.)"

July 31 DAY FIVE

Altar Offerings Day *Hapy is the Natur of this day.*

Those born this day will die making love. Do not leave your house by any roads this day. Do not make love.

"This is the day of offering before *Hedj-Hotpy* and *Montu.*"

Feast of Osiris.

August 1 DAY SIX

Sixth Day *Star Of His Mother is the Natur of this day.*

Anyone born on this day will die intoxicated.

"It is a happy day for Re in heaven, and the *Naturu* are calmed within his presence. The *Pot Natur* exalts before the Lord Of The Universe."

Feast of Thoth, Opet,
the marriage of Ammon Re to his wife Ammonet.

August 2 DAY SEVEN

First Quarter Day *Qebsenuf is the Natur of this day.*

Those born today will die in a foreign land. Do nothing today.

"Today Re goes (lost...) to the countries, which he created in order to slay the children of rebellion. He returns (lost...) his neck and executes them before the *Pot Natur*."

Monthly feast of Re.

(*Note*: Egyptians feared dying outside of Egypt, concerned about the proper rituals. They did not wish to spend eternity unable to reach the Nile.)

August 3 DAY EIGHT

Main Emergence *Ma'atef-f is the Natur of this day.*

Anything you see will be good.

(Lost...)

August 4 DAY NINE

Hidden One *He Does The Talking is the Natur of this day.*

Those born today will die of old age.

"There is joy in the heart of Re (Lost...) His *Pot Natur* is in celebration. All Re's enemies are overthrown."

Jubilation of the heart of Re.

August 5 DAY TEN

He Who Protects His Royal Name

He Makes A Name Himself is the Natur of this day.

(Lost...)

"The majesty of Bast, Lady of *Ankh-towe* (a city near Memphis) emerges, and his majesty Re of *Innu* inquires about her payment of tribute to the august tree. It is pleasing to his followers."

Procession of Bastet. The birth of Nut.

(*Note*: this may be the sacred *erica* tree of Osiris; the dawn tree which Re climbs like a cat, or the tree in Memphis with names of pharaohs on its leaves, or the World Tree.)

August 6 DAY ELEVEN

Great Lady Protector *Sekhmet is the Naturit of this day.*

All is good this day.

"This day they repair the front piece on the bow of the Sun Boat. Life! Prosperity! Health! Before the august (lost...) which is established behind him."

Monthly feast of Re.

August 7 DAY TWELVE

Making Love *Bring The Advocate is the Natur of this day.*

Do nothing this day.

"Today he who rebels his lord raises his head in hostility. His words drown out the speech of Sut, son of Nut. The rebel's head is removed for having conspired against his lord."

Birth of Hathor.

August 8 DAY THIRTEEN

Approach of Re *Re is the Natur of this day.*

(Lost...)

"The hearts of the *Naturu* are pleased by a feast and by honoring their lord, he who defeated the enemy so they will no longer exist."

Satisfying the hearts of the Pot Natur.

August 9 DAY FOURTEEN

Progress Of The Ba *Consider The Ba is the Natur of this day.*

Make offering to your *Naturu*. Pacify the spirits.

"The majesty of Horus receives the White Crown. The *Pot Natur* of his followers rejoice."

Horus receives the White Crown.

August 10 DAY FIFTEEN

Half Month Day *Amauai is the Natur of this day.*

Do not leave your house at night. If anyone sees them, he will pass away at once.

"The majesty of Re goes out at nightfall with his followers."

August 11 DAY SIXTEEN

Two Houses Fight *Horus and Sut are the Naturu of this day.*

Anything you see will be good.

"The *Naturu* attending the feast of Osiris are joyous. The hearts of the *Pot Natur* are pleased."

Feast of Osiris.

August 12 DAY SEVENTEEN

Second Arrival Day *Re is the Natur of this day.*

It is important to offer bread and beer, and to burn incense this day. It is necessary to make an invocation offering to the spirits so that your words will be heard by your sky *Naturu*.

"Smelling (lost...) on this day by the Great *Pot Natur* and the Lesser *Pot Natur* who comes out of Nun."

August 13 DAY EIGHTEEN
Moon Day *Ahi is the Natur of this day.*
Do nothing this day.
"On this day *Inpu* inspects the embalming tent, while performing the transformation into lizards in the sight of men. *Inpu* found all things being ready to care for the burial.
Then he started to weep. He repeated the inspection while still weeping. They begin to weep aloud. They place their hands upon their heads, both the *Naturu* and the *Naturitu*."
Ceremony of Transformation by Inpu. Mummification of Osiris.

August 14 DAY NINETEEN
Hear His Commands *Bring His Mother is the Natur of this day.*
(Lost...)
"Nun goes out to set the Noble One in his place, and to give redress to the *Naturu* who are in the presence of the Noble One."
Ceremony of raising the sacred Djed pillar.

August 15 DAY TWENTY
Offering Meat *Opener Of The Way is the Naturit of this day.*
(Lost...)
"It is the day of giving payment in the presence of Re, and the manner in which Thoth makes an example out of defeating the rebels of their lord. They are carried off by Sut, son of Nut, and they will be underneath. So say the *Naturu*."

August 16 DAY TWENTY-ONE
Apru's Day *Inpu is the Natur of this day.*
(Lost...)
"The *Naturit* Lady Net of Upper Egypt goes before the presence of Re. May he live and be prosperous! While appeasing and praising Lady Net, her eyes guide Thoth."
Lady Net emerges before Ra.

August 17 DAY TWENTY-TWO
Passing Of Sopdut *Nai is the Natur of this day.*
Do not bathe this day.
"It is the day they cut the tongue of Sobek's enemy."

August 18 DAY TWENTY-THREE
Last Quarter Day *Na-Ur is the Natur of this day.*
A crocodile will kill anyone born this day. (Lost...)

August 19 DAY TWENTY-FOUR
Darkness *Nekhbet is the Naturit of this day.*

Do not go out of your house in any wind until Re sets.
"On this day the executioners of *Saut* (Sais) go looking for the children of rebellion, when he is in the ocean. If any lion glances at them he will die immediately."

August 20 DAY TWENTY-FIVE
Departing *Shem is the Natur of this day.*
Do not leave your house or travel on any roads.
"This is the day they find the children of rebellion wrapped in a mat, on their sides. (Lost...) in his charge. (Lost...) if a lion looks for the *Naturu* today, he will suffer from the trampling of a bull and die."
(*Note*: this is an older form of burial, with the rebels corpses hung alongside Re's Boat.)

August 21 DAY TWENTY-SIX
House Of Appearance *Ma'atef-f is the Natur of this day.*
Build no house foundations. Put no ships in the shipyard. Do not work today.
"It is the day for opening and resealing the windows in the palace at the House Of Osiris."

August 22 DAY TWENTY-SEVEN
Funerary Offerings *Khnumu is the Natur of this day.*
Make a holiday. Avoid killing reptiles. Do not go out. Do not give your back to any work. Anyone born on this day will die from snakebite. (Lost...)

Lighting the fires of Lady Net.

August 23 DAY TWENTY-EIGHT
Jubilee Of The Sky *Nut is the Naturit of this day.*
Anything you see this day will be good. (Lost...)

August 24 DAY TWENTY-NINE
Weakness *Utettef-f is the Natur of this day.*
Anyone born this day will die honored by the people.
(Lost...)

August 25 DAY THIRTY
Awaken *Horus Advocates For Him is the Natur of this day.*
(Lost...)
"Last day. Found missing (lost...) by Nun, father of the *Naturu.* The land is joyous on this day. House Of Re. House Of Osiris. House Of Horus."

Sky Feast of Re.
Feasts of Osiris and Horus.

HATHYS

August 26 to September 24

Hathor is the Natur.

Third Month of *Akhet*

August 26 DAY ONE

New Month Day *Thoth is the Natur of this day.*

(Lost...)

"Feast of Hathor, Lady Of Heaven. (Lost...) *Naturu* (lost...) Lady of all the *Naturitu.*"

Month of Hathys begins.
Feast of Hathor. Feast of Re.

August 27 DAY TWO

New Crescent Day *Horus is the Natur of this day.*

Anything you see will be good.

"Return of the *Wadjet* Eye from *Dop* (pre-dynastic capital) In order to relate (lost...)"

August 28 DAY THREE

Arrival Day *Osiris is the Natur of this day.*

Anything you see will be good.

"(Lost...) by the noble *Naturu.*"

August 29 DAY FOUR

Zem Priests Emerge *Isis is the Naturit of this day.*

Anyone who sails this day will see his house destroyed.

"The Earth trembles under Nun."

August 30 DAY FIVE

Altar Offerings Day *Hapy is the Natur of this day.*

Put out the fires in your house. Avoid gazing at fire.

"This is the day the *Naturu* are blamed (lost...) by the majesty of these *Naturu.*"

Honor Hathor.

August 31 DAY SIX

Sixth Day *Star Of His Mother is the Natur of this day.*

(Lost...)

"The Encouragement of the *Naturu* of the two lands on this day (lost...) Encouragement of (lost...) the whole land."

Feast of the Naturu of the black mud of Egypt.

(*Note*: The "encouragement" is an command by Pharaoh to his soldiers, urging them on to fight, given here to the followers of Horus and Sut.)

September 1 DAY SEVEN

First Quarter Day *Qebsenuf is the Natur of this day.*

Anything you see will be good.
(Lost...)

Monthly feast of Re.

September 2 DAY EIGHT (omission)
Main Emergence *Ma'atef-f is the Natur of this day.*

(Lost...)
"Isis emerges. Her heart is pleased on this day. Horus's heritage is established."

September 3 DAY NINE
Hidden One *He Does The Talking is the Natur of this day.*

Do not leave your house by any road. Do not let light fall upon your face until Re sets.
"It is the day of blaming the Great Ones who are in his presence."

Isis emerges.

September 4 DAY TEN
He Who Protects His Royal Name
He Makes A Name Himself is the Natur of this day.

(Lost...) "There is great rejoicing in heaven. The crews of Re are at peace. His *Pot Natur* shouts with pleasure at seeing those working in the fields."

September 5 DAY ELEVEN
Great Lady Protector *Sekhmet is the Naturit of this day.*

All is good this day. Anything you see will be good.
(Lost...)

Monthly feast of Re.

September 6 DAY TWELVE (omission)
Making Love *Bring The Advocate is the Natur of this day.*

(Lost...)
"The appeasement of the *Natur's* hearts wherever they are. The *Wadjet* Eye is on the head of Re. Fixing (lost...) for the *Naturu*, raising those who are upon their thrones."

Osiris goes out of Ibtu.
Purification of the Naturu's and Naturitu's hearts.
Feast of Hapy. Offerings are given to the Nile this day.

September 7 DAY THIRTEEN
Approach of Re *Re is the Natur of this day.*

(Lost...) "The ferryman on the river is cut into pieces on this day, for not ferrying over the confederates of Sut. (Lost...) any (lost...) against the Boat Of Osiris, which was sailing upstream to *Ibtu*, the great city of Osiris.

Behold! He is transformed into a little old person carried in the arms of his nurse. (Lost...) giving gold as a reward to *Inty* as a fare, saying, 'Please ferry me over to the West.'

Then he (lost...) takes it from him.

Behold! The confederates were following like a swarm of reptiles. Thereupon he recognizes these, while Sut enters into the embalming booth to see the *Natur's* limbs. When they become fresh, Sut came (lost...) as an enemy on the water.

The rebels following him are transformed into small cattle. Horus and his followers slaughter the small cattle. They divide them among the crew.

An offering was made of the tongues of the enemy of *Inty*, in order to fix firmly the gold in the House Of *Inty* forever.

One was awed at the small cattle in the West. One was awed at the transforming of the small cattle into flocks of birds, until this day."

Hapy is created.

September 8 DAY FOURTEEN

Progress Of The Ba *Consider The Ba is the Natur of this day.*

Do nothing this day. Anyone born this day will die of (lost...)

"The hearts of the *Naturu* are saddened because of what was done by the enemy of Inty."

Jubilation of the Dead.

September 9 DAY FIFTEEN

Half Month Day *Amauai is the Natur of this day.*

(Lost...)

"Consideration by *Banob-Tet* (Osiris as the *Natur* of fertility, or the Ram of Mendes) (lost...) in the sacred House Of Life."

Fertility of Min.

A day of offerings to Min, especially by husbands wishing for sons.

September 10 DAY SIXTEEN

Two Houses Fight *Horus and Sut are the Naturu of this day.*

A happy day without end.

"The Great Ones appear in *Shmun*. Bringing of the ibis (Lost...) establishing (lost...) in *Shmun*, a joyous day in infinity and eternity."

Day of the appearance of the Eight Primordials.

(*Note*: *Shmun* is *Khemennu*, Thoth's town or the "City Of The Eight," was also called *Per Tehuty*, and Hermopolis by the Greeks. Today it is called *El-Ashmunein*. The Eight Primordials are the four paired*Naturu* of the creation story of Thoth's priests.)

September 11 DAY SEVENTEEN
Second Arrival Day *Re is the Natur of this day.*

(Lost...)

"The Great *Pot Natur* lands at *Ibtu.* Isis and Lady Of The House weep and wail loudly for Osiris in *Saut* (Sais.) It is heard in *Ibtu.*"

Lamentation of Isis and Lady Of The House for Osiris.

September 12 DAY EIGHTEEN
Moon Day *Ahi is the Natur of this day.*

If making a journey, do not go near roads.

"There is strife by Sut and Isis, the children of Geb. (Lost...)"

Feast of Hathor.

The statue of the Naturit is taken on a boating procession to the mortuary complexes, to visit the pharaoh's tomb.

September 13 DAY NINETEEN
Hear His Commands *Bring His Mother is the Natur of this day.*

Do not sail north or south. So not sail boats this day.

"The children of the storm of Apep (lost...)"

September 14 DAY TWENTY
Offering Meat *Opener Of The Ways is the Naturit of this day.*

Those born this day will perish during a year of pestilence.

"The emergence of Bastet, Lady of *Ankh-towe*, before Re. She is greatly angered. The *Naturu* could not stand near her. (Bastet has become a Great Flame.)"

Bastet appears before Re.

September 15 DAY TWENTY-ONE
Apru's Day *Inpu is the Natur of this day.*

(Lost...)

"The feast of Shu, son of Re. It is the day of Lady Net in the Evening Boat Of The Sun."

Feast of Ma'at.

September 16 DAY TWENTY-TWO (omission)
Passing Of Sopdut *Nai is the Natur of this day.*

(Lost...)

"When *Ma'at* is summoned before Re, the *Naturu* raise her up in order to see him. A Uraeus is placed upon her and another below her, being fixed at the front of the Evening Boat Of The Sun."

(*Note*: In every House Of The *Natur*, a figure of *Ma'at* is presented to the *Natur* by the priest or supplicant to the *Naturu* during rituals.)

September 17 DAY TWENTY-THREE

Last Quarter Day *Na-Ur is the Natur of this day.*

Those who were born this day will not survive.

"Nun drags (lost...) them from the flames by the hands. Behold! The majesty of these *Naturu* who judge in that great place (lost...) on the river."

The dispute between Horus and Sut judged by Re.

September 18 DAY TWENTY-FOUR

Darkness *Nekhbet is the Naturit of this day.*

(Lost...)

'Isis emerges. Her heart is happy and Lady Of The House is joyous. When they see Osiris (lost...) heart. He has given his throne to his son Horus in the presence of Re."

Isis emerges.

September 19 DAY TWENTY-FIVE

Departing *Shem is the Natur of this day.*

Anything you see will be pleasing to the *Naturu.*

(Lost...)

September 20 DAY TWENTY-SIX

House Of Appearances *Ma'atef-f is the Natur of this day.*

(Lost...)

"Raising the *Djed* of Re in the heaven and land of *Innu* at the time of uproar, and reconciliation of the Two Lords causes the land to be a peace. The Black Land is granted to Horus and the Red Land to Sut. Thoth emerges in order to judge in the presence of Re."

The Black Land is given to Horus, the Red Land to Sut.

September 21 DAY TWENTY-SEVEN

Funerary Offerings *Khnumu is the Natur of this day.*

"The judgment between Sut and Horus stops the hostility. They hunt down the followers of the two *Naturu,* and put an end to the tumult. It satisfies the Two Lords and causes the two doors to open."

The Autumn Equinox.

September 22 DAY TWENTY-EIGHT

Jubilee Of The Sky *Nut is the Naturit of this day.*

Anything you see this day will be good.

"All the *Naturu* are jubilant because the will is written for Horus, son of Osiris, to appease Osiris in the *Heh.* The land is joyous and the *Naturu* are pleased."

Horus is crowned King. The appearance before Ptah.

September 23 DAY TWENTY-NINE ☉♀♀♀

Weakness *Utettef-f is the Natur of this day.*

(Lost...)

"The emergence of the Three Noble Ladies who are in the *Tanent* Sanctuary in the presence of Ptah, beautiful of face, while they give praise to Re, he who belongs to the throne of *ma'at* of the Houses Of The *Naturitu*. For giving the White Crown to Horus and the Red Crown to Sut, their hearts are pleased."

September 24 DAY THIRTY ☉♀♀♀

Awaken *Horus Advocates For Him is the Natur of this day.*

Anything you see will be good.

"Last day. House Of Re, House Of Osiris, House Of Horus."

Feast of the Noble Ladies.

Sky Feast.

CHOIACH

September 25 to October 24

Sekhtet is the Natur. Last Month of *Akhet*

September 25 DAY ONE ☉♀♀♀
New Month Day *Thoth is the Natur of this day.*

(Lost...)

"The Great *Pot Natur* and the Lesser *Pot Natur* go to appease the majesty of Nun in the cavern. The majesty of Thoth orders Sia and his followers (lost...) saying, 'A copy of the command of the majesty of Re is brought to you. Re is joyful in his beauty. His *Pot Natur* is in celebration.

Every lion and all *inhy*-reptiles, the *Naturu, Naturitu*, spirits, dead and those who came into being in the primordial age, their form is in every one of you.'"

Month of Choiach begins.
Feast of Re and Sekhmet.

September 26 DAY TWO ☉♀♀♀
New Crescent Day *Horus is the Natur of this day.*

Anything you see will be good.

"The *Naturu* and *Naturitu* are joyous. Heaven and Earth are happy."

September 27 DAY THREE
Arrival Day *Osiris is the Natur of this day.*

Do nothing this day. Those born this day will die of his ears.

"It is the day of smashing the ears of *Bata* within his own inaccessible Houses Of Life."

(*Note*: *Bata* is the Lord of *Saka*, capitol of the nome *Atch*. He is mentioned in "The Tale Of Two Brothers." Offering-bread had molded ears so the *Naturu* could hear prayers. In the Old Kingdom, there was a practice of smashing ears off sculptured portrait heads.)

September 28 DAY FOUR ☉♀♀♀
Zem Priests Emerge *Isis is the Naturit of this day.*

Using all that is required, perform Sobek's rituals in your home and in his House Of Life.

"It will please the hearts of the *Naturu* on this day."

Feast of Sobek. Sacred crocodiles are honored this day.

September 29 DAY FIVE ☉♀♀♀
Altar Offerings Day *Hapy is the Natur of this day.*

(Lost...)

"The emergence of *Khentet-abet* (Hathor) in the presence of the Great Ones (Horus and Sut) in *Kher-Aaha*. Life, stability and welfare are given to her and the *Pot Natur.*

The *Naturu* of the *Kher-Aaha* and the majesty of Hapy, father of the *Naturu*, are joyous this day."

Procession of Hathor.

(*Note*: *Khentet-Abet* is Hathor. *Kher-Aaha* is the scene of the battles of Horus and Sut.)

September 30 DAY SIX
Sixth Day *Star Of His Mother is the Natur of this day.*

Do not go out on this day.
"The Sun Boat of Re is established in order to overthrow his foes from one moment to another this day."

October 1 DAY SEVEN
First Quarter Day *Qebsenuf is the Natur of this day.*

Do not eat or taste *mehit* fish this day.
"It is the day of (lost...) wind. (Lost...) death in (lost...) he will turn into a fish."

Feast of Sorqet.
Feast of Thoth.

October 2 DAY EIGHT
Main Emergence *Ma'atef-f is the Natur of this day.*

Anything you see will be good.
(Lost...)

Monthly Feast of Re.

October 3 DAY NINE
Hidden One *He Does The Talking is the Natur of this day.*

(Lost...)
"It is the day of action by Thoth. Re speaks in the presence of the Great Ones. Then together with Thoth, these *Naturu* cause the enemy of Sut to kill himself in his sanctuary. It is this that has been done by the executioners of (lost...) until this day."

October 4 DAY TEN
He Who Protects His Royal Name
He Makes A Name Himself is the Natur of this day.

Those born this day will die in old age, while beer enters into his mouth, face and eyes. Those born on this day will die in old age, choking to death swallowing beer.
(Lost...)

October 5 DAY ELEVEN
Great Lady Protector *Sekhmet is the Naturit of this day.*

(omission) Feast of Osiris in *Ibtu* in the Great *Neshmet* (the sacred boat of Re and Osiris) on this day.

"The dead are joyous."

Feast of Osiris in Abydos.

October 6 DAY TWELVE

Making Love *Bring The Advocate is the Natur of this day.*

Make offerings to the *Bennu*-phoenix in your home. Stay off windy roads this day.

"It is the day of transformation into the *Bennu*-phoenix."

Transformation of the Bennu Bird (Re).

October 7 DAY THIRTEEN

Approach of Re *Re is the Natur of this day.*

Make this a holy day in your house. Make a feast in your house on this day.

"The emergence of the White One of Heaven (Hathor). Their hearts are pleased for her in the presence of Re. The *Pot Natur* is in celebration."

Procession of Hathor and the Pot Natur.

October 8 DAY FOURTEEN

Progress Of The Ba *Consider The Ba is the Natur of this day.*

(Lost...)

"Lady Of The House and *Tait* come from the House Of The *Natur* of the *Benben* on this day. They present things to Lady Net. Their hearts are happy."

Feast of Naturu and Naturitu and Fate.

Emergence of the Transformed Bennu-phoenix.

(*Note*: *Tait* is Lady Of The House as the *Naturit* of weaving. Lady Of The House provided the role model for a woman's responsibilities as household manager. Women wove the cloth for their family's clothing and household goods as part of their daily chores.)

October 9 DAY FIFTEEN (Lost...)

Half Month Day *Amauai is the Natur of this day.*

(Lost...) Feast of Sekhmet and Bastet.

Feast of Sekhmet, Bastet and Re.

October 10 DAY SIXTEEN (Lost...)

Two Houses Fight *Horus and Sut are the Naturu of this day.*

(Day lost to papyrus damage.)

October 11 DAY SEVENTEEN

Second Arrival Day *Re is the Natur of this day.*

Stay home during the middle part of the day.

"The people and the *Naturu* judge the words of the crew in *Innu* when Horus arrives in *Kher-Aaha*."

Feast of the judging of the crew of the Sun Boat. Holy day of Hathor.

October 12 DAY EIGHTEEN
Moon Day *Ahi is the Natur of this day.*

(Lost...)

"It is the day of the overthrowing of the *Naturu's* boat on this day."

October 13 DAY NINETEEN
Hear His Commands *Bring His Mother is the Natur of this day.*

Drink no wine. Do not partake of bread or beer. Drink only the water of grapes until sunset.

"Offerings are presented in the *Hewit*-desert. Oinment is made for Osiris in the hall of embalming."

October 14 DAY TWENTY
Offering Meat *Opener Of The Way is the Naturit of this day.*

Stay off roads. Wear no ointments (perfumed oils.) Stay in when the Sun is at noon.

"It is the day of looking in the direction of the *Akhet* Eye of Horus."

October 15 DAY TWENTY-ONE
Apru's Day *Anubis (Inpu) is the Natur of this day.*

Do not leave your house during the hours of daylight.

"This is the day of the emergence of the Great Ones to look for the *Akhet* Eye Of Horus."

Ritual of raising the Djed pillar.

October 16 DAY TWENTY-TWO
Passing Of Sopdut *Nai is the Natur of this day.*

Anything you see will be good. (Lost...)

Feast of plowing the Earth.

October 17 DAY TWENTY-THREE
Last Quarter Day *Na-Ur is the Natur of this day.*

Do not go out during the hours of darkness. Should a lion see you if you go out this night, he will kill you.

"They (lost...) in order to defeat (lost...) Horus, who is the savior of his father."

October 18 DAY TWENTY-FOUR (Lost...)
Darkness *Nekhbet is the Naturit of this day.*

(Day lost to papyrus damage.)

October 19 DAY TWENTY-FIVE (Lost...)
Departing *Shem is the Natur of this day.*

(Day lost to papyrus damage.)

October 20 DAY TWENTY-SIX

House Of Appearance *Ma'atef-f is the Natur of this day.*

(Lost...)

"Thoth raised the nobles to an advanced position in the city of Sekhmet (Letopolis.) (Lost...)"

October 21 DAY TWENTY-SEVEN

Funerary Offerings *Khnumu is the Natur of this day.*

Anything you see in the daylight will be good. Do not go out during the hours of darkness this day.

(Lost...)

Feast of Isis seeking Osiris's body.

October 22 DAY TWENTY-EIGHT

Jubilee Of The Sky *Nut is the Naturit of this day.*

Eat no *mehit*-fish this day. Do not use it as an offering.

"It is the day of the emergence of the *ba-mehit*-fish, which is in the House Of Osiris, its form being the *iten*-fish."

Feast of the loss of Osiris by Isis.

October 23 DAY TWENTY-NINE

Weakness *Utettef-f is the Natur of this day.*

Avoid the scent of fish while throwing flame into the water from what is offered. Eat no *mehit*-fish. Do not let one touch you, or take one into your hands.

(Lost...)

Feast of rejoicing that Isis has found the body of Osiris.

October 24 DAY THIRTY

Awaken *Horus Advocates For Him is the Natur of this day.*

Anything you see will please hearts of the *Naturu* this day. Make offerings to them and their followers, and make invocation offerings to the spirits. Offer to the dead. Give food in accordance to the List.

It is a day of pleasure for the Great *Pot Natur.*

"House Of Re. House Of Osiris. House Of Horus."

Feast of the Pot of Re.

Feast of Osiris and Horus.

Offerings for the Ka. (Living memories.)

TYBY

October 25 to November 23

Khopry is the Natur.

First Month of *Poret*

October 25 DAY ONE

New Month Day *Thoth is the Natur of this day.*

Offer twice the usual amount. Give the gifts of *Hekenu*. Anything you see will be good.

"Double the offerings and bestow the gifts of *Hekenu* to the *Naturu* who attend Ptah in the *Tanent* shrings of the *Naturu* and *Naturitu*, protectors of Re and his followers and of the (lost...) of Ptah-Sokar, Sekhmet the Great, Nefertum and Horus Of The Two Horizons, *Mahes* (a lioness-headed form of Sekhmet,) Bastet the Great Fire (lost...) propitiating the *Wadjet* Eye."

The month of Tyby begins.
Feast of Re. Feast of Bastet.
The Heb-Sed (Jubilee) Festival.

(*Note*: The word *Heb* means "Festival," and *Sed* means "cloth," as well as "tail." During this festival the King had to run around the circumference of the House Of Life (temple) inner court, carrying ritual objects in his hands that performed his rejuvenation during his race. This feast took place every three years, with an even grander version occurring at a Pharaoh's Thirtieth Year Jubilee. The "tail" reference is an indication of the great age of the ritual, since priests continued to wear the bull or leopard tail as part of their ritual clothing, a practice dating back to the pre-dynastic days, and which is seen in petroglyphs all across Africa. The shift from "tail" to "cloth" shows how carefully this ancient ritual was maintained throughout the life time of the nation.)

October 26 DAY TWO (Lost...)

New Crescent Day *Horus is the Natur of this day.*

(Day lost to papyrus damage.)

October 27 DAY THREE (Lost...)

Arrival Day *Osiris is the Natur of this day.*

Light no fires to Re or in his presence.

(Lost...)

October 28 DAY FOUR

Zem Priests Emerge *Isis is the Naturit of this day.*

Those born this day will die in old age among his family. He will spend a long lifetime and will be received by his father. (He will be justified.) Anything you see will be good.

(Lost...)

October 29 DAY FIVE

Altar Offerings Day *Hapy is the Natur of this day.*

"It is the day of Sekhmet placing the flame before the Great Ones who preside in the sanctuary of Lower Egypt. She is fierce in

her manifestions because of her confinement in the sanctuary by *Ma'at*, Ptah, Thoth, Hu and Sia."
(Lost...)

October 30 DAY SIX
Sixth Day *Star Of His Mother is the Natur of this day.*
Offer twice the Horus Of The Two Horizons offerings to the *Naturu*. Offerings must be doubled. Repeat the food offerings of him who dwells in the Holy Place and return the food of the noble *Khenty-arty* (Horus.)
(Lost...)

Feast of Clothing Inpu.

October 31 DAY SEVEN
First Quarter Day *Qebsenuf is the Natur of this day.*
Do not make love with anyone in the presence of the Great Flame.
(Lost...)

Feast of Sekhmet and the purifying of the flame.

November 1 DAY EIGHT
Main Emergence *Ma'atef-f is the Natur of this day.*
Anything you see will be good.
(Lost...)

Monthly feast of Re.

November 2 DAY NINE
Hidden One *He Does The Talking is the Natur of this day.*
Repeat offerings using *Pot Natur* cakes, to please the *Naturu* and spirits.

"The *Naturu* are pleased with the offerings of Sekhmet this day."

Feast of Sekhmet.

(*Note*: *Pot Natur* cake is any special kind of dough prepared for offering.)

November 3 DAY TEN
He Who Protects His Royal Name
He Makes A Name Himself is the Natur of this day.
Do not burn papyrus this day.
"It is the day of the emergence of Horus and the Flame."

November 4 DAY ELEVEN
Great Lady Protector *Sekhmet is the Naturit of this day.*
Do not go near flame this day.
(Lost...)

November 5 DAY TWELVE
Making Love *Bring The Advocate is the Natur of this day.*

Do not go near any dogs this day.
"It is the day of answering the speech of Sekhmet."

Monthly Feast of Re.

November 6 DAY THIRTEEN
Approach of Re *Re is the Natur of this day.*
(Lost...)
"It is the day of prolonging the life and bringing about acts of benevolence from the *Naturit Ma'at* in the House Of The *Naturu.*"

Feast of Hathor and Sekhmet.
Day of prolonging life and the goodness of Ma'at.

November 7 DAY FOURTEEN
Progress Of The Ba *Consider The Ba is the Natur of this day.*
Avoid singers and chanting this day.
"This is the day Isis and Lady Of The House weep. This is the day they mourn Osiris in the House Of Osiris (Busiris) remembering what they had seen."

November 8 DAY FIFTEEN
Half Month Day *Amauai is the Natur of this day.*
Anything you see will be good.
"It is the day Nun goes through the cave to that place where the *Naturu* are (lost...) in darkness."

November 9 DAY SIXTEEN
Two Houses Fight *Horus and Sut are the Naturu of this day.*
"This is the day of the emergence of Shu in order to count the crew of the Evening Boat Of The Sun."

November 10 DAY SEVENTEEN
Second Arrival Day *Re is the Natur of this day.*
Do not wash yourself with water on this day.
"It is the day Nun emerges into the place where the *Naturu* are. Those who are above and below come into being. The land is still in darkness."

(*Note*: this is the day the *Naturu* are created. The Earth has yet to be created, and the cosmos is in a state of watery chaos. Nun is the primeval water from which the cosmos arose, and upon which it rests.)

November 11 DAY EIGHTEEN
Moon Day *Ahi is the Natur of this day.*
This day is a holiday in The Mouth Of The Far Horizon.
"The *Naturu* emerge from *Ibtu.*"

The Naturu leave Ibtu for Mouth Of The Far Horizon.

(*Note*: The Mouth Of The Far Horizon is the region in the western horizon where the

Sun sets, and is represented by the mouth of Nut swallowing the setting Sun. This is the beginning of the night journey of Re, and this is the first port of the dead on their journey to the Next Life, so the symbolism appears in many funeral scenes and texts.)

November 12 DAY NINETEEN

Hear His Commands *Bring His Mother is the Natur of this day.*

Those who are afflicted on this day, and do not mend before the day ends, will never recover.

"The Great *Naturu* are in heaven on this day, and mixed with the pestilence of the year. There are many deaths."

November 13 DAY TWENTY

Offering Meat *Opener Of The Ways is the Naturit of this day.*

Do nothing this day. Be ware of crossing over land. Do not cross land until Re sets.

"This day Bastet emerges to protect the Two Lands and to care for him who is in darkness."

Bastet leaves Bubastis to guard the Two Lands.

November 14 DAY TWENTY-ONE

Apru's Day *Inpu is the Natur of this day.*

Make spirit (*aabt*) offerings to the followers of Re on this day.

"Bastet guides the Two Lands."

Feast for the followers of Re.

(*Note*: *aabt* are the funeral or sacrifical offerings.)

November 15 DAY TWENTY-TWO

Passing Of Sopdut *Nai is the Natur of this day.*

Anything you see will be good.

(Lost...)

November 16 DAY TWENTY-THREE

Last Quarter Day *Na-Ur is the Natur of this day.*

Those born today will die rich in everything at an old age.

(Lost...)

Feast of Lady Net.

November 17 DAY TWENTY-FOUR

Darkness *Nekhbet is the Naturit of this day.*

There is joy in both heaven and Earth.

"Everything is put behind him in the presence of the *Pot Natur*, on the occasion of being loyal to the executioners of Re. There is happiness in heaven and on Earth this day."

November 18 DAY TWENTY-FIVE (omission)

Departing *Shem is the Natur of this day.*

Do not drink milk. Eat and drink honey.

"On this day the Great Divine Cow is brought before the presence of Re."

(*Note*: Hathor's role as *Meh-Urt,* who gave birth to the Sun each morning as she had given birth to the cosmos at the beginning of time. Milk was offered to her on this day, and used in ritual bathing to purify before ceremonies in the House Of The *Natur.*

November 19 DAY TWENTY-SIX ☉

House Of Appearances *Ma'atef-f is the Natur of this day.*

Do not go out on this day until Re sets, once the offerings are diminished in the House Of Osiris and while they are put on Earth towards heaven.

"They will be much blame for it."

November 20 DAY TWENTY-SEVEN ☉

Funerary Offerings *Khnumu is the Natur of this day.*

"Great festivity in (lost...) *Hefau (*Apep.)"

(Lost...)

November 21 DAY TWENTY-EIGHT ☉

Jubilee Of The Sky *Nut is the Naturit of this day.*

All the land is in festivity. Make a holiday at home.

"Thoth takes a solemn oath in *Khemennu* (Town Of The Eight) and the Noble One emerges. The land is in celebration."

Feast of Thoth's oath.

November 22 DAY TWENTY-NINE ☉

Weakness *Utettef-f is the Natur of this day.*

Anything you see will be good.

"Appearance in the sight of Hu. Thoth sends a command southward, by Bastet and Sekhmet The Great, to guide the Two Lands. The *Naturu* are happy."

Sky feast.

November 23 DAY THIRTY ☉

Awaken *Horus Advocates For Him is the Natur of this day.*

Forget no one when you offer incense in the Houses Of Re and Osiris and Horus. Do not forget any of them whle incense is on the fire, according to the list on this day.

"Last day. The crossing over in the presence of Nun from the House Of Hapy, father of the *Naturu* and of the *Pot Natur* lords of *Kher-Aaba.*

House Of Re. House Of Osiris. House Of Horus."

Feast in the House Of Life of Hapy.

MENCHIR

November 24 to December 23

Rekeh-Ur is the Natur.

Second Month of *Poret*

November 24 DAY ONE

New Month Day *Thoth is the Natur of this day.*

Be festive.

"The *Naturu* and *Naturitu* are festive this day. It is the feast of Ptah lifting Lord Re to heaven with his hands."

Month of Menchir begins.
Festival of Little Heat (left eye of Re.)
Feast of Ptah lifting up Re with his hands.

November 25 DAY TWO

New Crescent Day *Horus is the Natur of this day.*

(Lost...)

"This is the day the *Naturu* receive Re. The hearts of the Two Lands are festive."

Re returns to the sky.

November 26 DAY THREE

Arrival Day *Osiris is the Natur of this day.*

Do not go out on any road.

"Sut and his confederates go out to the eastern horizon, and *Ma'at* sails to where the *Naturu* are."

Sut emerges.

November 27 DAY FOUR

Zem Priests Emerge *Isis is the Naturit of this day.*

Honor the *Naturu*. Make offerings to the spirits. Devote your whole heart to your sky *Naturu*. Placate your spirits. Praise your crew on this day. (Lost...)

November 28 DAY FIVE

Altar Offerings Day *Hapy is the Natur of this day.*

Anything you see will be good.

November 29 DAY SIX

Sixth Day *Star Of His Mother is the Natur of this day.*

(Lost...)

"It is the day of putting up the *Djed* by Lord Osiris. The *Naturu* are saddened, with their faces downcast, when they remember the majesty of him."

Feast of Isis.

November 30 DAY SEVEN
First Quarter Day *Qebsenuf is the Natur of this day.*
Make spirit offerings. Make offerings to the *Naturu.*
(Lost...)

December 1 DAY EIGHT
Main Emergence *Ma'atef-f is the Natur of this day.*
Make a holiday.
(Lost...)
Feast of the Great Heat (Right Eye of Re). Feast of Hathor.

December 2 DAY NINE
Hidden One *He Does The Talking is the Natur of this day.*
Anything you see will be good.
"The *Naturu* enter. He will direct this *Septy* (i.e., give rations) to all the *Naturu* of *Kher-Aaha.*"
Monthly feast of Re.

December 3 DAY TEN
He Who Protects His Royal Name
He Makes A Name Himself is the Natur of this day.
(Lost...)
"The *Wadjet* Eye emerges for the singing in *Innu.* It is the day they raise up the Lady Majesty in the sanctuary of Osiris. Re raises *Ma'at* again and again to Atum."
Birth of Horus the Child (son of Isis and Osiris).

December 4 DAY ELEVEN
Great Lady Protector *Sekhmet is the Naturit of this day.*
You will see good from her hands.
"Feast of Lady Net in *Saut* (Sais.) Taking the writing material that was prepared in her house, she is guided there by Sobek."
Birth of Sobek
(*Note*: lady Net serves as letter-writer for the *Naturu* in the story of Horus and Sut.)

December 5 DAY TWELVE
Making Love *Bring The Advocate is the Natur of this day.*
Anything you see will be good.
(Lost...)
Feast of "Lifting the Sky."

December 6 DAY THIRTEEN
Approach of Re *Re is the Natur of this day.*
Do not go out of your house on this day.
"This day Sekhmet emerges from *Sekhemt* (Letopolis). Her great

executioners pass by their offerings."

Monthly feast of Re.

December 7 DAY FOURTEEN

Progress Of The Ba *Consider The Ba is the Natur of this day.*

Do not go out this day at the beginning of dawn.

"Seeing him, Sut kills the rebel at the bow of the great Sun Boat of Re."

December 8 DAY FIFTEEN (Lost...)

Half Month Day *Amauai is the Natur of this day.*

(Lost...)

"The *Naturu* emerge with him in heaven. He holds in his hands the ankh and the scepter to the nose to *Khenty-Irety* (Horus) at the time of his reckoning."

December 9 DAY SIXTEEN (Lost...)

Two Houses Fight *Horus and Sut are the Naturu of this day.*

(Lost...)

"Awakening of Isis by the majesty of Re (lost...) their hands when Horus saved his father. He has beaten Sut and his confederates."

December 10 DAY SEVENTEEN

Second Arrival Day *Re is the Natur of this day.*

(Lost...)

"It is the day of keeping those things of the *wabet* of Osiris which have been placed in the hands of *Inpu*."

The day of keeping Osiris in the hands of Inpu.

December 11 DAY EIGHTEEN

Moon Day *Ahi is the Natur of this day.*

(Lost...)

"This day the seven executioners search with their fingers for the *Akhet* Eye of Horus in the town of *Iy*t and in *Sekhemt*."

December 12 DAY NINETEEN

Hear His Commands

Bring His Mother is the Natur of this day.

Do not go out by yourself in daylight.

"It is the day of mourning the *Naturu*."

December 13 DAY TWENTY

Offering Meat *Opener Of The Way is the Natur of this day.*

(Lost...)

"The Lady Majesty of Heaven goes southward."

Day of Nut.

December 14 DAY TWENTY-ONE (omission)
Apru's Day *Inpu is the Natur of this day.*
(Lost...)
"It is the day of the birth of the cattle (lost...) to the place where the meadows are in the region of the foremost *Naturu.*"

December 15 DAY TWENTY-TWO
Passing Of Sopdut *Nai is the Natur of this day.*
Anything you see will be good.
Feasts of Horus and Ptah.

December 16 DAY TWENTY-THREE
Last Quarter Day *Na-Ur is the Natur of this day.*
Anything you see will be good.
(Lost...)
Festival of Isis.

December 17 DAY TWENTY-FOUR
Darkness *Nekhbet is the Naturit of this day.*
Do not sail on any boats. Anyone who approaches on the River will pass away.
"The *Naturu* are descending into the river."
Festival of Isis.

December 18 DAY TWENTY-FIVE
Departing *Shem is the Natur of this day.*
Anything you see will be good.
(Lost...)

December 19 DAY TWENTY-SIX (Lost...)
House Of Appearances *Ma'atef-f is the Natur of this day.*
(Lost...)
"It is the day of the emergence of Min from *Qebty* (Coptos.) He boasts of his beauty. Isis sees that his face is beautiful."
Feast of Min. Isis sees Osiris's face.

December 20 DAY TWENTY-SEVEN (omission)
Funerary Offerings *Khnumu is the Natur of this day.*
The feast of Sokar in heaven before Isis in *Ibtu.*
(omission)
Feast of Sokar.
Feast of Osiris.

December 21 DAY TWENTY-EIGHT
Jubilee Of The Sky *Nut is the Naturit of this day.*
(Lost...)

"Osiris is pleased. The spirits are joyful and the dead are in festivity."
The Winter Solstice.

December 22 DAY TWENTY-NINE ☉𓉐𓉐𓉐
Weakness *Utetteff is the Natur of this day.*
Do nothing this day.
"Encouragement of fighting spawns rebellion and tumult among the children of Geb."

December 23 DAY THIRTY ☉𓉐𓉐𓉐
Awaken *Horus Advocates For Him is the Natur of this day.*
Do not speak loudly to anyone this day.
"Last day. House Of Re. House Of Osiris. House Of Horus."

FAMENOTH

December 24 to January 22

Rekeh-Netches is the Natur.

Third Month of *Poret*

December 24 DAY ONE

New Month Day *Thoth is the Natur of this day.*

It is the day of feasting in heaven and on Earth.

"It is the feast of entering into heaven and the Two Riverbanks. Horus is jubilant."

The month of Famenoth begins.
Feast of entering heaven. Sky feast.

December 25 DAY TWO

New Crescent Day *Horus is the Natur of this day.*

Anything you see will be good.

(Lost...)

December 26 DAY THREE (Lost...)

Arrival Day *Osiris is the Natur of this day.*

(Lost to papyrus damage.)

December 27 DAY FOUR

Zem Priests Emerge *Isis is the Naturit of this day.*

(Lost...)

"Sut announces the coming conflict. His voice is so angered it is heard in heaven and on Earth."

December 28 DAY FIVE

Altar Offerings Day *Hapy is the Natur of this day.*

Do not go out during these hours.

"lady Net goes to *Saut* (Sais) where they see her beauty during the night for four and one-half hours."

Festival of Lights of Lady Net.

December 29 DAY SIX

Sixth Day *Star Of His Mother is the Natur of this day.*

Make ritual this day!

"Osiris is in the House of Osiris (Busiris). *Inpu* emerges with his worshippers. He receives everyone in the hall."

Procession of Inpu. Jubilation of Osiris.

December 30 DAY SEVEN

First Quarter Day *Qebsenuf is the Natur of this day.*

Do not leave your house until Re sets. Take heed of it.

"It is the day when the Eye Of Re summons his followers. They reach him at nightfall."

December 31 DAY EIGHT ☉

Main Emergence *Ma'atef-f is the Natur of this day.*

Anything you see will be good.

"It is the day of making way for the *Naturu* by Khnum, who presides over those who remove themselves from him."

Festival for Khnum.

January 1 DAY NINE ☉

Hidden One *He Does The Talking is the Natur of this day.*

(Lost...)

"Judgment in *Innu.*"

Day of Hathor.

January 2 DAY TEN ☉

He Who Protects His Royal Name

He Makes A Name Himself is the Natur of this day.

Any who approach her cannot be taken from her by force.

"This day Thoth comes. They guide the Great Flame into her House Of The Desert Of Eternity which has been set up for them."

Day of Thoth.
Monthly feast of Re.

January 3 DAY ELEVEN ☉

Great Lady Protector *Sekhmet is the Naturit of this day.*

(Lost...)

"As to those dead who go about the *Heh* this day, they do so to repel the anger of the enemies who are in this land."

January 4 DAY TWELVE ☉

Making Love *Bring The Advocate is the Natur of this day.*

Give food. Foodstuffs are given on this day.

"Hapy The Nile comes from Nun this day."

January 5 DAY THIRTEEN ☉

Approach of Re *Re is the Natur of this day.*

Any ritual performed this day will be good.

"The arrival of Thoth with his followers on this day. Replacing (lost...) in the seats of the *Naturu.*"

January 6 DAY FOURTEEN ☉

Progress Of The Ba *Consider The Ba is the Natur of this day.*

Do not go out on any road this day.

"It is the day of making health in *Sekhemt* (Letopolis.)"

Monthly feast of Re.

January 7 DAY FIFTEEN
Half Month Day *Amauai is the Natur of this day.*

Do no work this day.
"There is uprising in the shrine."

January 8 DAY SIXTEEN
Two Houses Fight *Horus and Sutekh are the Naturu of this day.*

Do not look at anything in darkness this day. Do not see darkness.
"This day they open the doors and courts of *Nest-tauy* (Karnak.)"
Day of opening the doors and courts of Karnak.

January 9 DAY SEVENTEEN
Second Arrival Day *Re is the Natur of this day.*

Anyone who speaks Sut's name will fight eternally in his house. He will not stop quarreling in his house.
(Lost...)

January 10 DAY EIGHTEEN
Moon Day *Ahi is the Natur of this day.*

Make holiday in your house.
"It is the feast of Nut who counts the days."
Feast of Nut.

January 11 DAY NINETEEN (omission)
Hear His Commands *Bring His Mother is the Natur of this day.*

Do not go out of your house. Do not look into the light.
"Birth of Nut anew (lost...) any dead on this day (lost...) Bastet the majesty of the foreign land."
Birth of Nut.

January 12 DAY TWENTY
Offering Meat *Opener Of The Way is the Naturit of this day.*

Do not go out of your house by road. Do not look into the light.
(Lost...)

January 13 DAY TWENTY-ONE (Lost...)
Apru's Day *Inpu is the Natur of this day.*

(omission.)

January 14 DAY TWENTY-TWO
Passing Of Sopdut *Nai is the Natur of this day.*

Do not think about or pronounce the names of snakes. It is the day of catching his children.
"Birth of the Mysterious One (Apep) with his limbs."
Birth of Apep.

January 15 DAY TWENTY-THREE ☉𓋹𓋹𓋹
Last Quarter Day *Na-Ur is the Natur of this day.*
(Lost...)
"Feast Of Horus on this day of his years in his beautiful images."
Feast of Horus. Offerings made for the Dead.

January 16 DAY TWENTY-FOUR ☉𓅪𓅪𓅪
Darkness *Nekhbet is the Naturit of this day.*
Do not go out of your house on any road.(Lost...)

January 17 DAY TWENTY-FIVE (omission.)
Departing *Shem is the Natur of this day.*
Do nothing on this day.
"The *Naturu* make a great cry in desert places on this day."

January 18 DAY TWENTY-SIX ☉𓅪𓅪𓅪
House Of Appearances *Ma'atef-f is the Natur of this day.*
(Lost...)
"This day he was sent into the cave without the knowledge of the Great Ones, to look for the time of coming."
Day for those in the West.

January 19 DAY TWENTY-SEVEN ☉𓅪𓅪𓅪
Funerary Offerings *Khnumu is the Natur of this day.*
Do nothing on this day.
(Lost...)

January 20 DAY TWENTY-EIGHT ☉𓋹𓋹𓋹
Jubilee Of The Sky *Nut is the Naturit of this day.*
(Lost...)
"The feast of Osiris in *Ibtu.* The majesty of Osiris puts up the (tree or plank) (lost...)"
Feast of Osiris.

January 21 DAY TWENTY-NINE ☉𓋹𓋹𓋹
Weakness *Utettef-f is the Natur of this day.*
Anything you see will be good.
(Lost...)

January 22 DAY THIRTY ☉𓋹𓋹𓋹
Awaken *Horus Advocates For Him is the Natur of this day.*
(Lost...)
"Last day. Feast in the House Of Osiris (Busiris.) The names of the doors come into existence.
House Of Re. House Of Osiris. House Of Horus."
Festival of the Opening Of The Doorways of the Horizon. Sky feast.

PARMUTHY

January 23 to February 21

Rennutet is the Natur.

Last Month of *Poret*

January 23 DAY ONE ☉☥☥☥

New Month Day *Thoth is the Natur of this day.*

(Lost...)

"There is a great feast in heaven. This day they overthrow those who rebelled against their mistress."

Month of Parmuthy begins.

Feast of Re.

January 24 DAY TWO ☉☥☥☥

New Crescent Day *Horus is the Natur of this day.*

(Lost...)

"The majesty of Geb goes to the House Of Osiris to see Inpu who instructs the council on the day's requirements."

Procession of Geb to see Anubis.

January 25 DAY THREE ☉

Arrival Day *Osiris is the Natur of this day.*

Any lion who pronounces the name of the *Sah* (Orion constellion) will die at once. Do nothing this day.

"The Great Ones fight with the Uraeus. She is appointed to create the Eye Of The Original Horus."

January 26 DAY FOUR ☉

Zem Priests Emerge *Isis is the Naturit of this day.*

Anything you see will be good.

"The *Naturu* and *Naturitu* are pleased when they see the children of Geb sitting in their places."

January 27 DAY FIVE (Lost...)

Altar Offerings Day *Hapy is the Natur of this day.*

Anyone who approaches on this day, anger will come of it.

"The majesty of Horus is sound when the Red One (*Wadjet*) sees his form."

January 28 DAY SIX ☉

Sixth Day *Star Of His Mothers the Natur of this day.*

Anyone seeing small cattle will die immediately.

"It is the going forth of the Red Star openly."

Feast of "Chewing Onions For Bast."

January 29 DAY SEVEN ☉☥☥☥

First Quarter Day *Qebsenuf is the Natur of this day.*

Pay attention to the fire. Smell sweet myrrh.
"In celebration, Min goes into his tent. Life! Prosperity! Health! The *Naturu* are joyous."

Feast of Min.

January 30 DAY EIGHT
Main Emergence *Ma'atef-f is the Natur of this day.*

(Lost...)
"The *Pot Natur* are in adoration when they see the Eye Of The Original Horus in its place. It is perfect in all its parts, 1/2, 1/4, 1/8, 1/16, 1/32, 1/64 in the counting for its master."

Monthly feast of Re. Counting the parts of the Wadjet eye.

(*Note*: the familar icon of the Horus Eye was used to represent the common fractions. Since Horus was the *Natur* of the integrity of unique identity, the whole that is the sum of its parts, each section of the Eye, or "fraction" of the whole, was a symbol for a particular fraction.)

January 31 DAY NINE
Hidden One *He Does The Talking is the Natur of this day.*

Do not go out in the darkness once Re sets.
(Lost...)

February 1 DAY TEN
He Who Protects His Royal Name
He Makes A Name Himself is the Natur of this day.

Anything you see will be good.
"It is the day of introducing the Great Ones of Re to the whole *Wadjet*."

February 2 DAY ELEVEN
Great Lady Protector *Sekhmet is the Naturit of this day.*

(Lost...)
(Lost...)

February 3 DAY TWELVE
Making Love *Bring The Advocate is the Natur of this day.*

Do not watch dancers or anyone who is digging the ground.
"As to him who sees dancing or digging on any roads, do not approach the majesty of *Montu*. Do not dance or dig this day."

Monthly feast of Re.

February 4 DAY THIRTEEN
Approach of Re *Re is the Natur of this day.*

Avoid any wind this day. Do not sail on any wind this day.
"This day they conduct Osiris on this boat to *Ibtu*."

Feast of Nut.

February 5 DAY FOURTEEN
Progress Of The Ba *Consider The Ba is the Natur of this day.*
Do not be courageous this day.
"Re's followers go about the *Naturu* in search of Sut's confederates."

February 6 DAY FIFTEEN
Half Month Day *Amauai is the Natur of this day.*
(Lost...)
"It is a great day in the eastern horizon, where the followers of the *Naturu* who are in their Houses receive their instructions before the majesty of the Great One of the Two Horizons."

February 7 DAY SIXTEEN
Two Houses Fight *Horus and Sut are the Naturu of this day.*
Rejoice.
"This day Khepry hears the words of his followers. Every town rejoices."
Procession of Khepry.

February 8 DAY SEVENTEEN
Second Arrival Day *Re is the Natur of this day.*
(Lost...)
"Sut, son of Nut, emerges to disturb the Great Ones who restrain him in his town. Now these *Naturu* who recognized him drive away his followers. None of them remain."
Procession of Sut.

February 9 DAY EIGHTEEN
Moon Day *Ahi is the Natur of this day.*
Do not approach in the morning. Do not wash yourself with water.
"Do not approach when the majesty of Re emerges."

February 10 DAY NINETEEN
Hear His Commands *Bring His Mother is the Natur of this day.*
Anything you see will be good.
"The majesty of Re emerges in his Sun Boat to feast in *Innu*."
Feast of Re.

February 11 DAY TWENTY
Offering Meat *Opener Of The Way is the Natur of this day.*
The soul of anyone who passes rebels will suffer from weakness for eternity. Do not work.
"He casts down those who rebel against their master."

February 12 DAY TWENTY-ONE
Apru's Day *Inpu is the Natur of this day.*
Do not go out of your house on any road this day.
(Lost...)

February 13 DAY TWENTY-TWO
Passing Of Sopdut *Nai is the Natur of this day.*
Anyone born this day will not live.
"It is the day of slaying the children of rebellion."

February 14 DAY TWENTY-THREE
Last Quarter Day *Na-Ur is the Natur of this day.*
(Lost...)
"It is the day of offering foodstuff in *Ibtu* to the spirits."

February 15 DAY TWENTY-FOUR
Darkness *Nekhbet is the Naturit of this day.*
Do not say Sut's name. Should you forget and do so, you will have quarreling in your home forever.
"It is the day Sut rises up against Osiris."

February 16 DAY TWENTY-FIVE
Departing *Shem is the Natur of this day.*
Do not eat anything which is on or which swims in the water.
"It is the day they cut the tongue from Sobek."
(*Note*: the tongue is is for the murder of the Ferryman *Inty*.)

February 17 DAY TWENTY-SIX (Lost...)
House Of Appearance *Ma'atef-f is the Natur of this day.*
(Lost to papyrus damage.)

February 18 DAY TWENTY-SEVEN
Funerary Offerings *Khnumu is the Natur of this day.*
Do not go out until Re sets.
"Sekhmet is angry in the land of *Temhu* (or *tenu*) Behold! She went about walking."
Feast of Sekhmet destroying mankind.

February 19 DAY TWENTY-EIGHT
Jubilee Of The Sky *Nut is the Naturit of this day.*
Anything you see will be good.
(Lost...)

February 20 DAY TWENTY-NINE
Weakness *Utettef-f is the Natur of this day.*
It will be pleasant on this day. Offer myrrh to your sky *Naturu*.

"The *Naturu* are pleased when they give praise to Osiris. There is incense on the fire."

Adoration of Beautiful Being (Osiris.)
Sky Feast.

February 21 DAY THIRTY ☉𓋹𓋹𓋹
Awaken *Horus Advocates For Him is the Natur of this day.*

Make offerings to all the *Naturu.*

"Last day. Make offerings to Ptah-Sokar-Osir. (Lost...) Re, Lord of the Two Lands of *Innu* this day. Offer to all the *Naturu* on this day.

House Of Re. House Of Osiris. House Of Horus."

Offerings to Re, Osiris, Horus, Ptah, and Sokar.

PACHONS

February 22 to March 23

Khonsu is the Natur.

First Month of *Shomu*

February 22 DAY ONE

New Month Day *Thoth is the Natur of this day.*

Anything you see this day will be good.

"Feast of Horus, Son of Isis, and his followers this day."

First Day of Pachons.

Feast for Re, Horus, and Renemutet.

February 23 DAY TWO

New Crescent Day *Horus is the Natur of this day.*

Do not sail on this day in any wind.

(Lost...)

February 24 DAY THREE

Arrival Day *Osiris is the Natur of this day.*

Anything you see this day will be good.

(Lost...)

February 25 DAY FOUR

Zem Priests Emerge *Isis is the Naturit of this day.*

Do not go out of your house.

"It is the day of (Lost...) follow Horus this day."

February 26 DAY FIVE

Altar Offerings Day *Hapy is the Natur of this day.*

Anyone who goes out of his house will waste away from disease until he dies.

"This day is the Feast Of The Golden *Ba* (*Ba* Of Osiris)."

Feast of Sexual fertility of Min.

February 27 DAY SIX

Sixth Day *Star Of His Mother is the Natur of this day.*

Anything you see this day will be good.

"The Great Ones and their followers arrive from the House Of Re, rejoicing as they receive the *Wadjet* Eye."

Harvest festival.

Festival of the Great One of the House of Re.

February 28 DAY SEVEN

First Quarter Day *Qebsennuf is the Natur of this day.*

Every heart is glad. The land is happy.

"The crew follows Horus into the foreign land. There he examines the list, and smites those who rebelled against their master."

March 1 DAY EIGHT (Lost...)

Main Emergence *Ma'atet-f is the Natur of this day.*

Anything you see this day will be good.

(Lost...)

Festival of Isis.

March 2 DAY NINE

Hidden One *He Does The Talking is the Natur of this day.*

Anything you see this day will be good.

(Lost...)

Monthly feast of Re.

March 3 DAY TEN

He Protects His Royal Name

He Makes His Name Himself is the Natur of this day.

"The White One Of Heaven goes upstream to search among those who rebelled gainst their master in the Delta."

(Lost...)

Festival Of Clothing Anubis.

March 4 DAY ELEVEN (Lost...)

Great Lady Protector *Sekhmet is the Naturit of this day.*

(Lost...)

(Lost...)

March 5 DAY TWELVE

Making Love *Bring The Advocate is the Natur of this day.*

(Day lost...)

March 6 DAY THIRTEEN (Lost...)

Approach Of Re *Re is the Natur of this day.*

(Day lost to papyrus damage...)

Monthly feast of Re.

March 7 DAY FOURTEEN

Progress Of The Ba *Consider The Ba is the Natur of this day.*

"(Lost...) Apep in (lost...) They cut the tongue of the enemy of Sobek."

The day of cutting out the tongue of Sobek, the crocodile Natur.

March 8 DAY FIFTEEN (Lost...)

Half Month Day *Armauai is the Natur of this day.*

(Day lost to papyrus damage...)

March 9 DAY SIXTEEN

Two Houses Fight *Horus and Sut are the Naturu of this day.*

Anyone born this day will die. Do not go out of your house until

Re sets in the horizon.
(Lost...)

March 10 DAY SEVENTEEN
Second Arrival Day *Re is the Natur of this day.*
Anything you see this day will be good..
(Lost...)

March 11 DAY EIGHTEEN
Moon Day *Ahi is the Natur of this day.*
Anything you see this day will be good.
"The *Pot Natur* is joyous and the crew of Re makes merry."

Day of joy for Re and his Pot Natur.

March 12 DAY NINETEEN
Hear His Commands *Bring His Mother is the Natur of this day.*
(Lost...)
"This day Thoth counts in the presence of Re, who hears the Great One Of Reality."

The day of the counting of Thoth.

March 13 DAY TWENTY
Offering Meat *Opener Of The Ways is the Natur of this day.*
(Lost...)
"*Ma'at* judges in the presence of the *Naturu* in the island sanctuary of Sekhmet (Letopolis,) who become angered.
The Lord Horus changes it."

Lady Ma'at judges souls.

March 14 DAY TWENTY-ONE
Apru's Day *Anubis (Inpu) is the Natur of this day.*
(Lost...)
"Vomit up the things that returned with the boat, so that no follower of Re remains who was in attendance."

March 15 DAY TWENTY-TWO
Passing Of Sopdut *Nai is the Natur of this day.*
Anyone born on this day will live to old age.
(Lost...)

March 16 DAY TWENTY-THREE
Last Quarter Day *Na-Ur is the Natur of this day.*
Anything you see this day will be good.
(Lost...)

March 17 DAY TWENTY-FOUR (Lost...)
Darkness *Nekhbet is the Naturit of this day.*
(Day lost to papyrus damage...)

March 18 DAY TWENTY-FIVE (Lost...)
Departing *Shem is the Natur of this day.*
(Day lost to papyrus damage...)

March 19 DAY TWENTY-SIX
House Of Appearances *Ma'atef-f is the Natur of this day.*
Anything you see this day will be good.
(Lost...)

March 20 DAY TWENTY-SEVEN
Funerary Offerings *Khnum is the Natur of this day.*
(Lost...)

March 21 DAY TWENTY-EIGHT
Jubilee Of The Sky *Nut is the Naturit of this day.*
Anything you see this day will be good. (Lost...)
The Spring Equinox.

March 22 DAY TWENTY-NINE (Lost...)
Weakness *Utettef-f is the Natur of this day.*
(Day lost to papyrus damage...)

March 23 DAY THIRTY
Awaken *Horus Advocates For Him is the Natur of this day.*
(Lost...)
"Last Day (lost...)
House Of Re, House Of Osiris, House Of Horus."
Celebrations for Re, Osiris, and Horus.

PAONY

March 24 to April 22

Khenthy is the Natur. Second Month of *Shomu*

March 24 DAY ONE

New Month Day *Thoth is the Natur of this day.*

(Lost...)

The Month of Paony begins. Feasts for Re, Horus and Bast.

March 25 DAY TWO (omission)

New Crescent Day *Horus is the Natur of this day.*

(omission...)

"The hearts of the *Naturu* listen very well. The crew of Re is in celebration."

Holy to Re and his followers.

March 26 DAY THREE

Arrival Day *Osiris is the Natur of this day.*

(Lost...)

"The followers of Re fix this day in heaven as a feast."

March 27 DAY FOUR

Zem Priests Emerge *Isis is the Naturit of this day.*

Anything you see this day will be good.

(Lost...)

March 28 DAY FIVE

Altar Offerings Day *Hapy is the Natur of this day.*

Shout at no one on this day.

"That which Geb and Nut have done is counted in the presence of the *Naturu.*"

March 29 DAY SIX (omission...)

Sixth Day *Star Of His Mother is the Natur of this day.*

(Lost...)

"Horus goes to avenge what was done against his father, and to question the followers of his father Osiris on this day."

March 30 DAY SEVEN

First Quarter Day *Qebsennuf is the Natur of this day.*

While Re is in the horizon (during waking time) do not go out of your house.

"It is the day that the executioners of Sekhmet (*khatbu*) count by names."

Feast Of The Wadjet Eye.

March 31 DAY EIGHT
Main Emergence *Ma'atet-f is the Natur of this day.*
Make a holiday for Lord Re and his followers on this day. Make this a good day.
(Lost...)

April 1 DAY NINE
Hidden One *He Does The Talking is the Natur of this day.*
Make different kinds of incense from sweet herbs for the followers of Re. This will please him today.
(Lost...)

Feast of Re.

April 2 DAY TEN
He Protects His Royal Name
He Makes His Name Himself is the Natur of this day.
Those born on this day will be noble.
(Lost...)

April 3 DAY ELEVEN
Great Lady Protector *Sekhmet is the Naturit of this day.*
Do not sail this day. Anyone who sails on the river won't live.
"It is the day of catching birds and fish by the followers of Re."

April 4 DAY TWELVE
Making Love *Bring The Advocate is the Natur of this day.*
Anything you see this day will be good.

April 5 DAY THIRTEEN
Approach Of Re *Re is the Natur of this day.*
Make offerings.
"Feast of the *Wadjet* Eye. Her followers are also in festival when singing and chanting on the day of offering incense and all manner of sweet herbs."

Feast Of Re.

April 6 DAY FOURTEEN
Progress Of The Ba *Consider The Ba is the Natur of this day.*
Anything you see this day will be good.
(Lost...)

April 7 DAY FIFTEEN
Half Month Day *Armauai is the Natur of this day.*
Do not judge yourself. It is the day of fighting (lost...) their rebellion.
(Lost to papyrus damage...)

April 8 DAY SIXTEEN
Two Houses Fight *Horus and Sut are the Naturu of this day.*
Anyone born this day will die as a great magistrate to all people. (Lost...)

April 9 DAY SEVENTEEN
Second Arrival Day *Re is the Natur of this day.*
Do not go out. Do not do anything on this day. Do no work. (Lost...)

April 10 DAY EIGHTEEN
Moon Day *Ahi is the Natur of this day.*
Do not eat the meat of lions. Any who smell the stench of death and has a skin, will never be healthy.
"It is the day of the emergence of *Khenty (Osiris)* from the *Naturu's* house, when he goes on to the august mountain."

Feast of Osiris.

April 11 DAY NINETEEN
Hear His Commands *Bring His Mother is the Natur of this day.*
If you see a lion, he will pass away.
"The *Pot Natur* sails throughout the land. There are many departures of the *Pot Natur* throughout the land on this day. This day is day of the judging of the Great Ones."

April 12 DAY TWENTY
Offering Meat *Opener Of The Ways is the Natur of this day.*
Do not sail in any wind this day.
"Many die because they come on an unfavorable wind."

April 13 DAY TWENTY-ONE
Apru's Day *Inpu is the Natur of this day.*
Stay in until Re appears on his horizon.
"It is the day of the living-legs, the children of Nut."

Feast of the Children of Nut.

(*Note*: The Yearly Five Days are the children of Nut, her limbs, as in a family tree.)

April 14 DAY TWENTY-TWO
Passing Of Sopdut *Nai is the Natur of this day.*
Do not go out on this day.
"There is a disturbance below, and turmoil among the *Naturu* of the *Ka*-shrines on this day, when Shu finds fault with the Great Ones of infinity."

April 15 DAY TWENTY-THREE ☉♁♁♁
Last Quarter Day *Na-Ur is the Natur of this day.*
(Lost...)
"The crew rest when they see the enemy of their master."

April 16 DAY TWENTY-FOUR ☉♁♁♁
Darkness *Nekhbet is the Naturit of this day.*
Anything you see this day will be good.
(Lost to papyrus damage...)

April 17 DAY TWENTY-FIVE ☉♁♁♁
Departing *Shem is the Natur of this day.*
(Lost...)
"The *Akhet* Eye pacifies everything and everyone. It is pleasant to the *Naturu*."

Holy to Re.

April 18 DAY TWENTY-SIX ☉
House Of Appearances *Ma'atef-f is the Natur of this day.*
(Lost...)
"Lady Net goes forth walking in the flood this day, searching for the things of Sobek. If a lion sees them, he will pass away."

Procession of Lady Net.

April 19 DAY TWENTY-SEVEN ☉
Funerary Offerings *Khnum is the Natur of this day.*
Do not work on this day.
"There is fighting among the *Naturu* this day, with the cutting of heads and the binding of the necks. "

April 20 DAY TWENTY-EIGHT ☉♁♁♁
Jubilee Of The Sky *Nut is the Naturit of this day.*
Act in acordance with the events of the day.
"It is the day of purifying things and making offerings in the House Of Osiris."

Day of purifying all things.

April 21 DAY TWENTY-NINE (Lost...)
Weakness *Utettef-f is the Natur of this day.*
Anything you see this day will be good.
(Lost to papyrus damage...)

April 22 DAY THIRTY ☉♁♁♁
Awaken *Horus Advocates For Him is the Natur of this day.*
(Lost...)
"Last Day. The emergence of Osiris in the form of Shu, with the

intention of bringing back the *Wadjet* Eye. This day Thoth appeases her.
House Of Re. House Of Osiris. House of Horus."

Holy to Thoth. Feast of Re.

EPIPY

April 23 to May 22

Ipt is the Natur.

Third Month of *Shomu*

April 23 DAY ONE ☉ (hieroglyphs)

New Month Day *Thoth is the Natur of this day.*

(Lost...)

"There is a great feast in the southern heaven for Hathor, Mistress Of Heaven, and everyone and everything are festive."

Month of Epipy begins.
Festivals to Hathor and Bast.
Day of the great feast of the southern heavens for Re.

April 24 DAY TWO ☉ (hieroglyphs)

New Crescent Day *Horus is the Natur of this day.*

(Lost...)

"The *Naturu* and *Naturitu* spend the day in festivity, and in great astonishment in the sacred House Of The *Naturu*."

The Naturitu feast in their Houses Of Life.

April 25 DAY THREE ☉ (hieroglyphs)

Arrival Day *Osiris is the Natur of this day.*

Do nothing on this day.

"The divine majesty is angered."

(*Note*: this refers to Hathor, in her form as the *Wadjet* Eye.)

April 26 DAY FOUR ☉ (hieroglyphs)

Zem Priests Emerge *Isis is the Naturit of this day.*

Anything you see this day will be good.

(Lost...)

April 27 DAY FIVE ☉ (hieroglyphs)

Altar Offerings Day *Hapy is the Natur of this day.*

Do not go out. Do not sail or proceed by boat. Do no work.

"It is the day of the departure of this *Naturit* (Hathor) to the place from where she came. The *Naturu* are downcast."

Hathor sails for Punt.

(*Note*: Feast of the Beautiful Reunion. Hathor's Boat, Mistress of Love, leaves Dendera and sails to Horus in Edfu. She visits the House Of the *Natur* Mut. On the second day she visits Anukis. On the third day she is joined by the local *Natur* of *Nehan* (a form of Horus.) She ends her travels at the great House Of Horus. Horus sets out in his boat to meet Anukis. The two statues are enshrined together for 14 days, then taken to the roof of the House Of the *Natur* to greet Re.)

April 28 DAY SIX ☉ (hieroglyphs)

Sixth Day *Star Of His Mother is the Natur of this day.*

Do not fight or make uproar in your house.
"Every House Of The *Naturit* (Hathor) is in like manner."

April 29 DAY SEVEN

First Quarter Day *Qebsennuf is the Natur of this day.*

(Lost...)
"The *Naturu* sail after the *Naturit* (Hathor.) There is great flame in front of them."

The other Naturu follow.

April 30 DAY EIGHT

Main Emergence *Ma'atet-f is the Natur of this day.*

Do not strike anyone. Do not beat anyone this day.
"This day the followers of the majesty of the *Naturit* are slaughtered."

May 1 DAY NINE

Hidden One *He Does The Talking is the Natur of this day.*

(Lost...)
"The *Naturu* are content and all are happy. Re is at peace with the *Akhet* Eye Of Horus. All the *Naturu* are in celebration this day."

May 2 DAY TEN

He Protects His Royal Name

He Makes His Name Himself is the Natur of this day.

(Lost...)
"Creating enmity (hostility) over the event. The *Naturu* who are in the shrine are sad."

Monthly feast of Re.

May 3 DAY ELEVEN

Great Lady Protector *Sekhmet is the Naturit of this day.*

Do not perform any rituals this day.
"Bring the Great Ones to the booth. Re makes known to them what he observed through the Eye of Horus The Elder. They bow their heads when they see the Eye of Horus being angry before Re."

May 4 DAY TWELVE

Making Love *Bring The Advocate is the Natur of this day.*

"Holiday (lost...) reception of Re. His followers are all festive." (Lost...)

May 5 DAY THIRTEEN

Approach Of Re *Re is the Natur of this day.*

(Lost...)
"The majesty of the *Naturu* sails west to see the beauty of Osiris."

May 6 DAY FOURTEEN

Progress Of The Ba *Consider The Ba is the Natur of this day.*

Do not burn in your house anything of burning flame, with its glow.

"On this day of the anger of the Eye of The Original Horus."

May 7 DAY FIFTEEN

Half Month Day *Armauai is the Natur of this day.*

Anything you see this day will be good. You will see every good thing in your house.

"This day Horus hears your words in the presence of all the *Naturu* and *Naturitu*."

Horus hears the supplications of the Natur.

May 8 DAY SIXTEEN

Two Houses Fight *Horus and Sut are the Naturu of this day.*

(Lost...)

"It is the day the majesty of Re in *Innu* sends *Ma'at* out to the shrine. The *Naturu* learn why he is angry. She is blamed."

Ma'at appears before Re.

May 9 DAY SEVENTEEN

Second Arrival Day *Re is the Natur of this day.*

(Lost...)

"The escape of the fugitive (Eye) and the *Naturu* are deprived of Re, who had come to hand the rebels over to them."

May 10 DAY EIGHTEEN

Moon Day *Ahi is the Natur of this day.*

Do not travel by road. Do not go out of your house. Anyone who is outside (lost...) the trampling of a bull.

"*Ma'at* and Re go forth in secret."

Ma'at and Re leave in secret.

May 11 DAY NINETEEN

Hear His Commands *Bring His Mother is the Natur of this day.*

Do not embrace anyone a second time nor do any work.

(Lost...)

May 12 DAY TWENTY

Offering Meat *Opener Of The Ways is the Natur of this day.*

Do not go out on any road this day.

(Lost...).

May 13 DAY TWENTY-ONE ☉𓄤𓄤𓄤
Apru's Day *Inpu (Inpu) is the Natur of this day.*
Anything you see this day will be good.

May 14 DAY TWENTY-TWO ☉𓆱𓆱𓆱
Passing Of Sopdut *Nai is the Natur of this day.*
Do not look at anyone with fevers or rashes. Do not watch anyone digging this day.
"It is the day of the coming of Sepa of In to *Innu*."

(*Note*: *Sepa* is a reptile-*Natur*, chief of the seven spirits who guard Osiris. Innu or the limestone quarries opposite Memphis are referred to, the location now of a village called *Tura*.)

May 15 DAY TWENTY-THREE ☉𓆱𓆱𓆱
Last Quarter Day *Na-Ur is the Natur of this day.*
Anyone born on this day will die.
"It is the day of quarrelling and reproaching by Osiris."

May 16 DAY TWENTY-FOUR ☉𓄤𓄤𓄤
Darkness *Nekhbet is the Naturit of this day.*
(Lost...)
"It is the day of (lost...) children of rebellion. The *Naturu* have slain them because he came and then he sailed south."

May 17 DAY TWENTY-FIVE ☉𓄤𓆱𓄤
Departing *Shem is the Natur of this day.*
Do not go out at midday.
"The great enemy (Apep) is in the House Of Life Of Sekhmet."

May 18 DAY TWENTY-SIX ☉𓄤𓄤𓄤
House Of Appearances *Ma'atef-f is the Natur of this day.*
Anything you see this day will be good.
(Lost...)

May 19 DAY TWENTY-SEVEN ☉𓆱𓆱𓆱
Funerary Offerings *Khnum is the Natur of this day.*
(Lost...)
"It is the day of sailing on the river, and of overthrowing the enclosure wall."

May 20 DAY TWENTY-EIGHT ☉𓆱𓆱𓆱
Jubilee Of The Sky *Nut (The Sky) is the Naturit of this day.*
(Lost...)
"Creating misery and bringing fear into agreement with the habit of this time of year."

(*Note*: this passage refers to the Nile's lowest water levels of the year)

May 21 DAY TWENTY-NINE ☉♁♁♁
Weakness *Utettef-f is the Natur of this day.*
It is the day of feeding the *Naturit* and her followers.
"This day is the feast of Mut in *Sheta*."
Festival of Mut. Sky feast.

May 22 DAY THIRTY ☉♁♁♁
Awaken *Horus Advocates For Him is the Natur of this day.*
Anything you see this day will be good.
"Last Day. House Of Re. House Of Osiris. House Of Horus."
Ceremony of Horus Of The Winged Disk.

MESORE

May 23 to June 21

Final Month of *Shomu*, Last Month of the Year

Horus Of The Two Horizons is the Natur.

May 23 DAY ONE

New Month Day *Thoth is the Natur of this day.*

This day is the feast of Osiris.

"Send *Aabt*-offerings to those who are in heaven. All the *Naturu* and *Naturitu* spend the day in feasting Osiris."

Month of Mesore begins. Festivals for Re.

May 24 DAY TWO

New Crescent Day *Horus is the Natur of this day.*

(Lost...)

"*Ma'at* (lost...) and all the *Naturu* perform the rites as one who is in heaven."

Sacred to Ma'at.

May 25 DAY THREE

Arrival Day *Osiris is the Natur of this day.*

Do not go out, and do nothing on this day.

"The majesty of this *Naturit* proceeds to *Innu*. A feast was made on this day."

Feast of Raet. Feast of Hathor as Sopdut.

May 26 DAY FOUR

Zem Priests Emerge *Isis is the Naturit of this day.*

(Lost...)

"It is the day of the procession of *Sopdut* and her followers, being in a state of youth and remaining in the course of the day. She will never be able to find a living soul...(lost...)'

Processional Day of Sopdut.

May 27 DAY FIVE

Altar Offerings Day *Hapy is the Natur of this day.*

Anything you see this day will be good.

"*Maner* (possible the name of Min's sanctuary) is in festivity, Min being at *Khent-min*."

Day of the appearance of Min.

(*Note*: *Khent-min* was known as Panopolis, and is now called *Akhmim*.)

May 28 DAY SIX

Sixth Day *Star Of His Mother is the Natur of this day.*

Do nothing on this day.

"Send the restored one into Mouth Of The Far Horizon, and hide the mysteries of the conspirators on this day."

May 29 DAY SEVEN
First Quarter Day *Qebsennuf is the Natur of this day.*
Any who draws near him will be trampled by a bull and die.
"The Dead One goes about the Heh and appears on Earth."
Inpu travels to the necropolis.

May 30 DAY EIGHT
Main Emergence *Ma'atet-f is the Natur of this day.*
Anything you see this day will be good.
(Lost...)
Wadjet's Summer Solstice.

May 31 DAY NINE
Hidden One *He Does The Talking is the Natur of this day.*
Those born today will possess noble honor.
(Lost...)

June 1 DAY TEN
He Protects His Royal Name
He Makes His Name Himself is the Natur of this day.
(Lost...)
"This day the crew in the Delta is repulsed. It is the day the Eye of Re enters the horizon when he sees his beauty."
Monthly feast of Re. Holiday of Inpu.

June 2 DAY ELEVEN
Great Lady Protector *Sekhmet is the Naturit of this day.*
Do not perform any rituals this day.
"There is disturbance in the presence of Re's followers and the driving back of the confederates of Sut into the eastern country."

June 3 DAY TWELVE
Making Love *Bring The Advocate is the Natur of this day.*
(Lost...)
"There is joy throughout the whole world on this day. The hearts of those in the shrine are happy."

June 4 DAY THIRTEEN
Approach Of Re *Re is the Natur of this day.*
(Lost...)
"It is a holiday because of defending the son of Osiris. (Lost...) at the portal by Sut."
Feast of the followers of Horus.

June 5 DAY FOURTEEN
Progress Of The Ba *Consider The Ba is the Natur of this day.*

(Lost...)

"Establish her throne and hall (lost...) the *Naturu's* portal for the first time on this day."

June 6 DAY FIFTEEN
Half Month Day *Armauai is the Natur of this day.*

(Lost...)

"Re emerges on this day to appease Nun (lost...) in his cavern, in the presence of his followers and the *Pot Natur* of the Evening Boat Of The Sun."

Re emerges to honor Nun.

June 7 DAY SIXTEEN
Two Houses Fight *Horus and Sutekh are the Naturu of this day.*

Ritually give water to those ancestors who are in the West.

"(Lost...) *Pot Natur* of the West. It is pleasant to your divine Father and Mother who are in the *Heh.*"

June 8 DAY SEVENTEEN
Second Arrival Day *Re is the Natur of this day.*

Anything you see this day will be good. (Lost...)

June 9 DAY EIGHTEEN
Moon Day *Ahi is the Natur of this day.*

Do not go out during the morning. Any lions that go out will be blind and will not live.

"The crew who is leading the rebels. If any lion goes out on top of the Earth this day, he will go blind, and they say he will not live."

June 10 DAY NINETEEN
Hear His Commands *Bring His Mother is the Natur of this day.*

Feast your nome *Naturu.* Placate your spirits.

"Appease your spirit, for the *Wadjet* Eye of Horus has returned complete. Nothing is missing from it."

Day of the return of the complete Eye of Re (Wadjet eye).

June 11 DAY TWENTY
Offering Meat *Opener Of The Ways is the Naturit of this day.*

Kill no *inhy*-reptiles this day.

"It is the day of the purification and transformation of the noble ones. There is silence on Earth because of it, to appease the *Wadjet* Eye."

(*Note*: *inhy*-reptiles protect the dead. Killing one would be killing a divine creature.)

June 12 DAY TWENTY-ONE
Apru's Day *Inpu is the Natur of this day.*
Anything you see this day will be good.
(Lost...)

June 13 DAY TWENTY-TWO
Passing Of Sopdut *Nai is the Natur of this day.*
(Lost...)
"The feast of *Inpu*, who is on his mountain this day. The children of Geb and Nut spend the day in festivity, which is a holiday after the good bath of the *Naturu*."
Inpu feasts with the children of Nut and Geb.

June 14 DAY TWENTY-THREE
Last Quarter Day *The Original (Ur) is the Natur of this day.*
Eat no bread and drink no beer this day. Do not taste bread or beer.
"Because of what was done before him who rebelled against his master on this day."

June 15 DAY TWENTY-FOUR
Darkness *Nekhbet is the Naturit of this day.*
Make offerings to Re. Make a holiday in your house this day.
"Make *aabet*-offerings to the *Naturu* in the presence of Re."

June 16 DAY TWENTY-FIVE
Departing *Shem is the Natur of this day.*
(Lost...)
"The *Naturu* are established in front of the crew of Re, who is happy in the *Hiwet*-desert."

June 17 DAY TWENTY-SIX
House Of Appearances *Ma'atef-f is the Natur of this day.*
Stay in at midday. Do not go out of your house at midday.
"The *Naturu* sail with all winds. (Lost...)"

June 18 DAY TWENTY-SEVEN
Funerary Offerings *Khnum is the Natur of this day.*
Do not do anything this day.
(Lost...)

June 19 DAY TWENTY-EIGHT
Jubilee Of The Sky *Nut is the Naturit of this day.*
Anything you see this day will be good.
"(Lost...) feast of Min."
Feast day of Min.

June 20 DAY TWENTY-NINE ☉♁♁♁
Weakness *Utetteff is the Natur of this day.*

(Lost...)

'There is a holiday in the House Of Sokar, in the estate of Ptah. Those who are in his estate are in great festivity, being healthy ... (lost...)"

Feast in the House Of Life of Sokar.
Feast of Ptah.

June 21 DAY THIRTY ☉♁♁♁
Awaken *Horus Advocates For Him is the Natur of this day.*

Rites performed or anyone born on this day, or anything done this day, will be good all year. Make numerous offerings, and sing this day.

"Last Day. Anything that comes from the estate of Ptah will be good. House Of Re. House Of Osiris. House Of Horus."

Birthday Of Re.
Final Day Of The Year.

Summer Solstice.

THE ANCIENT HOROSCOPE AT A GLANCE

June 22 *The Pure One*	☉☥☥☥ **Lord Osiris is born.**
June 23 *Powerful Is The Heart*	☉☥☥☥ **Lord Horus The Original is born.**
June 24 *Powerful Of Arm*	☉☥☥☥ **Lord Sut is born.**
June 25 *He Who Makes Terror*	☉☥☥☥ **Lady Isis is born.**
June 26 *The Child Who Is In His Nest*	☉☥☥☥ **Lady Of The House is born.**

June 27	DAY ONE	
June 28	DAY TWO	
June 29	DAY THREE	
June 30	DAY FOUR	
July 1	DAY FIVE	
July 2	DAY SIX	
July 3	DAY SEVEN	
July 4	DAY EIGHT	
July 5	DAY NINE	
July 6	DAY TEN	
July 7	DAY ELEVEN	
July 8	DAY TWELVE	
July 9	DAY THIRTEEN	
July 10	DAY FOURTEEN	(Lost...)
July 11	DAY FIFTEEN	
July 12	DAY SIXTEEN	
July 13	DAY SEVENTEEN	
July 14	DAY EIGHTEEN	
July 15	DAY NINETEEN	
July 16	DAY TWENTY	
July 17	DAY TWENTY-ONE	
July 18	DAY TWENTY-TWO	
July 19	DAY TWENTY-THREE	
July 20	DAY TWENTY-FOUR	
July 21	DAY TWENTY-FIVE	
July 22	DAY TWENTY-SIX	
July 23	DAY TWENTY-SEVEN	
July 24	DAY TWENTY-EIGHT	
July 25	DAY TWENTY-NINE	
July 26	DAY THIRTY	

July 27	DAY ONE	
July 28	DAY TWO	(omission)
July 29	DAY THREE	
July 30	DAY FOUR	
July 31	DAY FIVE	
August 1	DAY SIX	
August 2	DAY SEVEN	
August 3	DAY EIGHT	
August 4	DAY NINE	
August 5	DAY TEN	
August 6	DAY ELEVEN	
August 7	DAY TWELVE	
August 8	DAY THIRTEEN	
August 9	DAY FOURTEEN	
August 10	DAY FIFTEEN	
August 11	DAY SIXTEEN	
August 12	DAY SEVENTEEN	
August 13	DAY EIGHTEEN	
August 14	DAY NINETEEN	
August 15	DAY TWENTY	
August 16	DAY TWENTY-ONE	
August 17	DAY TWENTY-TWO	
August 18	DAY TWENTY-THREE	
August 19	DAY TWENTY-FOUR	
August 20	DAY TWENTY-FIVE	
August 21	DAY TWENTY-SIX	
August 22	DAY TWENTY-SEVEN	
August 23	DAY TWENTY-EIGHT	
August 24	DAY TWENTY-NINE	
August 25	DAY THIRTY	

August 26	DAY ONE	𓇳𓄤𓄤𓄤
August 27	DAY TWO	𓇳𓄤𓄤𓄤
August 28	DAY THREE	𓇳𓄤𓄤𓄤
August 29	DAY FOUR	𓇳𓂚𓂚𓂚
August 30	DAY FIVE	𓇳𓂚𓂚𓂚
August 31	DAY SIX	𓇳𓄤𓄤𓄤
September 1	DAY SEVEN	𓇳𓄤𓄤𓄤
September 2	DAY EIGHT	(omission)
September 3	DAY NINE	𓇳𓂚𓂚𓂚
September 4	DAY TEN	𓇳𓄤𓄤𓄤
September 5	DAY ELEVEN	𓇳𓄤𓄤𓄤
September 6	DAY TWELVE	(omission)
September 7	DAY THIRTEEN	𓇳𓂚𓂚𓂚
September 8	DAY FOURTEEN	𓇳𓂚𓂚𓂚
September 9	DAY FIFTEEN	𓇳𓂚𓂚𓂚
September 10	DAY SIXTEEN	𓇳𓄤𓄤𓄤
September 11	DAY SEVENTEEN	𓇳𓄤𓄤𓄤
September 12	DAY EIGHTEEN	𓇳𓂚𓂚𓂚
September 13	DAY NINETEEN	𓇳𓂚𓂚𓂚
September 14	DAY TWENTY	𓇳𓂚𓂚𓂚
September 15	DAY TWENTY-ONE	𓇳𓄤𓄤𓄤
September 16	DAY TWENTY-TWO	(omission)
September 17	DAY TWENTY-THREE	𓇳𓂚𓂚𓂚
September 18	DAY TWENTY-FOUR	𓇳𓄤𓄤𓄤
September 19	DAY TWENTY-FIVE	𓇳𓄤𓄤𓄤
September 20	DAY TWENTY-SIX	𓇳𓄤𓄤𓄤
September 21	DAY TWENTY-SEVEN	𓇳𓄤𓄤𓄤
September 22	DAY TWENTY-EIGHT	𓇳𓄤𓄤𓄤
September 23	DAY TWENTY-NINE	𓇳𓄤𓄤𓄤
September 24	DAY THIRTY	𓇳𓄤𓄤𓄤

September 25	DAY ONE	𓇳𓄤𓄤𓄤
September 26	DAY TWO	𓇳𓄤𓄤𓄤
September 27	DAY THREE	𓇳𓂚𓂚𓂚
September 28	DAY FOUR	𓇳𓄤𓄤𓄤
September 29	DAY FIVE	𓇳𓄤𓄤𓄤
September 30	DAY SIX	𓇳𓂚𓂚𓂚
October 1	DAY SEVEN	𓇳𓂚𓂚𓂚
October 2	DAY EIGHT	𓇳𓄤𓄤𓄤
October 3	DAY NINE	𓇳𓄤𓄤𓄤
October 4	DAY TEN	𓇳𓄤𓄤𓄤
October 5	DAY ELEVEN	𓇳𓄤𓄤𓄤
October 6	DAY TWELVE	𓇳𓂚𓂚𓂚
October 7	DAY THIRTEEN	𓇳𓄤𓄤𓄤
October 8	DAY FOURTEEN	𓇳𓄤𓄤𓄤
October 9	DAY FIFTEEN	(Lost...)
October 10	DAY SIXTEEN	(Lost...)
October 11	DAY SEVENTEEN	𓇳𓂚𓂚𓂚
October 12	DAY EIGHTEEN	𓇳𓂚𓂚𓂚
October 13	DAY NINETEEN	𓇳𓂚𓂚𓂚
October 14	DAY TWENTY	𓇳𓂚𓂚𓂚
October 15	DAY TWENTY-ONE	𓇳𓂚𓂚𓄤
October 16	DAY TWENTY-TWO	𓇳𓄤𓄤𓄤
October 17	DAY TWENTY-THREE	𓇳𓄤𓄤𓂚
October 18	DAY TWENTY-FOUR	(Lost...)
October 19	DAY TWENTY-FIVE	(Lost...)
October 20	DAY TWENTY-SIX	𓇳𓄤𓄤𓄤
October 21	DAY TWENTY-SEVEN	𓇳𓄤𓄤𓂚
October 22	DAY TWENTY-EIGHT	𓇳𓂚𓂚𓂚
October 23	DAY TWENTY-NINE	𓇳𓂚𓂚𓂚
October 24	DAY THIRTY	𓇳𓄤𓄤𓄤

October 25	DAY ONE	
October 26	DAY TWO	(Lost...)
October 27	DAY THREE	(Lost...)
October 28	DAY FOUR	
October 29	DAY FIVE	
October 30	DAY SIX	
October 31	DAY SEVEN	
November 1	DAY EIGHT	
November 2	DAY NINE	
November 3	DAY TEN	
November 4	DAY ELEVEN	
November 5	DAY TWELVE	
November 6	DAY THIRTEEN	
November 7	DAY FOURTEEN	
November 8	DAY FIFTEEN	
November 9	DAY SIXTEEN	
November 10	DAY SEVENTEEN	
November 11	DAY EIGHTEEN	
November 12	DAY NINETEEN	
November 13	DAY TWENTY	
November 14	DAY TWENTY-ONE	
November 15	DAY TWENTY-TWO	
November 16	DAY TWENTY-THREE	
November 17	DAY TWENTY-FOUR	
November 18	DAY TWENTY-FIVE	(omission)
November 19	DAY TWENTY-SIX	
November 20	DAY TWENTY-SEVEN	
November 21	DAY TWENTY-EIGHT	
November 22	DAY TWENTY-NINE	
November 23	DAY THIRTY	

November 24	DAY ONE	
November 25	DAY TWO	
November 26	DAY THREE	
November 27	DAY FOUR	
November 28	DAY FIVE	
November 29	DAY SIX	
November 30	DAY SEVEN	
December 1	DAY EIGHT	
December 2	DAY NINE	
December 3	DAY TEN	
December 4	DAY ELEVEN	
December 5	DAY TWELVE	
December 6	DAY THIRTEEN	
December 7	DAY FOURTEEN	
December 8	DAY FIFTEEN	**(Lost...)**
December 9	DAY SIXTEEN	**(Lost...)**
December 10	DAY SEVENTEEN	
December 11	DAY EIGHTEEN	
December 12	DAY NINETEEN	
December 13	DAY TWENTY	
December 14	DAY TWENTY-ONE	**(omission)**
December 15	DAY TWENTY-TWO	
December 16	DAY TWENTY-THREE	
December 17	DAY TWENTY-FOUR	
December 18	DAY TWENTY-FIVE	
December 19	DAY TWENTY-SIX	**(Lost...)**
December 20	DAY TWENTY-SEVEN	**(omission)**
December 21	DAY TWENTY-EIGHT	
December 22	DAY TWENTY-NINE	
December 23	DAY THIRTY	

December 24	DAY ONE	
December 25	DAY TWO	
December 26	DAY THREE	(Lost...)
December 27	DAY FOUR	
December 28	DAY FIVE	
December 29	DAY SIX	
December 30	DAY SEVEN	
December 31	DAY EIGHT	
January 1	DAY NINE	
January 2	DAY TEN	
January 3	DAY ELEVEN	
January 4	DAY TWELVE	
January 5	DAY THIRTEEN	
January 6	DAY FOURTEEN	
January 7	DAY FIFTEEN	
January 8	DAY SIXTEEN	
January 9	DAY SEVENTEEN	
January 10	DAY EIGHTEEN	
January 11	DAY NINETEEN	(omission)
January 12	DAY TWENTY	
January 13	DAY TWENTY-ONE	(Lost...)
January 14	DAY TWENTY-TWO	
January 15	DAY TWENTY-THREE	
January 16	DAY TWENTY-FOUR	
January 17	DAY TWENTY-FIVE	(omission.)
January 18	DAY TWENTY-SIX	
January 19	DAY TWENTY-SEVEN	
January 20	DAY TWENTY-EIGHT	
January 21	DAY TWENTY-NINE	
January 22	DAY THIRTY	

January 23	DAY ONE	
January 24	DAY TWO	
January 25	DAY THREE	
January 26	DAY FOUR	
January 27	DAY FIVE	(Lost...)
January 28	DAY SIX	
January 29	DAY SEVEN	
January 30	DAY EIGHT	
January 31	DAY NINE	
February 1	DAY TEN	
February 2	DAY ELEVEN	
February 3	DAY TWELVE	
February 4	DAY THIRTEEN	
February 5	DAY FOURTEEN	
February 6	DAY FIFTEEN	
February 7	DAY SIXTEEN	
February 8	DAY SEVENTEEN	
February 9	DAY EIGHTEEN	
February 10	DAY NINETEEN	
February 11	DAY TWENTY	
February 12	DAY TWENTY-ONE	
February 13	DAY TWENTY-TWO	
February 14	DAY TWENTY-THREE	
February 15	DAY TWENTY-FOUR	
February 16	DAY TWENTY-FIVE	
February 17	DAY TWENTY-SIX	(Lost...)
February 18	DAY TWENTY-SEVEN	
February 19	DAY TWENTY-EIGHT	
February 20	DAY TWENTY-NINE	
February 21	DAY THIRTY	

February 22	DAY ONE	𓇳𓄤𓄤𓄤
February 23	DAY TWO	𓇳𓂚𓂚𓂚
February 24	DAY THREE	𓇳𓄤𓄤𓄤
February 25	DAY FOUR	𓇳𓂚𓂚𓂚
February 26	DAY FIVE	𓇳𓂚𓂚𓂚
February 27	DAY SIX	𓇳𓄤𓄤𓄤
February 28	DAY SEVEN	𓇳𓄤𓄤𓄤
March 1	DAY EIGHT	(Lost...)
March 2	DAY NINE	𓇳𓄤𓄤𓄤
March 3	DAY TEN	𓇳𓂚𓂚𓂚
March 4	DAY ELEVEN	(Lost...)
March 5	DAY TWELVE	𓇳𓂚𓂚𓂚
March 6	DAY THIRTEEN	(Lost...)
March 7	DAY FOURTEEN	𓇳𓂚𓂚𓂚
March 8	DAY FIFTEEN	(Lost...)
March 9	DAY SIXTEEN	𓇳𓂚𓂚𓂚
March 10	DAY SEVENTEEN	𓇳𓄤𓄤𓄤
March 11	DAY EIGHTEEN	𓇳𓄤𓄤𓄤
March 12	DAY NINETEEN	𓇳𓄤𓄤𓄤
March 13	DAY TWENTY	𓇳𓂚𓂚𓂚
March 14	DAY TWENTY-ONE	𓇳𓂚𓂚𓂚
March 15	DAY TWENTY-TWO	𓇳𓄤𓄤𓄤
March 16	DAY TWENTY-THREE	𓇳𓄤𓄤𓄤
March 17	DAY TWENTY-FOUR	(Lost...)
March 18	DAY TWENTY-FIVE	(Lost...)
March 19	DAY TWENTY-SIX	𓇳𓄤𓄤𓄤
March 20	DAY TWENTY-SEVEN	𓇳𓂚𓂚𓂚
March 21	DAY TWENTY-EIGHT	𓇳𓄤𓄤𓄤
March 22	DAY TWENTY-NINE	(Lost...)
March 23	DAY THIRTY	𓇳𓄤𓄤𓄤

March 24	DAY ONE	𓇳𓄤𓄤𓄤
March 25	DAY TWO	(omission)
March 26	DAY THREE	𓇳𓄤𓄤𓄤
March 27	DAY FOUR	𓇳𓂚𓂚𓂚
March 28	DAY FIVE	𓇳𓄤𓄤𓄤
March 29	DAY SIX	(omission...)
March 30	DAY SEVEN	𓇳𓂚𓂚𓂚
March 31	DAY EIGHT	𓇳𓄤𓄤𓄤
April 1	DAY NINE	𓇳𓄤𓄤𓄤
April 2	DAY TEN	𓇳𓂚𓂚𓂚
April 3	DAY ELEVEN	𓇳𓂚𓂚𓂚
April 4	DAY TWELVE	𓇳𓄤𓄤𓄤
April 5	DAY THIRTEEN	𓇳𓄤𓄤𓄤
April 6	DAY FOURTEEN	𓇳𓄤𓄤𓄤
April 7	DAY FIFTEEN	𓇳𓂚𓂚𓂚
April 8	DAY SIXTEEN	𓇳𓄤𓄤𓄤
April 9	DAY SEVENTEEN	𓇳𓂚𓂚𓂚
April 10	DAY EIGHTEEN	𓇳𓂚𓂚𓂚
April 11	DAY NINETEEN	𓇳𓂚𓂚𓂚
April 12	DAY TWENTY	𓇳𓂚𓂚𓂚
April 13	DAY TWENTY-ONE	𓇳𓂚𓂚𓄤
April 14	DAY TWENTY-TWO	𓇳𓂚𓂚𓂚
April 15	DAY TWENTY-THREE	𓇳𓄤𓄤𓄤
April 16	DAY TWENTY-FOUR	𓇳𓄤𓄤𓄤
April 17	DAY TWENTY-FIVE	𓇳𓄤𓄤𓄤
April 18	DAY TWENTY-SIX	𓇳𓂚𓂚𓂚
April 19	DAY TWENTY-SEVEN	𓇳𓂚𓂚𓂚
April 20	DAY TWENTY-EIGHT	𓇳𓄤𓄤𓄤
April 21	DAY TWENTY-NINE	(Lost...)
April 22	DAY THIRTY	𓇳𓄤𓄤𓄤

April 23	DAY ONE	𓇳𓄤𓄤𓄤
April 24	DAY TWO	𓇳𓄤𓄤𓄤
April 25	DAY THREE	𓇳𓂚𓂚𓂚
April 26	DAY FOUR	𓇳𓄤𓄤𓄤
April 27	DAY FIVE	𓇳𓂚𓂚𓂚
April 28	DAY SIX	𓇳𓂚𓂚𓂚
April 29	DAY SEVEN	𓇳𓂚𓂚𓂚
April 30	DAY EIGHT	𓇳𓂚𓂚𓂚
May 1	DAY NINE	𓇳𓄤𓄤𓄤
May 2	DAY TEN	𓇳𓂚𓂚𓂚
May 3	DAY ELEVEN	𓇳𓂚𓂚𓂚
May 4	DAY TWELVE	𓇳𓄤𓄤𓄤
May 5	DAY THIRTEEN	𓇳𓂚𓂚𓂚
May 6	DAY FOURTEEN	𓇳𓂚𓂚𓂚
May 7	DAY FIFTEEN	𓇳𓄤𓄤𓄤
May 8	DAY SIXTEEN	𓇳𓂚𓂚𓂚
May 9	DAY SEVENTEEN	𓇳𓂚𓂚𓂚
May 10	DAY EIGHTEEN	𓇳𓂚𓂚𓂚
May 11	DAY NINETEEN	𓇳𓂚𓂚𓂚
May 12	DAY TWENTY	𓇳𓂚𓂚𓂚
May 13	DAY TWENTY-ONE	𓇳𓄤𓄤𓄤
May 14	DAY TWENTY-TWO	𓇳𓂚𓂚𓂚
May 15	DAY TWENTY-THREE	𓇳𓂚𓂚𓂚
May 16	DAY TWENTY-FOUR	𓇳𓄤𓄤𓄤
May 17	DAY TWENTY-FIVE	𓇳𓄤𓂚𓄤
May 18	DAY TWENTY-SIX	𓇳𓄤𓄤𓄤
May 19	DAY TWENTY-SEVEN	𓇳𓂚𓂚𓂚
May 20	DAY TWENTY-EIGHT	𓇳𓂚𓂚𓂚
May 21	DAY TWENTY-NINE	𓇳𓄤𓄤𓄤
May 22	DAY THIRTY	𓇳𓄤𓄤𓄤

May 23	DAY ONE
May 24	DAY TWO
May 25	DAY THREE
May 26	DAY FOUR
May 27	DAY FIVE
May 28	DAY SIX
May 29	DAY SEVEN
May 30	DAY EIGHT
May 31	DAY NINE
June 1	DAY TEN
June 2	DAY ELEVEN
June 3	DAY TWELVE
June 4	DAY THIRTEEN
June 5	DAY FOURTEEN
June 6	DAY FIFTEEN
June 7	DAY SIXTEEN
June 8	DAY SEVENTEEN
June 9	DAY EIGHTEEN
June 10	DAY NINETEEN
June 11	DAY TWENTY
June 12	DAY TWENTY-ONE
June 13	DAY TWENTY-TWO
June 14	DAY TWENTY-THREE
June 15	DAY TWENTY-FOUR
June 16	DAY TWENTY-FIVE
June 17	DAY TWENTY-SIX
June 18	DAY TWENTY-SEVEN
June 19	DAY TWENTY-EIGHT
June 20	DAY TWENTY-NINE
June 21	DAY THIRTY

ANCIENT TIME AND THE EGYPTIAN CALENDAR

"Now are born Shu and Tafnut together with Nut. Now are born Geb, and Nut, and Osiris, and Horus Without Eyes, and Sut, and Isis, and Lady Of The House in the flesh. Each one is behind the one inside them. They are born. They multiply in this earth."

Eternal Skies

The earliest ancestors of Egypt's ancient civilization studied the day and night skies just as intently as they studied their own souls. They accumulated considerable knowledge and wisdom about both the daylight world and the dream-time of the night sky, and they established and maintained the long-enduring foundations of their empire with this wisdom.

In the Twenty-first Century, the sky is no longer just the mundane, light-washed display of constellations learned in childhood. Our own wisdom has transformed the night sky into a place once again as vast and mysterious as it was for the ancients. The astounding photographs of the cosmos from NASA and the Hubble Space Telescope Project have restored the value of the heavens as both mystery and source of wisdom, because the images and data gathered from the sky have revealed the deeper structures of reality and taken humankind's knowledge up to the instant of creation itself.

There is, once again, a living mythology about the relationship between the heavens and our daily life on Earth. We truly *are* made of "star stuff," and it *is* in heaven as it is on Earth.

It is easy, however, to become lost in so vast and stupendous a cosmos. A functioning mythology must provide a sense of place and purpose as well as a cosmic viewpoint. It would seem that the belief system of ancient Egypt is emerging as useful for our own times. The Western world's ancient European, pre-Roman sensibilities regarded the nature of the individual as inviolate. They believed in the struggle of honor versus obedience to blind faith. These are apparently finding a more detailed and practical application within the ethical field of the Egyptian's civilized world-view.

A fundamental and universal principle in every religion and mythology is that there is an invisible world or dimension supporting the visible world that we know. This is the divine plane of the Australian "Dream Time," and the *Duat* of ancient Egypt. It is Heaven and Hell in every religion. It is the modern "Twilight Zone," and the "Force."

This other dimension is as real as reality but of a wholly other kind, the reality behind all definitions and experiences of divine-as-counterpoint-to-physical. It is the source of *manna*, the reality behind the Grail, defined by and made manifest in the soul of every living thing.

The night sky above Egypt was that mystery of starlight and dreams through which the world and reality turned between sunset and dawn, the *Duat*, the dazzling display of the night sky, embodied in the star-spangled figure of Nut enfolding the world.

The calendar text translated by Diana Janeen Pierce has revealed a wealth of connections between their belief in that divine, eternal dimension and the everyday life of the ancient people of the Nile. The patterns of the sky and river that shaped their lives serve today as valid metaphors of the eternal patterns of human behavior and human nature.

The growing fascination with the world of ancient Egypt is evidence that the images, stories and mysteries of humankind's first civilization have the power to function as a living mythology today much as they did in the ancient world, teaching us how to walk through reality knowing that eternity is held carefully inside.

We have grown up with the image of ancient Egypt as a mysterious world obsessed with death and mummification. In truth their obsession was with life. In the western world today, we view death as separation from life, as being cut off from this world, possibly even as total extinction. In ancient Egypt, death was viewed as simply the next stage of life, the "Great Journey," the "Great Pathway," a journey not to a separate, unknown place. Death is the ultimate inward journey to the self, back to the divine source from which life sprang at birth.

Their culture was based on living a life worth taking with them on that journey into eternity. The beauty of their art, the practical and comfortable nature of their daily life were grounded in this belief that the perfect memory of the images and experiences of this life would accompany them on the journey to the next world. The stars in the night sky were believed to be good souls shining in eternity. The night sky itself was the visible presence of that next world beyond the horizon.

This belief provides for a profound change in morality and ethics as well. You cannot escape from yourself, not even in death. The memory of your actions and the consequences of your actions and choices will also accompany you on that journey.

At the core of Egyptian spiritual philosophy are Osiris, Re and Horus. The horoscope and the calendar play out the events of their mystery stories, the round of their interaction in the human community. Osiris is the personification of the divine and eternal soul that is at the center of each of us. The deceased person receives the title "Osiris" because death is the return to pure soul being. We put off the garment of flesh, store it away carefully in its tomb in gratitude for a lifetime of loyal service to the soul, and go on to eternity. Re is the light of conscious awareness, lighting the inner world of the soul just as the sun lights the outer world of reality. Horus represents the unique and divine identity of each individual soul defined in the field of time.

The rest of this book places the bewildering array of names and divine personalities into their proper relationship with the soul and the conscious awareness of the soul, the two fundamental concepts of their religion. Isis is the soul in love. Ptah, the craftsman, is the soul engaged in work, making the invisible plans of the soul visible, solid, real and functional. And so on.

I address the question of "multiple souls" in chapter five, "Why The Cat Has Nine Lives: The Essential Egyptian View Of The Self." The issue of "multiple souls" in most text books demonstrates the theological orientation of the person writing the testbook, not the ancient Egyptian belief. There was just the one soul, that is Osiris. (The generic for soul is *Akh*, or *Khu*, depending on how a modern scholar decides to pronounce the stork hieroglyph.) The other terms are psychological in nature, defining the layers of the soul's experience, such as the inner life that only you can know, your secret self inside (the *ba*) and the outer life in which others see you, knowing you in ways that you cannot (the *ka*). The ancient Egyptians defined the nature of the soul most carefully, and defined energy differently from substance. Our modern theological teaching does very little to define the nature of the soul. Indeed, we seem no longer capable of acknowledging the soul's existence. Maybe we have one. Maybe we do not. The Egyptians had no doubt, and that belief defined their world.

The Egyptians also had a resounding answer to the question of existence. Why are we here if not to talk to one another, to *be* together? The divine plane has the satisfaction of divine essence, divine presence, divine consciousness, eternal being, yet we find our souls compelled one by one in our billions over and over to return to this "vale of sorrows," to this realm of *Maya's* delusion where all things are sorrowful and time passes—and we can talk to one another.

The two greatest religious spheres of our modern world, the Buddhist religion and the Western religions, share the idea that life is a form of punishment or at least of a severe educational process. By contrast, life to the Egyptian mind possessed the supreme spiritual value of our living communion with each other.

Why do we give up the peace and connection of the divine plane in endless round to play the game of life? Is it because we have no choice? Or could it be precisely because we *do* have the choice? Could it be that life is *better* than eternity? In eternity, we yearn for time. While alive in space/time, we aim ourselves at eternity. The wheel of time, of being, turns on this forever movement from one plane to another and back.

These are two radically different views of life and bring with them radically different appreciations and values of existence. By the Egyptian point of view, the Internet is the most powerful spiritual expression of our time, for it brings us together not just by family or village, by city or state, but *globally*. Souls of a like mind can commune across inseparable distances. People who could never travel to meet soul mates can find them online, not just for sexual congress but for every kind of communion.

Apparently, it is not only naturally human to walk like an Egyptian, but to talk and to work like one as well.

OUT OF TIMELESSNESS AND INTO THE DAYLIGHT: THE ANCIENT EGYPTIAN CALENDAR

"An Introduction To The Beginning Of Infinity
And The End Of Eternity..."

(From the title of the calendar of ancient Egypt, *Cairo Papyrus.*)

Measuring time in seconds is a modern fascination, and the measure of a civilization's technological level can be made by the quality and quantity of its clocks. This has not always been so. Prehistoric humans lived by the circadian rhythms of their own bodies, the seasonal behavior-patterns of their animal companions, and by the regular transformations of their environment. Days and months, even years, could go by uncounted, especially when survival was moment by moment and one step in front of the other.

Civilization provides peace and security, but the price paid for that security is attention to a calendar, obedience to a clock. Hardly a day goes by that you do not find yourself needing to know, for one reason or another, the date of the month. It's easy to keep track of the days of the week, especially with the lure of the weekend drawing you forward, but the date of the month–that's trickier. A global industry has been developed, employing millions of people, to provide you with a paper or electronic calendar that orders the days of the year for you and keeps the date at your fingertips.

Our modern lifestyle ticks along in mutual progression because we have collectively agreed to live our individual lives by this annual pattern. Chinese New Year included, whatever variations we create within the multi-cultural strata of our lives, that 365.25-day round has been pinned down to the nanosecond, and the date printed on your business invoice will be accepted around the world.

We began as human beings, however, in a timeless world. Your day started when you and your family awoke, and it ended when the night became too dark for work. Until we had migrated far enough northward, we did not even need to worry too much about when to unpack our winter woolens. We followed the herds; we danced animal-patterned dances and we wondered at the sky.

The phases of the Moon were humankind's first time-keeper, the first calendar. No matter where our nomadic lifestyle took us across the face of the Earth, we could look up to the same face of the Moon. The patterns of the stars might change in confusing array and, if we wandered too close to the cold realms of the North Star even the Sun behaved strangely, but the Moon was always the Moon. The calendar made its first appearance in the late Paleolithic when women worked out the relationship between the Moon's phases and their own bodies, counting the days of the Moon's changes with nicks carved into pieces of antler, bone or shell. The days and months were yet unnamed and the years went by on their own, but we had begun to count time, keeping track of the regularly irregular Moon.

Plants grow according to the Sun's cycles, not the Moon's, so the round of the agricultural season—the gestation not of women but of the Earth—became the pattern of survival. The introduction of farming and the regular village life that grew up alongside the fields created fixed points on the horizon by which the patterns of the Sun could be marked. This solar calendar was more difficult to mark than the Moon's, however, with the result that we have always used both calendars side-by-side, interweaving the patterns and teaching ourselves complex mathematics along the way. In this new millennium, fewer of us live by the Moon's phases, yet we celebrate our holidays, religious and civil, by complicated algorithms of the Full Moon/New Moon cycle and the days of the week.

Ancient Egypt was the first great civilization of humankind and our first agricultural empire, and a cornerstone of their success was that they were the first to use the 365-day calendar. The inconsistencies in their method did allow the calendar to drift through the seasons, making it seem primitive compared to our own. Nevertheless, it was the most sophisticated of its era, and kept the Two Lands of Egypt ticking along comfortably for thousands of years.

The Roman calendar, by comparison, had an unfixed number of days, from 304 to 354 or 355. The Romans used only three day-names, *Kalendae*, *Idus*, and *Nonae*. The rest of the days were related to these by counting, for example, "three days before the *ides*." The calendar began on March 1, but only covered ten months.

Winter was evidently so discouraging a period that they did not even bother to count those days. It was not until the time of the Emperor Augustus, when Egyptian influence was strong in Rome, that the 365-day Egyptian-style system was adopted as the official Roman calendar. The modern world inherited the Egyptian calendar through this decree of Augustus.

Our seven-day week arose with Judaism and Christianity and the introduction of Sabbath days. The Egyptians did not have the concept of the Sabbath, since their system predates that religious movement. The Egyptian time-sense was dominated by the longer cycles of plant growth and animal husbandry, thus the round of thirty repeated day-names was an adequate time-span for ordering their social and spiritual interactions.

There was, in addition, regular attention in the temples to the patterns of the thirty-six decan stars, astronomical signs that changed regularly every ten days. This pattern became the basis of the ten-day market-week that remains in use in rural Africa even today. The stellar pattern of the decan stars was a backup measurement that made it possible to weave together the patterns of the Moon, the Sun and the Nile.

Whatever happened in the sky, the year in Egypt was controlled by the Nile. "Egypt is a gift of the Nile," has been said about the land for millennia, but the gift of the Nile can become a muddy, sticky curse without the organized cooperation of the people living by its bounty. The necessary spirit of cooperation was created by the beauty and majesty of their spiritual training. The organization was provided by the beauty of their calendar system and by the faithful, methodical work of the priests.

FIVE DAYS OUTSIDE OF TIME: THE YEARLY FIVE DAYS AND THE BIRTH OF THE DIVINE RECYCLING THE CIRCLE OF THE YEAR

In The Legend Of The Yearly Five Days, Nut is ready to give birth to the five divine children of Geb, but Re has discovered the prophecy (or curse) that Nut's children cannot be born on any day of the year. Thoth makes a bet with Ahi, the Moon, and they play a board game together. The actual game varies from era to era. Several board games were invented in Egypt, and such games were popular. The meaning of the game is the interaction of the Sun and Moon; the intellectual exercise of keeping count, planning and the throw of the dice, elements which are vital to calendar keeping and the horoscope. Thoth wins the game five times, winning each time a day "outside of time" in which one of Nut's children can be born. Osiris is first born, Isis second, with The Original Horus followed by Sut, and then Lady Of The House, *Nobt Hut.*

The dynamic tension by which Egyptian religion sustained the nation was a careful balance between the timelessness of the eternal, immortal dimension that existed "below the horizon," and the rounds of time in mortal existence "on top of the Earth."

The rich, black silt deposited by the Nile was the foundation of Egypt's farming wealth, and its annual return sustained the entire nation. This silt was considered to be the actual matter of Osiris' sacrificed body as it decayed, the manifest residue of divine existence, and it is during the Yearly Five Days that this divine substance pours into the world. The Yearly Five Days served a unique purpose, one which has no true counterpart in the Western world. The closest we can get is our regular New Year celebrations, reaching its most enthusiastic and dramatic expression recently in the events accompanying the start of the new millennium. Our deeply rooted cultural superstitions about New Year's Eve and New Year's Day are echoes of the spiritual value once attributed to the completion of the magical round of time.

The Egyptian Yearly Five Days ceremonies ended the year and started of the next year, but they were not really part of the annual round. These days were "outside of time," eternity pouring into time/space, the world dipping below the horizon to become saturated, once more, with divine energy.

The divine dimension of eternity enfolding the space/time dimension was envisioned as the sky enfolding the Earth, and the blazing star-field of the night sky was the divine counterpoint to daily life beneath the Sun. The horizon is the final dividing line between these two dimensions, between the eternal and the everyday. The world, indeed, turns on the wheel of the horizon, and the measure of time is in the enormous turning of that sky-sized clock-face around the fixed horizon.

Once a year, as the turning of that clock-face turns around to its beginning point, the horizon "tilts" into or passes through the divine dimension for five, magical, transforming days that are outside of time, outside of the everyday, and which function as the link between the dimensions. Divine energy pours into the world during those five days as water pours over the rim of a full bowl that has been tilted.

This is the energy that pours through the land of Egypt in the

Nile River, and through the body of every living person as the divine energy of their souls. These are the Yearly Five Days that are neither the end of the old year nor the beginning of the new, but the immersion of reality into the divine.

It is in these Yearly Five Days that we find the ancient faith. Within the span of these days the gods were born. Divine energy pours into the human sphere through this break in the circle that is not a break, but rather an intersection between dimensions, giving a spin to the spiritual gyroscope that maintained society's balance. Properly directed, this intersection provided the psychic, emotional, spiritual and living energies that sustained the round of the year ahead.

Osiris was *Khent Imentiu*, "Foremost Of The Westerners," and he gave a human shape to the divine dimension symbolized by the unreachable nature of the land to which the setting Sun descends "below the horizon." No matter how far you travel across the face of the Earth, the horizon moves with you, keeping you in the field of space/time. The land "below the horizon" was the ultimate metaphor of the experience of the internal territory of the psyche, the heart and the soul.

Returning to Osiris below the horizon was the ultimate inward withdrawal, and the ceremonies of the Yearly Five Days celebrated and established the outpouring of energy from that same source, filling the land with the stuff and substance of life- recycling death into new life in the circle of the year.

Even as the Yearly Five Days were a national celebration of religious belief, the very personal nature of that belief is shown in the name for the amulet created each year as part of the ending ceremony: "This charm is called *Self-dedication Contract*."

The ceremonies and rituals of these events were not performed in order to make the divine intersection happen. The Nile will flood with or without prayer and ritual. The human rituals were designed to focus this outpouring of spiritual energy into channels of human intention, to direct its flow toward human purpose, human enlightenment, human comfort and peace. Just as the Egyptians had learned how to use the natural forces of the river currents and winds to carry human traffic, they had also learned how to use the natural forces of spiritual energy to carry them through daily life.

The Three Seasons Of The Nile

Egypt is the gift of the Nile. The cycles, the moods and the landscape of the Nile were the backdrop of the Egyptian view of the universe and of humanity. The heartbeat of Egypt was the Nile's ceaseless round of Inundation, Emergence and Harvest. The name, "Nile," is from the Romans. *Itru* is the Egyptian word for "river," and the Nile was the Mother Of All Waters. When an Egyptian used *itru*, it likely referred to only one River.

No matter what they called it, the River flowed through the center of their lives. It is not surprising then that the Egyptian calendar is based on the seasons of the River. Converting the bounty of rich, black silt into rich, green fields requires carefully coordinated effort, and the formal structure of the seasonal calendar provided common ground for agreement in the chaos of mud.

The Egyptians linked the beginning of the inundation to the appearance of Isis' star, Sirius, *(Sopdut)* but they had to go to some effort to keep their methodical 365-day calendar count aligned. There is record of pharaohs officially shifting the calendar around to "reset" the alignment of the seasonal pattern of names with the actual seasons.

No matter when Sirius makes its appearance, however, the Nile's Inundation begins in summer and culminates in September (by our modern dates). An "ideal" year is one in which the Nile's inundation actually does coincide with the appearance of the star.

Akhet: The Inundation, The Season Of Hapy, The Nile's Abundance.

Months: *Thuthy, Paopy, Hathys, Choiach.*

The season of Inundation was the beginning of the year's cycle, a time for public works and prayers. Offerings were dropped into the Nile to assure that the coming flood would be neither too high nor too low. Temporary levees and canals guaranteed that the water would leave its rich silt behind. This was so important that one of the Forty-Two Negative Confessions reads, "I have not held back water in its time."

The cooperative irrigation of the fields was the backbone of the nation. The greatest weight of responsibility of one citizen to the community and to the nation was the contribution of time and effort to maintain the irrigation system. Families went hungry if the Nile did not reach the fields.

No farming could be done during the inundation because the fields were flooded, and the greatest wealth of the Pharaoh was the workforce of farmers freed during these months. This workforce was ready, willing and able to dig irrigation canals, to build levees, wharves, palaces, tombs and temples.

Relief from farm duties gave women the opportunity to concentrate on craft-skills: weaving, spinning, knitting, sewing, sandal- and basket-making, pottery, etc.

The word *akhet* is related to words for horizon, for the divine soul and for the greening fields. The opening season of their year was dedicated to and ruled over by Hap, Divine Force Of The Nile's Abundance. "Egypt is the Land Of The Nile" may be a cliché, but it is true in every respect. No aspect of their daily lives or their anticipation of eternity was untouched by the River. Every metaphor of their religion has the resonance of these sacred waters as a subtle harmonic.

Hap (Hapy in the dual aspect) is one of the most ancient deities of Egypt. Hap is mentioned in texts as old as that of Unas. Hap is the energy and flow of that inundation, and therefore the energy of the nation.

Hap was associated with *Ipuwait*, or "Opener Of The Ways." These two were called upon to activate the annual inundation, opening the waters of heaven to pour through the Nile. Opener Of The Ways is represented by a pair of bull horns. This suggests not an opening of a door or gate, but rather a natural process of opening, just as the points of the bull's horns spread open gradually in the natural expansion of growth. A door or gate can be opened at will, but the water of the Nile can be opened only in proper season.

Their perception of the dual nature of reality was reflected in Hapy. Hap is shown as a man with the pendulous breasts of a women, a symbol of the Shaman that hearkens back to prehistoric times and is among the oldest expressions of humanity's relationship with the forces of the world.

There was a Hap Of The North, *Hap Meht*, and a Hap Of The South, *Hap Reset.* "Hapy" is the dual mode, that which is two but united in purpose and function, as the two eyes, or the two banks of the river. The Hap of the North is represented by a cluster of papyrus plants, and the South by a cluster of lotus plants.

The unification of Upper and Lower Egypt is often shown as these two standing with lotus and papyrus stems knotted around the hieroglyph for "unity," This symbol was an emblem of the nation just as the eagle or the flag are emblematic of America. It was part of the ornamentation of the pharaoh's throne.

Poret: Emergence, The Season Of Khepry, The Awakening Land.

Months: *Tyby, Menchir, Famenoth, Parmuthy.*

The season of Emergence began as soon as the water receded. Boundaries were established by "String Stretchers," ancestors of the modern surveyor, using string and strict record-keeping to measure out and to re-assign private fields in the flat, featureless mud. Evidence of sophisticated fiber technology has been discovered around the world, dating as far back as the Paleolithic. The Egyptians developed this technology with great success, using a wide variety of fibers and techniques. String was as all-purpose a tool then as duct-tape is today. Their use of string to define field boundaries demonstrates their ability to apply simple, practical solutions to complex social concerns.

While the land was muddy, they sowed the crops. To assure that these would flourish, the Egyptian farmers spent countless hours lifting Nile water onto the fields, using *shadufs*, levers made of long poles with a bucket at one end and a heavy rock to balance at the other. Smaller crops of a variety of herbs, vegetables and flowers were planted in household plots and alongside the roads. Fod supplies were supplemented by goods stored the previous year.

It has been suggested that the name of the third month of this season, *Famenoth*, is the root of the modern word "famine," via the Latin. In bad times of low inundation, the last weeks of this season could be filled with hungry days, as stored supplies dwindled and crops were not yet ready to harvest.

The word *poret* (also spelled *peret, pert* or *proyet,*) is related to words for the emergence of that which is contained, as a person emerges from the container of the home, as frogs, snakes and insects emerge from the black mud, as plants emerge from the container of the seed, as leaves emerge from the stem. The divine substance of Osiris flows into the world from the divine dimension during the season of *Akhet*, and its spiritual energy "pours forth" from the black mud into the many forms of life, both plant and animal, that grow there in the season of *Poret.*

Khepry, the god of this season, is represented most often by the now-familiar scarab. Khepry was manifest in the moment of the Sun's rising, the birth of new light, of revelation and of enlightenment. "Light dawns" as an expression of awakening consciousness is the psychological revelation of Khepry. His most sublime expression is as the moment of the awakening of the Cosmos itself.

Shomu: The Harvest, Season Of Re, Wealth And Taxes

Months: *Pachons, Paony, Epipy, Mesore.*

The season of Harvest brought bounty, happiness and, if the flood had been a good one, taxes. Harvest was the season of bread, beer and festivals. The fields were harvested; the grain thrashed, winnowed and stored away. Excess grain was stored outdoors in time of great abundance, covered by straw mats to prevent birds from stealing it. There was a great deal of work to be done. Even the cats had to work, protecting the harvest. Taxes were assessed and paid. The Houses Of The *Naturu* gave thanks for the harvest and made ready for the most important festival of the year, the Yearly Five Days. *Sopdut,* (modern Sirius) rose on the horizon at the end of *Shomu,* marking the Birth of Re and his Ennead and leading to the start of the next New Year.

The word *shomu* is related to words for heat and dryness, the shimmer of heat rising off the desert sand. *Shomu* could well be the root of our modern word "summer."

This is the season of Re, when his days begin lengthening.

THE NAMES AND THE DIVINE GUARDIANS OF THE MONTHS

Akhet, season of Hapy.

Thuthy. The deity is Thoth.
Paopy. The deity is Ptah.
Hathys. The deity is Hathor.
Choiach. The deity is Sekhmet.

Poret, season of Khopry.

Tyby. The deity is Min.
Menchir. The deity is *Rekeh-Ur.*
Famenoth. The deity is *Rekeh-Netches.*
Parmuthy. The deity is *Rennetet.*

Shomu, season of Re.

Pachons. The deity is Khonsu.
Paony. The deity is *Khenthy.*
Epipy. The deity is *Ipt.*
Mesore. The deity is Horus Of The Two Horizons.

The Egyptian Calendar Today

The modern Copts of Egypt are the surviving descendents of the actual citizens of ancient Egypt. Even though they have adopted the Christian religion, they have done so in Egyptian fashion. They retain, within the sacred calendar of their Church, the ancient month names. The pronunciation has softened through the centuries, but they are yet recognizable: "*Tout, Paopy* (pronounced "Baba,") *Hator, Kiahk, Twby* (pronounced "Toba,") *Meshir* (pronounced "Amshir,") *Paremhat* (pronounced "Baramhat,") *Farmothy* (pronounced "Baramouda,") *Bashans, Paona, Epep, Mesra, Nasie*."

The most immediate difference between the modern Coptic calendar and the ancient calendar also demonstrates the most immediate difference between the ancient religion and modern Christianity. The Coptic Church calendar still uses these same twelve months of thirty days each, but the Yearly Five Days have been demoted to being simply a thirteenth month, extended to six days during Leap-year. The circle of the horizon has been closed, and the last day of the old year opens only into the first day of the new year. There is no spiritual immersion in the timeless realm below the horizon, no outpouring of divine energy to revitalize the round of the coming year.

The Ancient Egyptian Book Of Days

Thirty days has September, April, June and November, but every month of the Egyptian year had thirty days. We have carved our month into four weeks of seven repeated day-names, Monday, Tuesday and so on. The child in ancient Egypt had to learn thirty day-names, one for each of the thirty days of the twelve months of the yearly round. The first day of every month was named "New Month Day." The fifteenth day of each month was named "Half Month Day." The sixth day was always named "Sixth Day," followed by "First Quarter Day," which seems simple enough, but the days in between were as mythological in their source as our references to Sun and Moon and various Roman and Norse gods.

This regular round of twelve times thirty (plus the Yearly Five Days outside of time) was only one of the calendar rounds by which the Egyptians measured time. Since their entire civilization was born, existed and vanquished before the birth of Christianity, the "B.C./A.D." system which we have used for two thousand years to establish the count of years did not exist. The passage of years was marked by the "civil calendar," based on the reign on the currently living Pharaoh. (Similar calendars are still in use in the Far East today.) The first year of a Pharaoh's reign was "Year One Of Pharaoh X." Clearly, the ancient Egyptians were immersed in an environment of eternity.

The other major calendar-system they worked with was the seasonal round of planting and harvest, and the annual inundation of the River's silt deposit was the central theme of this calendar. The ceremonies of the agricultural year were based on the events in the story of Osiris, Isis, Sut and Horus. Re, creator of the cosmos of space and time, led the rounds of changing stars that mark the progress of that story. We ourselves have several types of calendar superimposed one upon the other, but we are so accustomed to it that we do not think of them as different calendars. We have the seven days of the week in their unchanging succession, and we have the twelve months, also in their unchanging round and unchanging count. Those two rounds do not match up, so there is a constantly changing interaction of dates of the month and days of the week. Holidays that are tied to the monthly calendar are on different days of the week every year. Holidays and events that are tied to specific weekdays, such as weekend events and "church on Sunday" fall on different dates of the month each year. There is the current practice in some states in America of assigning the official day off to the Monday before a holiday which is tied to a specific date of the month, such as President's Birthdays or Independence Day. That is one of the ways in which these differing calendar-systems are reconciled. We have even incorporated different New Year days, in that the fiscal year begins in July and the school year in September. We have even begun to celebrate Chinese New Year, and every single person has their own, personal New Year's Day on their birthday, measuring out the years with their own lives.

The Egyptian calendar system created the first successful overlay of such measurement systems. The subtle complexity of the mythological interactions of days and months, Moon, stars and Sun, gave great depth to their cultural experience and to their daily lives, as well as unifying the nation in rhythmic participation in the universal dance of the days. Every hour of the day and night had its own set of divine guardians who watched over that span of time, and each day of the month and each month of the year, as well as each season. The primary divinities of the calendar are the five who are born during the Yearly Five Days of the Epagomenal, the opening in eternity through which the New Year arrives. These are Osiris, The Original Horus (Horus The Elder) Sut, Isis and Lady Of The House *(Nobt Hut.)*

These five *Naturu* rule throughout the year, and the stories from which the names, festivals, ceremonies and auspices arise are the stories of these five, their struggles, loves, births and deaths.

The calendar tells the eternal story of the round of time in the human community, and the divinities featured in its round are those which form the core of each human being.

The Name And The Divine Guardian Of Each Day

1. **New Month Day**. Thoth is the deity.
2. **New Crescent Day**. Horus is the deity.
3. **Arrival Day**. Osiris is the deity.
4. **Zem Priests Emerge**. Isis is the deity.
5. **Altar Offerings Day**. Hapy is the deity.
6. **Sixth Day**. Star Of His Mother is the deity.
7. **First Quarter Day**. *Qebsennuf* is the deity.
8. **Main Emergence**. *Ma'atet-f* is the deity.
9. **Hidden One**. He Does The Talking is the deity.
10. **He Who Protects His Royal Name**.
    He Makes His Name Himself is the deity.
11. **Great Lady Protector**. Sekhmet is the deity.
12. **Love Making**. Bring The Advocate is the deity.
13. **Approach of Re**. Re is the deity.
14. **Progress Of The Ba**. Consider The *Ba* is the deity.
15. **Half Month Day**. *Amauai* is the deity.
16. **Two Houses Fight**. Horus and Sut are the gods.
17. **Second Arrival Day**. Re is the deity.
18. **Moon Day**. Ahi The Moon is the deity.
19. **Hear His Commands**.
    Bring His Mother is the deity.
20. **Offering Meat**. Opener Of The Ways is the deity.
21. **Apru's Day.** *Inpu* is the deity.
22. **Passing Of Sopdut.** *Nai* is the deity.
23. **Last Quarter Day**. *Na-Ur* is the deity.
24. **Darkness**. Nekhbet is the deity.
25. **Departing**. Shem is the deity.
26. **House Of Appearances**. *Ma'atef-f* is the deity.
27. **Funeral Offerings**. Khnum is the deity.
28. **Jubilee Of The Sky.** Nut is the deity.
29. **Weakness**. *Utettef-f* is the deity.
30. **Awaken**. Horus Advocates For Him is the deity.

PLACING THE ANCIENT CALENDAR TODAY

The Egyptian civilization was long-lived and successful enough that the stars and the Sun had time to shift in their patterns around the horizon. The calendar of the river's inundation had to be adjusted to the written date on official documents and to dates literally carved in stone. The empire had become wide-spread enough that they needed matching dates on letters and on written documents relating to business and government in order to maintain the smooth functioning of society. They survived these necessary calendar-adjustments with little disruption themselves, but they have left us with a dilemma once we try to layer the grid of our modern 365.25-day year upon the ancient structure.

The Egyptians used two benchmarks for the calibration of their system, one on the Earth, in the day-to-day world and one in the sky, a fixed point in eternity. The earthly marker was the annual rising of the Nile at about the time of the Summer Solstice. The celestial marker was the rising of the brilliant star, Sirius. (*Sopdet* in Egyptian, *Sothis* in Greek.) The "rising" here is the *heliacal* rising, which means that the star first appears over the horizon just before the rising of the Sun. *Acronychal* rising is the opposite, in which the star first appears just as the Sun sets.

In 4,000 to 3,000 B.C., the rising of the Nile and the rising of Sirius coincided, which suggests the era in which the calendar originated. In our times, in the Twenty-first Century and the new milenium, Sirius rises in August.

Our modern dilemma stems from the debate of which of these benchmarks should be aligned with our own calendar, the rising of the Nile in summer or the modern heliacal rising of Sirius in August. This dilemma is deepened by modern interference, since the building of the Aswan Dam has disrupted the ancient cycle. The question then is whether the calendar is more "authentic" if it begins in June, when the Nile begins its flood, or in August, the current time of the rising of Sirius.

The Nile Rising Calendar begins on June 27, and the Sirius Rising Calendar begins on August 1.

There is evidence within the nature of the mythological story that drives the round of the year that the last day of their year would be our June 21, the day of the Summer Solstice. This is the day of the most hours of sunlight and the time during which the Sun reaches its highest point in the sky. The word "solstice" comes from the Latin, and means the "Sun Standing Still."

From this point of paramount ascension and fullest power, Re the Creator, father of the gods, is able to "stop time" for the Yearly Five Days when the world dips below the horizon to let the divine silt of the river flow into the world. During these Five Days outside of time the gods are born into the world, crossing the threshold from eternity into daily life to begin the round of the year once again. The Solstices are also known as the "Poles Of The Year," the axis around which the year turns, and it is from this still point that divine energy enters. Horus Of The Two Horizons is the god of the last month of the year, *Mesore.* Horus Of The Two Horizons is represented by the Sun at zenith, ruling the horizons of both dimensions of reality, the daily and the eternal. On the last day of the year, time stands till and Re reaches the topmost point of heaven. From that lofty place he brings forth the *Naturu*, and he gives the wheel of the year another spin.

Modern text books, most notably Bob Brier's *Egyptian Magic*, align the ancient calendar with the modern date of the heliacal rising of Sirius, beginning on August 1 and placing the omens and auspices of each day in the Egyptian calendar according to this template. Anyone interested in the decan cycle and their relationship to the texts would do best to use this August 1 New Year's date. (Students should keep in mind that this August 1 date will be the reference point of any Egyptian dates used in most text books.)

Those who are interested in the ceremonies, rituals and annual round of daily life in ancient times might want, instead, to use the Nile Rising Calendar alignment. The Nile's flood has been disrupted and the agriculture of Egypt no longer functions in the ancient style, yet the underlying principles of the faith remain unchanged. The symbol of divine energy annually renewing spiritual life is more powerful than the Nile and more enduring than the houses or the images of the diivinities.

For example, ending the year on the Summer Solstice not only puts Re's birthday on the longest day, it also aligns the Autumn Equinox, Winter Solstice and Spring Equinox with days and ceremonies more appropriate to these events in the story of the year. The Autumn Equinox in the Nile Rising Calendar system falls on *Hathys* 27, and the ceremonies of this day and the days before and after are focused on the tension between Sut and Horus:

"The judgment between Sut and Horus stops the hostility. They hunt down the followers of the two *Natury*, and put an end to the tumult. It satisfies the Two Lords and causes the doors to open."

This is the time in which the night and day are of equal length, and Sut and Horus represent, in their most primal form, the darkness and the daylight. There are three days of ceremonies involved in the division of the world between Sut and Horus, and the Nile Rising Calendar places the Autumn Equinox right in the middle of these events relating to the balance of dark and light.

By contrast, the Autumn Equinox in the Sirius Rising Calendar (beginning August 1) falls on *Paopy* 22, and the omen is "Do not bathe this day. It is the day they cut the tongue of Sobek's enemy."

The ceremonies and events of the Spring Equinox and Winter Solstice events also fit more appropriately in the Nile Rising Calendar, occurring on days named "Jubilee Of The Sky." For the Winter Solstice, the shortest day and the longest night of the year, the ceremonies are for Osiris: "Osiris is pleased. The spirits are joyful and the dead are in festivity."

Elaborate festival days lead up to the Winter Solstice, ceremonies of the silence and of the heart, the places in the inner world of the soul. Alas, the details of the calendar on the days in March around the Spring Equinox have been lost to papyrus damage, so this evidence is incomplete.

Again, by contrast, the Sirius Rising Calendar places these events on days named "Last Quarter Day," and the ceremonies are out of context with the solar events.

After the Yearly Five Days that are the bridge of the old year and the new, the first day of the new year is listed in the calendar as "The birth of Re." Having achieved his fullest status in the Solstice, and having brought the gods into the world, Re himself enters the world to begin the year again, descending and ascending in his annual round. The divine substance of the eternal dimension, manifest in the black silt of the River, begins to flow into the world. The divine energy of the eternal pours into the world in the form of the Sun quickening the plant and animal life in the black mud, providing the bounty of Egypt. Re, indeed, is the god dedicated to the final season, *Shomu*. It is during the days of *Shomu* that the hours of daylight lengthen once again, culminating in the Solstice.

In the Nile Rising Calendar, Re's birthday falls on the Summer Solstice. In the Sirius Rising Calendar, Re's birthday is July 26, diminishing the importance of Re's role in the round of time.

The heliacal rising of Sirius does mark the beginning of the round of the thirty-six decan stars, the ten days that measure out the turning of the night sky around the horizon. The astronomical clock of the decan stars measures out the turning of the *Duat*, the divine realm of the gods and of the dead that is the night sky and stars enfolding our waking world. This night-sky calendar measured out the mathematics of the solstice, since the timelessness of the *Duat* overhead is not interrupted by the Yearly Five Days of timelessness that reign on Earth. There are 72 half-decan counts in the 360 days of the mundane year, and the seventy-third half-decan count during those sacred Five Days. Sut has 72 minions who put Osiris in his coffin, and it is specifically this betrayal of one brother by another that is the opening of the divine drama which underlies the agricultural cycle of River and land.

The Egyptian mind did not perceive these discrepancies between the decan count and the Nile Rising count as contradictory or, indeed, as discrepancies. The dual dimensions of the land below the Sun and the eternity of the sky below the horizon were part of the Egyptian world-view. The calendar-count was seen as a triumph of humankind's mentality, finding our proper place in the divine plan of the Cosmos. The first month of the year is dedicated to Thoth and, although the first day of the year is the birth of Re, the day itself is dedicated to Thoth. Thoth is the personification of the divine nature of human intellect. The *Naturu* established the round of the year and the physical expressions of our daily journey through time, ordering both realities into orderly patterns, but the mind of man was needed to harness that divine pattern for the service of civilized life.

Modern Dates For The Nile Rising Calendar

Akhet, season of The Inundation, June 27 to October 24.

The deity is Hapy, the Nile in flood.

- *Thuthy* — June 27 to July 26.
- *Paopy* — July 27 to August 25.
- *Hathys* — August 26 to September 24.
- *Choiach* — September 25 to October 24

Poret, season of The Emergence, October 25 to February 21.

The deity is Khepry, the Rising Sun.

- *Tyby* — October 25 to November 23.
- *Menchir* — November 24 to December 23.
- *Famenoth* — December 24 to January 22.
- *Parmuthy* — January 23 to February 21

Shomu, season of The Harvest, February 22 to June 21.

The deity is Re, the creator of consciousness and space/time.

- *Pachons* — February 22 to March 23.
- *Paony* — March 24 to April 22.
- *Epipy* — April 23 to May 22.
- *Mesore* — May 23 to June 21.

"ANYTHING YOU SEE THIS DAY WILL BE GOOD." THE DAILY AUSPICE

In addition to this layering of lunar, solar, civil and agricultural time patterns, every day of the month also had its feasts and celebrations, as well as omens, prophecies and psychological dangers. There are shorthand references to these in the surviving material.

The Egyptian day was divided into three portions of roughly eight-hours each. Most calendars simply rank each eight-hour portion as either favorable or adverse, without explanation.

In the *Sallier* Papyrus, the auspice of each portion was illustrated with the hieroglyph for *nefer,* 𓄤, the symbol of the heart and respiratory system, to mean favorable, and the hieroglyph *aha,* 𓂚 , an arm bearing a shield, to mean adverse or challenging. Three nefers 𓇳𓄤𓄤𓄤 meant a good day all day long, while a *nefer* and two *ahas* 𓇳𓄤𓂚𓂚 meant the day would have ups and downs, and so on.

The position of the hieroglyphic symbols told the ancients which part of the day was good or bad, joyful of heart or challenging to the spirit. The Cairo Calendar is important because it explains why a certain day is good or bad and advises an appropriate course of action. Some daily recommendations warn you not to travel by road or boat, or tell you not to eat certain foods, while others tell you, straight out, "Stay home."

It must be remembered that these are shorthand and idiomatic, rather than enigmatic for the sake of being mysterious. "Do not sail in a boat," for example, could be a reference to going out on the Nile, but if everyone in Egypt regularly avoided boats on the same day annually, it would have been noted elsewhere in their writings.

More likely such language was idiomatic, much like our modern phrases "Go with the flow," or "Make up your own mind." In that ancient world there were, for the most part, only two ways of getting from place to place: walking on your own two feet or sailing on the river. As metaphors of progress through daily life, these are opposites forms of movement: you sit in a boat and are carried along either by wind or water, i.e., by the natural flow of events. You are not making decisions about the direction and speed of your course. Even navigating a boat, although more active than being a passenger, is nonetheless participation in the natural flow.

Walking on your own two feet, however, is an act of self-determination that can go against the natural flow, and can lead you into unknown places. Thus, there are days when you are safest letting events carry you along without protest, and there are days when you have to put your foot down and have it your way.

Similarly, being killed by a crocodile, within their mythological structure, was a metaphor of succumbing to depression, grief or mental illness: the Great Crocodile, Sobek, was Lord and Master of the psychic waters below the level of consciousness and upon which Re-consciousness must float.

There are other similar auspices, relating to the lighting of fire, making love, and eating. The mythology behind the omens is not given in complete forms, but only in glimpses, the high points, if you will, of the *Naturu's* lives. The entries may seem enigmatic to us, but at the time they were written, the ancients had idiom, metaphor and imagery grown out of environment, lifestyles and mutual experiences that we no longer share, making their references seem at times mysterious and unfathomable. This book is intended to be a resource for the background of the imagery and intention of the calendar entries.

Egyptian children learned their first lessons in spirituality, duty and civic pride from their mothers and from the people who cared for them. The natural curiosity of a child asking, "What does today's name mean?" was certainly the opening for many long and happy hours of telling the stories of the divinities and for discussion of their roles in human life. Above everything else, it is clear that the ancient Egyptians loved to talk together, to share their thoughts and feelings and words with each other, and the rich tapestry of the calendar must have been the ground of many conversations and of much meditation.

The Patterns Of Lucky, Unlucky And Mixed Days Of Each Month

The number of lucky (𓇳𓄤𓄤𓄤) and unlucky (𓇳𓂡𓂡𓂡) days is roughly equal, with lucky days leading. There are 172 𓇳𓄤𓄤𓄤 days and 131 𓇳𓂡𓂡𓂡 days, although the 35 days lost to papyrus damage or scribal omission do make the count less certain. Even if all 35 lost days were unlucky 𓇳𓂡𓂡𓂡, however, the good days would still be in the majority. This is another indication of the average Egyptian's positive outlook on life.

The central months of the *Cairo Calendar* papyrus suffered the most damage, with the month of *Pachons* losing nearly a quarter of its days, although fortunately not in a single stretch. Only the last two months, *Epipy* and *Mesore*, are complete. They represent the extremes as well, with *Epipy* having 18 unlucky 𓇳𓂡𓂡𓂡 days and *Mesore* having 19 lucky 𓇳𓄤𓄤𓄤 days.

The first and last days of each month are ☉𓄤𓄤𓄤 lucky days, with a single exception, the last day of the sixth month *Menchir* (December 23) which is ☉𓂡𓂡𓂡. This day is the midpoint of the year, the furthest from the outpouring of divine energy at the Yearly Five Days. Perhaps there was some concern that the year could become difficult at this point, or that it could not make the return. The admonition is "Do not speak loudly to anyone on this day." On such a dangerous day, it is sensible to remain quiet and calm with one another. This is also the furthest point from the bounty of last year's harvest, and emotional tension can rise as belts get tighter.

The following month is *Famenoth*, and there is reason to believe that our word "famine" comes from the name *Famenoth*, via Rome. Indeed, if the previous harvest had been lean, this would be the point in the year at which food supplies were running at their lowest, with the next harvest only greening in the fields.

A primary duty of the priests and ultimately the pharaoh himself was the storage, care and distribution of food supplies for the times when these unlucky days became truly tragic.

As the calendar shifted through the patterns of layered time-counting systems, the omens also went through a similar shuffling around the year. This sense of relationship to their environment, religion and lifestyle must be considered when evaluating and interpreting these cryptic statements.

Thuthy	☉𓄤𓄤𓄤•13	☉𓂡𓂡𓂡•8	☉𓂡𓂡𓄤•4	
			☉𓂡𓄤𓂡•1	
			☉𓄤𓄤𓂡•3	lost•1
Paopy	☉𓄤𓄤𓄤•15	☉𓂡𓂡𓂡•10	☉𓂡𓂡𓄤•1	
			☉𓂡𓄤𓂡•1	
			☉𓄤𓂡𓂡•2	lost•1
Hathys	☉𓄤𓄤𓄤•17	☉𓂡𓂡𓂡•10		lost•3
Choiach	☉𓄤𓄤𓄤•13	☉𓂡𓂡𓂡•10	☉𓂡𓂡𓄤•1	
			☉𓄤𓄤𓂡•2	lost•4
Tyby	☉𓄤𓄤𓄤•17	☉𓂡𓂡𓂡•9	☉𓂡𓄤𓂡•1	lost•3
Menchir	☉𓄤𓄤𓄤•15	☉𓂡𓂡𓂡•9	☉𓂡𓄤𓂡•1	lost•5
Famenoth	☉𓄤𓄤𓄤•14	☉𓂡𓂡𓂡•11	☉𓂡𓄤𓂡•1	lost•4
Parmuthy	☉𓄤𓄤𓄤•11	☉𓂡𓂡𓂡•16	☉𓂡𓂡𓄤•1	lost•2
Pachons	☉𓄤𓄤𓄤•13	☉𓂡𓂡𓂡•10		lost•7
Paony	☉𓄤𓄤𓄤•14	☉𓂡𓂡𓂡•12	☉𓂡𓂡𓄤•1	lost•3
Epipy	☉𓄤𓄤𓄤•11	☉𓂡𓂡𓂡•18	☉𓄤𓂡𓄤•1	
Mesore	☉𓄤𓄤𓄤•19	☉𓂡𓂡𓂡•8	☉𓂡𓂡𓄤•2	
			☉𓄤𓂡𓄤•1	

Astrology as we know it today has its most solid roots in Mesopotamian, Babylonian, Hindu and Greek mythologies, rather than in the Egyptian. The authors consider that this calendar is a horoscope of daily auspice, chosen by human events rather than as tool of star shapes. In that sense, it can be placed among the world's older horoscopes. The word "horoscope" derives ultimately from Horus' name via the root for "horizon." The purpose of the calendar is to bring about a working relationship between events on both sides of the horizon.

History Of The Cairo Calendar Papyrus

In 1943, the **Cairo Museum** purchased a set of scrolls of uncertain provenance from an antiques dealer, on the recommendation of the celebrated **Dr. Cerny.** It turned out to be a lucky find, the now-celebrated *Cairo Calendar.* The papyrus had been discovered with the writing palette of *Semendes,* dating to the Twenty-second dynasty. Experts who later studied and translated it believe the artists' colony at *Deir-el-Medina* to be the likeliest source for the work.

The scroll is twenty centimeters wide (a little over seven inches) and nearly seven meters long (almost thirty feet). It is written in red and black ink. The scroll appears to have been cleaned in some places, and shows signs of regular use. There are errors, and the predation of ants can be blamed for missing entries. Despite these ravages, however, the papyrus contains a nearly complete calendar.

The *Cairo Calendar* shares almost identical entries with its very damaged cousin, the *Sallier IV* Papyrus, of which only four months remain intact. There is the possibility that the scribe who wrote the *Cairo* scroll was taking dictation at the time of its writing. There are several instances where the writer used the wrong hieroglyph, or wrong determinative for the intended phrase. The language of the calendar is not late Egyptian. The lack of mention of the Theban Triad suggests that the calendar was dictated from an older document. The scribe, therefore, may have made mistakes because he did not know the vocabulary.

The first English translation was undertaken by **Dr. Adb EL-Mohsen Bakir** in 1943, and finally published in 1966 in Cairo by the Egyptian government. This volume is no longerin print.

In 2001, Diana Janeen Pierce and Ramona Louise Wheeler began the project of assembling and designing a modern presentation of this invaluable information, rediscovering an important element of the ancient religion that has long been neglected.

REALITY AND THE SOUL: BASIC CONCEPTS OF THE ANCIENT PHILOSOPHY

"I have been given my name
in the Register of the Shrine of the House Of The *Naturu*,
and I remember my name in the Common House.
It is the night of counting years, not adding up months.

I am that which is within the dual *Natur.*
I have stationed the face properly
upon the eastern horizon of heaven.
The totality of every *Natur* is behind me, and I say his name."

What If Love Goes On Forever? Ancient Egypt, Land Of Love On The Nile

The Ancient Egyptians asked the biggest "what if" question ever: what if your soul truly *is* eternal? What if you *do* continue? What would it be like? What are the expectations of an immortal and divine soul? What if awareness *truly* goes on forever? It is the ultimate "desert-island game:" What if you were stuck on a desert island forever? What would you want to have with you?

Death is that desert island, stuck in the ocean of eternity.

The ancient Egyptians played this "desert-island game" with elaborate intensity, devoting their lives to living a life worth living for eternity. They began with the basics: air, water, light, a place to stand, making love, breathing, bread, beer and onions. Their tomb paintings are references to the activities they loved, to those precious moments of life in which they sighed contentedly and wished that the moment could go on forever. On this private desert island of the next life, these moments *are* forever.

The more deeply you inhale the images and joys of the outer world into your soul, the more deeply you will relive them in the next world. These images of life taken into the next world are imaged upon the substance of your soul. You are the film, the cameraman, the actor, director and audience of the story of your life. In the next life you are every moment of your own existence.

The images of everything and everyone around you are from the reality of your own life "on top of the Earth." Do you really want to watch yourself telling that lie for all eternity? Do you want to see the faces of your victims for eternity? Do you want to live forever in fear of revenge from those you have injured? These issues, too, must be addressed in the baggage you bring to the next life.

Your actions are now and forever. Not in the way of the Levant–Jehovah-ordained and Allah-controlled–but as the considered behavior of the self-aware, civilized adult. That is the goal of learning how to "Walk like an Egyptian," knowing that your footsteps will lead you to eternity, no matter where you go or how long it takes to get there.

Africa is the cradle of our humanity. The civilization which blossomed at the crown of Africa was the prototype of all humanity's struggles to be civilized. The nation that once flourished along the Nile River was named "Egypt" only after her actual civilization had been destroyed. The ancient Egyptians saw themselves as "The Children of the Sun," and the nation was often referred to as *Ta Mery,* meaning both "Land of Love" and "Beloved Land." *Kkemmet,* the riverbanks and rich fields of the Delta, was "The Black Land." We derive the modern term "chemistry" from this name, via alchemy in the Middle Ages and Renaissance. *Deshert,* "The Red Land," was the name for the sandstone desolation that surrounded them, a region called "desert" to this day. There is still much debate over exactly how and why Egypt went from being the land of "The Children of the Sun," to "Egypt," which is the misspelling of a mispronunciation of *Hikuptah,* the native name of a Temple of Ptah. The Greeks and Romans who were the nation's destroyers gave us this name for her, as well as their own view of what she had been. Just as we know Egypt by a name that she did not give herself, we are each seeing her from a point of view she would not have used.

Ancient Egypt is accused of having been a static culture locked into the rhythms of the Nile, yet dynamic changes throughout the nation's history are dramatically evidenced in their lives and in their art. Theirs was, however, the single most stable culture humanity has ever produced; this alone warrants closer examination of the principles by which they managed their lives.

"The Children of the Sun" fell, not to stagnation, but to Alexander the Great.

Wherever possible Diana Janeen Pierce and I have drawn from direct sources from the artwork and words of the ancient peoples themselves. What is most impressive about the stubborn persistence of their words and images is that even now, thousands of years later, their message survives despite how much time and the desert have buried. Much has changed since the days of Egypt's greatness, but the art of being human is timeless. This art was never more timelessly expressed than in Egypt's ancient culture.

We must never lose sight of the fact that however strange or nonsensical any of this ancient material may seem to modern eyes, in its day it made perfect sense to the people who lived it. We forget this easily in the face of such a seemingly confused and confusing array of images and ideas. They made sense in their time, and it is that sense we must pursue.

The spiritual teachings of ancient Egypt are similar to Buddhism in that each produced a religion grounded in the practice of meditation, in which actions in this world "on top of the Earth" have transcendent, symbolic significance to the divine essence of being that is the eternal soul within. Their living world was a divine landscape, shaped by divine forces for the experience of the divine soul within its garment of flesh. The ancient Egyptian religion is an elegant philosophy of dancing, of joy, of pageants, and of serenity, nurtured by a secure, relaxed worldview and by some familiarity with the sense of boredom grown out of leisure time. It was not a religion developed at the point of a spear. Their serene, elegant vision of reality reflects the relatively comfortable circumstances in the Nile Valley, carried by the river of time, always on schedule, the divine soul experiencing the riverboat journey of real life.

The surviving mythology of ancient Egypt is personal and human. The stories about their gods are not hollow tales of wars or battles with giants. Humankind does not fight the gods, struggle with them, or oppose them. Their stories are individualized sagas suffused with a dreamy magic that elevates them to the realm of myth. There is no Armageddon, no *Gotterdammerung*; just betrayal by a trusted friend, a murder committed in jealousy, and the evil of loneliness. There are no avenging armies of celestial hosts, just the judgments of a family about the actions of one of their own against another; in short, the archetypal human family. The heart and soul of their "greatest story ever told," that of Isis and Osiris, is the deeply abiding loyalty of a woman for her man, and her grief at his death. In bonding the lost Osiris together, Isis bonded the entire nation, humanity united by a single vision of reality. Their mythology and their literature are people stories with enough magic thrown in to plant the events firmly in the fertile ground of the inner psyche.

Their mythology was not lost up in the sky–they were looking at each other.

THE POWER OF MA'AT: THE REALITY OF REALITY

MA'AT is most often translated as "truth," or "cosmic order." Her ostrich-plume symbol as the "Feather of Truth." The modern term "reality," however, is closer to the nuance of the ancient meaning. Truth is a relative concept, easily abused, and one's truth is another's delusion; yet all share a common physical reality. That is *ma'at*, the reality of reality. The practically-minded Egyptians knew that the world of human sense perception is grounded in immutable laws that even the gods cannot subvert or deny. Their remarkable technological triumphs and observations of the environment became the foundation of the early sciences.

The word for this fundamental, unchanging reality, *ma'at*, derives from the same ancient root word as "mother," "matter," "material," "mathematics," "measure," and "meter"; from *mater*, which is the physical body of the World Mother. It is a subtle but meaningful difference in attitude in that it has the Egyptian asking not, "Is it true?" but "Is it real?"

Ma'at is sometimes described as "ethics" or "truth," but it is a modern assumption that *Ma'at* was merely a philosophy of ethics. The Levant, after the fall of Egypt, separated Creator and Created, reduced the divine world to dirt and ashes and sin, and made mankind into servants of the God. This is a very different attitude from the Egyptian. *Ma'at* is more than just Truth. *Ma'at* is reality, the solid grounding of reality that makes the Sun rise, the stars shine, the river flood and mankind think. The universe itself, all the world around them, was sacred in the ancient view. "Ethics" is an issue of human will and human permission. It is a function of the human world of duality. What is "ethical" for one group is "sin" for another. *Ma'at*, the reality that made all groups what they are is transcendent of ethics, just as a rock or a flower is amoral, a-ethical, without truth or falsehood. How can a flower be false or ethical. It just is. How can the universe be ethical or moral, right or wrong? It simply is. That is *Ma'at.*

For mathematics to be "the measure of reality and the reality of the measure" is perfectly understandable in that world view, particularly for as practically minded and empirical a people as the ancient Egyptians.

A single ostrich plume is the identifying crown for reality personified, and Lady *Ma'at* is shown as a woman wearing the feather crown. Death is the final reality of life; therefore Lady *Ma'at* is a major player in funeral rituals, but she is represented everywhere in their lives as well.

Ma'aty: The Dual Realities, The Land Under The Horizon: Inner And Outer Landscapes Of The Soul

The philosophy of ancient Egypt is organized on a doctrine of duality, similar to the Oriental concept of the *Yin* and *Yang*. This philosophy is dominated by the concept of the union of opposites, the balance of opposing tensions that creates the harmony and movement of real life. The hieroglyphic symbol of the union of opposites is a stylized graphic of the human windpipe and lungs. The ancients were deeply fascinated by the incomprehensible magic of the living breath, and used it frequently as a symbol of ultimate mystery. The living breath in the lungs is the interface of the outer world of inanimate air and the inner world of living breath. The divine energy force of life is created at the interface of those opposites, air and lung, and symbolizes the powerful magic created by that one-out-of-two.

This graphic image, combined with the interwoven stems of lotus and papyrus plants, comprised the symbol of the nation, representing the unification of Upper and Lower Egypt into one kingdom. This combination hieroglyph stood for the nation, as the eagle emblem stands for America today.

The language of the ancient Egyptians clearly reflected their fascination with the concept of duality. They rarely used the neuter gender; everything in the world was either male or female, either *yang* or *yin*. This sense of duality is expressed by a separate grammatical structure called "the dual voice." There are few English equivalents, only such phrases as "the two eyes," "the two riverbanks." The dual voice is not just two things, and not just two halves of one thing, but two which are one, at once separate and united, each single yet incomplete without the other.

Reality itself, *ma'at*, has two equal but opposite forms: the reality of the outer world of space/time; and the reality of the inner world of the soul. These are referred to as *tauy*, the "dual worlds," or as *ma'aty*, "the dual realities." The Nile River served as the primary metaphor for this dual reality. The two banks of the river are separated and united at the same instant by the body of the river, just as the reality of the soul is separated from, and united with, outer reality by the body of flesh. This inner world of the soul's reality is the balance of the outer world's reality. Our lives are the interface of the two.

The western horizon where the Sun set was one of the many entrances of the *duat*, this interior landscape of the soul. The laws of this inner world are as real as the laws of physics. Inner is related to outer in the same way that a thing is related to its image reflected in a mirror; in other words, there is no image until the lens of a living eye focuses the light. Every image of the interior landscape is filtered through a living person; every detail is related to the life and experiences of the individual. *Duat* is the collected experiences of being alive. It is that place within where those experiences are lived: the inner *Twilight Zone.*

Imenta is also known as the land hidden under the horizon, that place of absolute "otherness" through which the Sun must pass between sunset and dawn.

The Sun enters the horizon, swallowed by the sky, Nut. The horizon is the dividing line between that which can be known and the unknowable. It is the most immediate perception of primal duality, since the circle of the horizon is an impassable boundary. No matter how quickly you travel, the horizon moves with you, away from you, forever unreachable, always present; containing you and yet utterly separate.

Compare "Plato's cave" to the descriptions of the *duat,* of *Imenta,* the Hidden Land inside that is Osiris, inside the soul. The reality of the soul's inner dimension was the counterpoint to physical reality, partner in "the dual realities" and "the two worlds" *(ma'aty, tauy).* It has mountain walls that cut it off from Earth on one side and from heaven on the other, curving mountain walls–the skull. Through the valley of this place a river runs, and Re in his solar barque sails on these psychic waters. The only light which penetrates "comes through the two eyes," and some places are so dark that only the light of Re consciousness passing can bring life to the unconscious elements there. Compare Plato's light, projecting shadows.

What is the light? From where is it projected? The Greeks did not ask. The Egyptians did. "Who" is projecting and "who" is perceiving the projection? The Greeks just could not get past this conundrum, having removed the Divine Eye from the inner world of each living individual, reduced it to a single vision, then further sequestered that vision atop a fabled mountain, Mount Olympus.

The broad scope of Egyptian religion grew out of the most ancient roots in our world and time. They were the inheritors of humanity's oldest religious philosophies, and represent a continuity of thought and religious training that goes back to the days of the great cathedrals of cave art. The earliest images of their philosophy are more intensely sky-related, demonstrating the widespread geography which was the natural environment out of which the images grew. These images are the iconography of the Divine evolved by the nomadic plains peoples of Neolithic Africa. The Nile took over the imagery once it became their primary environment. The layers of stellar, solar and horizon related images as metaphor of the transition through dimensions indicate the older, prehistoric strata of this philosophy. In the days of the First Kingdom, there are images of climbing stairs or a ladder to heaven, an image surviving from the days of the first villages, which were built so that the door was on the roof and entry was gained only by ladder.

The ease with which they later fit the marshland, riverside and river journey imagery into this philosophy demonstrates the move from the full Saharan environment to the restriction of the river and marsh environments for survival when the climatic changes expanded the desert regions of Africa, destroying entire cultural realms and burying them under sand.

NATUR: THE METAPHOR OF METAPHOR, METAPHORS OF THE DIVINE, THE "GODS" OF EGYPT

Spelled "*Neter*" or "*netjer*" in older textbooks on Egypt.

The concept of the *Natur* is one of the most controversial in our understanding of this ancient world, and few Egyptologists today agree on its exact definition. This very fact helps point to its use in Egyptian thought.

The hieroglyph *n*t*r* is a flag on a pole, spread out by the breeze. Flags were a regular sight in that ancient world. Huge, colorful banners waved on poles high over the temples and palaces in their cities, visible from great distances. Flags were a welcome sign to the traveler, aids to navigation, markers of life. The ancient language is filled with visual punning, graphic word games, and metaphors. Metaphor abounds in every text, creating a rich, vibrant literature. Like the flag over the city, the *Natur* flag-hieroglyph means "This stands for something. Fill in the blank." It is a flag, also, because a flag is "alive" in the air, moved by the breeze: the inanimate given lifelike energy and motion by invisible forces, particularly by the divine force of life which is in the atmosphere. *Natur* is also represented by the Horus falcon perched on the flagpole; a focus of divine presence, that which descends out of heaven.

To translate the concept of *n*t*r* as polytheistic "gods," however, is to underestimate the studied sophistication of the ancient mind. In the belief that the best translation is no translation, I prefer to use the original term. Its ancient meaning is revealed by its use in their writings. (The vowels are uncertain but "*Natur*" has gained currency.) In fact, it is quite possible that the Latin root of our word "nature" originatedfrom the Egyptian . The Latin culture is two-thousand years younger than the Egyptian, and there was considerable contact between the two from the earliest times. Egyptian theological teaching is so much more sophisticated than the Roman that concepts were garbled in the translation. We have lost the evidence of more direct connections. Egypt was the America of the ancient world and, just as it happens today, not everyone who borrowed their ideas acknowledged the source.

The *Natur* are the archetypes of reality personified, metaphors transformed into recognizable people in order to make stories of how the world works. There is nothing primitive or polytheistic about them. The *Natur* are teachers and teaching aids, inanimate art yet vibrant with the living energy of the minds who created them. In this larger context, the ripples of feedback by which the ancient "*n**t*r*" becomes the modern "Nature" are obvious, and make clearer both the ancient and the modern meanings. For example, Osiris is the nature of the soul's mysterious substance. Isis is the nature of the soul's bonding integrity. Horus is the nature of divine identity, "The Face of Heaven." *Hapy* is the nature of the Nile. And so on. Every category of meaning that is applied to the modern word "Nature" and all the routes it took from then to now function logically together. The *Natur* in their hosts are the many faces of the nature of Nature. Their images sprang out of the nature of human nature. At the same time, they show the personal natures of the peoples who lived by the Nile. Egypt's finest art has the breath of naturalism, yet shows clearly the nature of their remarkable capacity for abstract understanding.

"God The Creator" is *The Natur,* the Archetype of archetypes, Metaphor of metaphors, unnamable, invisible, without form, the pattern of all patterning, and is often referred to in religious texts. The ancient Egyptians, however, like the Buddhists, believed that the eternal divine is beyond names and beyond personality. The soul needs no mediator or liaison between itself and the divine. The soul *is* divine. Therefore the world itself is sacred in the Egyptian mind. They did not feel the separation of divine and mundane that was introduced by their conquerors, the Persians and the Greeks.

The human soul is the ultimate expression of divine experience in Egyptian religion. Metaphors, embodied as the *Natur,* are divine images of the soul's understanding, relating the inner divine and its capacity to create and use the iconography of the living, extant system of mythological understanding. Just as Unas and Pepi "ate back the gods" as they ascended to heaven, the human soul is the source and field of action for the symbols of the divine imagery.

The Houses Of The *Naturu* (temples) represented the inner life of each living person. They were solid, tangible symbols of the intangible inner landscapes which each of us encompass. The figures of the *Natur*, the gods, were kept in golden shrines deep inside, symbolic of the golden shrine inside each person in which awareness of the divine nature of that *Natur* dwells. The Houses Of The *Naturu* were referred to as "sky." Each morning the priest opened the doors to the sky when he opened the doors of the shrine. These were consecrated gateways to the *duat*, to the divine dimension made visible in the sky above and invisible in the inner world. Just as the priests kept a living focus on the *Natur* in the shrine, each of us must keep a living focus on the *Natur* inside us. A generic term for these temples, known as the House Of The *Natur*, was *ro-per*, translated as "Mouth Of The House." The image of Nut swallowing the Sun each sunset at the western horizon was powerful in their world, and the entrance to the House of a *Natur* was also the entrance to that world "below the horizon" where the divine plane existed, linking the daily world to the eternal. The offering to *Ma'at* was important in the House of every *Natur*. Awareness of the dual realities was the prime teaching of each. Inner and outer realities are equally real, and each must be dealt with in its proper place. Depression, boredom, stress, anxiety, fear and even madness are the results of allowing the darkness of inner reality to overwhelm outer reality, or of allowing the light of outer reality to wash away the forms of the inner landscape.

Pot *Natur*: The Ennead, Organizations of Human And Divine

Spelled "*paut neter*" in earlier textbooks.

The *Natur* are most often encountered in groups or families, known as *Pot* (*paut*) and referred to in translation as the "pantheon or Ennead of gods." *Pot* is translated most simply as "bread," although bread is only the beginning of the meaning of *Pot*. It is one of the most complex spiritual concepts in the ancient world.

The *Pot* is expressed in terms of two groups of *Natur* known as the "*Lesser and Greater Pot*." The *Greater Pot Natur* consists most often of Osiris, Isis, Re, Thoth, Horus, Sut, Nepthys, Shu, and Tafnut in various combinations. The group comprising the *Lesser Pot* varies more in personnel, but the basic premise is that the divine forces of the soul interact and work together within the world. The *Greater Pot Natur* are the divine metaphors of the living soul within; the

Lesser Pot Natur are of the space/time world in which the fleshly garment of the soul lives. The use of the number nine here connected with the Ennead shows the deep roots of Egyptian thinking. The "Sacred Number" of the World Mother Goddess of the older mythological stratum is always nine. There has been much speculation about this, leading to formal structures based on 432, 108, etc. Comparative mythologists, such as Joseph Campbell, tie it in with the average number of heartbeats in 24 hours. I myself think the original fascination with nine and the reason it is associated with the Self-Created World Mother (*mater*) who creates the world out of herself is the nearly magical way in which nine is always the sum of its parts. 2X9=18, 1+8=9. 3X9=27, 2+7=9 and so forth.

The number one, the monad, is the starting point, and the next three numbers, 2,3,4, add up to 9. That is because ours is a ten-base system, yes. We, in our "Modern Math" enlightenment, consider such things to be children's games for remembering mathematical principles, but that is actually the point. The World Mother has mathematical games as an intrinsic part of the "playground of reality" she made for her children, humanity. The modern mind must stretch to grasp his attitude of delight about reality, yet it is precisely this delight in the true miracles of reality represented in every gesture of the Egyptian world.

This delight in the natural miracles of the world is demonstrated with great energy and elegance in the conception of the *Pot Natur.* Its initial meaning is "bread." The divine metaphor of bread comes from the earliest days of mankind. Fire was a profoundly new metaphor for the mysterious forces of the world that surround us, but fire, for all its magic, is wholly of the natural world. It is spontaneous magic, creating itself, raining down from the heavens or bursting out of the Earth. It is a metaphor of divine force only nominally under our control. Bread, however, is wholly a human invention, no matter how natural the source of the grain. The new metaphors of human experience that rise out of bread have endured for ten thousand years and more. Bread is as unique a thing as the human being who bakes it. Grass will nourish only animals, and thus grass, like fire, is entirely of the natural realm; but the seeds of grass will feed humans as well as animals. Flour made from these grass seeds is itself a new substance, a substance that is not like grass or seeds. It is like the substance of the Earth itself, but edible, and it is a product of the hand and energy of humans, not magic.

When water is mixed with flour it becomes remarkably like flesh, not only in its color, but also in that it yields like flesh, warm to the touch. Like flesh, it is better to eat when cooked. Bread can be molded to any shape. Once baked, it holds that shape. Too much or too little heat can spoil it but, once baked, it has become "of one flesh."

Here we stumble onto suspicions of a miracle. Baked bread is not anything like its parts. It is not like green grass, not like yellow grain, nor brown flour. It is neither gaseous like fire, wet like water, nor dry like flour, yet these elements combine to make bread. The human hand has made something "wholly other," something wholly human. Best of all, it is good to eat. This marvelous secret is locked up in the nourishing World Mother Earth as a prize for her curious child.

This is the beginning of the metaphor of baked bread as divine substance.

When earth in the form of clay is used instead of precious flour, and baked just like bread, another miracle is found: pottery. The more flour-like the clay, the finer the quality of the pot. Once more, the human hand transforms elements of the natural world into something wholly other and wholly human. Thus the solid substance of the Earth, in loose grains or parts, mixed with moisture, is transformed by heat into a single, coherent body. In other words, transformed by the experience of the union of opposites: dry and wet, shattered and whole, natural and human. These mysterious relationships of bread, clay, and flesh are the basis of the bread metaphor of The *Pot Natur*, the holy pantheon of The Children of The Sun. The echo remains today in our word for such clay vessels: "pottery." It is the power in "potency" and "potential."

The interior cohesion of flesh, bread, and pottery that maintains the individual integrity is a magical metaphor for the power of the divine. This cohesion withstands much stress and use, but, once broken, it is as permanently broken as before it was whole. Pottery cannot be remolded once shattered; bread cannot be re-baked. Dead flesh will not rise.

This magic of cohesion is the meaning of the *Pot Natur*, the gathered forces of the *Natur* that define a human being in life. It is the magic of the divine presence made manifest. For centuries, ancient Egypt was the breadbasket of the western world, suppliers of grain for all the ovens of the Mediterranean. Every ceremony and ritual in Egypt involved bread in one form or another throughout the life of their civilization. The hieroglyph for the verb "to give offering" is a loaf of bread on a woven reed tray.

The magical metaphor of baked bread was never lost, and the *Pot Natur* nourished the millennia of success enjoyed by the world's first civilization.

Egyptian Divinity: "Who's In Charge Here?"

There is no one "head God" in the Egyptian pantheon.

This fact has mystified, frustrated, confused, puzzled, amused and outraged monotheists for 2,500 years. As a result, Egyptian philosophy has been labeled with the curious oxymoron, "spiritual materialism," and dismissed as primitive.

The "divine" forces of Nature are mysterious and seem miraculous, but are nevertheless bound by their own rules of logic and reality and are subject to scientific comprehension. In the ancient view, that is their *divine* nature. In our modern view, that is simply their *physical* nature. In our modern theological training, we tend to equate divine and magical, as though God were some divine conjurer messing about with reality for whimsy's sake. Conscious will, however, *can* change the laws of Nature. By all the laws of divine reality, only winged beings can fly; but we have mastered the art in our way, defying such divine law. Yet, because of our religious training, we deny ourselves the miracle of it since it is not levitation. Egyptians were less concerned with magical tricks than in a deeper understanding of the miracle of existence.

In our modern, monotheistic world view, divinity is separated out from everyday life, and concentrated in the single personality of the anthropomorphised deity to whom we are related–"Our Father"–Zeus and family remote on Mount Olympus, Yahweh/Jehovah/Allah in Their/His celestial isolation. The physical world in which we live is seen as somehow "corrupted" in comparison to this celestial place. We are supposedly here on Earth to act as servants to this God on High. To see the path of the Egyptian in his/her lifetime, you must recognize how different from this was their sense of the miracle of existence. Egypt preferred the divine nature of their own life-experience to contemplation of a distant deity. They saw reality as a manifestation of the Divine. The only "corruption" was in intentions and act, those expressions of free will for which only living souls have the capacity. The Egyptian is ruled by his divine soul, not by a divine being separated and remote from the world.

A more modern example of the profound and profoundly subtle difference in world view between the Egyptian nature of the divine, and monotheism, rests in the Bible story of Jesus converting water into wine. In modern terms, a "god" is one who can perform, as a divine conjuring trick, a miracle such as turning water into wine. All divinity is concentrated in that one being. We can be a servant to that divinity, but we cannot *be* that divinity.

For a man to do this is sleight-of-hand. Yet, the "miracle" of converting water into wine is accomplished without ceasing by the humblest of creatures, the simple yeast cells which "create wine out of water" as a natural gesture of their existence. As monotheists, we are unimpressed by this natural miracle. The nature of yeast is to create alcohol. Where's the miracle?

The Egyptian considers the existence of the yeast cell creating wine, and sees in that a manifestation of the divine presence enclosed in reality. They do not "worship the yeast cell" but a universe that would accommodate both such a creature as the yeast cell and a human being to appreciate the wine. The Egyptians related the human to the divine of the entire universe, not just to a remote, isolated deity of arbitrary will.

This is also not an isolated nor indeed even an antiquated world view. This sense of the divinity of reality is the underlying principle of Oriental religion today. There is, however, a primary difference between the modern Orient and the ancient Egyptian mind. The *erasure* of ego-identity is the goal of Oriental meditation, the complete dissolution of self into the bliss of undifferentiated consciousness. Egypt saw the uniqueness of identity as the ground of divine nature. Identity is the divinity of the soul. The purpose of life is to achieve and to groom your own identity, polishing yourself into the finest image of yourself of which you are capable, your "Golden Horus name," then to carry that polished image into eternity, to shine there in the next life as illuminated as the stars themselves.

The difficulty with this philosophy for the peoples outside of Egypt was the problem of the "spiritual democracy" implied in the Egyptian doctrine of "I am divine as you are divine and we are divine together." The difficulty with that is when you have something that I want to take, like desert tribes who want to stole crops to feed their children. If we are spiritual equals, then I must earn what I need from you. If we are both servants of the One Divine Being, then that Master can direct one of his servants to take the possessions of another servant, and the loser has to declare it "the will of God." I can storm in, take what I want, believing that "God instructed me." Which is, alas, what the tribes of the desert, swelled into nations of barbarian splendor, did to Egypt.

The Egyptologist John Romer, in his *Ancient Lives* series, has made the observation that everyone brings their own interpretation of ancient Egypt with them. He has worked with archaeologists from three different nations, America, England, and Germany, and each has a different Egypt. Like the elephant of the seven blind men, ancient Egypt is too enormous for a single point of view.

Egyptologists, however, all have a common point of view: we are descendants of Egypt's conquerors, ancient and modern. The emotional need to reduce the extent of the destruction has led to a general devaluation of her timeless philosophy. That trend has been compensated for in modern times by the opposite need to see that ancient world as a nation of supermen, in touch with aliens and the technology of the stars.

No other civilization, modern or ancient, has successfully maintained as coherent and as evenly sustained a cultural identity as the peoples of ancient Egypt. Even China is three thousand years younger. This remarkable integrity has been attributed to the stable environment of the Nile River valley, yet no modern nation has made the Nile work for them as did The Children Of The Sun. *Khemmet,* the Black Land, does not yield forth her bounty for the Arab-based culture as she once did for The Land of Love.

Her ancient stability has been called stagnation. Her universality of image-based communication is dismissed as primitive and one-dimensional. They did not build lasers in ancient Egypt, but neither did they worship animals nor multiple souls or gods. They were humanity's first true civilization, and they, themselves, want us to know that. The pride which they felt for their nation, their civilization, their lives was deep, innocent and beautifully expressed in their art and writings. This pride and joy of living has been ignored and misinterpreted by scholars, ancient and modern.

The primary, basic premise is that only a logical, practical-minded philosophy could hold together a nation with such total and magically enduring coherency for so many millennia through so many changes in the world around them. If their images seem irrational, it must be in *our* interpretation not in *their* original intention and understanding. Seen with this author's prejudice, the ancient imagery is as coherent and logical as *Scientific American* magazine–grounded, however, in their absolute faith in the divine and eternal nature of the soul: Osiris. That is the only unprovable, illogical feature of their philosophy, transforming it with sudden, transcendent light into a deeply spiritual teaching.

They also believed, utterly, in the vital necessity of education and this was their undoing: the peoples who conquered them never quite got the story right. The resonance of their beliefs became the fragmented images of genuinely primitive cultures, copies of copies of copies...

Even my interpretation is corrupt; trust no one except the ancients themselves to tell their story. If you look at their world, their works and their art using this guide, you will see their story more clearly, erasing some of the years and distance between. Their images speak most directly. Whatever the actual, absolute nature of the human soul, no one has ever pursued the language and imagery of it with greater eloquence, art and style than The Children Of The Sun.

The Egyptian Trinity

The Egyptian Trinity is a complex issue, and one that I address in my work only indirectly. The most well known are the triads of Osiris, Isis and Horus, of Amon-Mut-Khons, and of Ptah-Sekhmet-Nefertum. There were many variations on the theme as the temple systems evolved. Each triad is a complex set of relationships. Fundamental to every triad is the relationship itself, the concept of the two poles of duality and the dynamics of the energy flowing between them. Energy must have two "poles to move between, otherwise it is only potential, static, grounded in one place. The duality of the mother/father is the creation of the two poles between which the dynamic of life-energy can flow, represented by the child. The Egyptians tended to arrange the deities in Father-Mother-Child triads, since that was their primary trinity, an element that remained largely unchanged from the most ancient of times to the end. The specific archetype fulfilling each role as Father/Mother/Child varied from city to city and temple to temple, depending on the pattern being defined. A farmer, for example, would be more likely to have the Hathor-Osiris-Horus triad at the center of his pattern because these are linked with the primary, raw cycling of life-force through the world, imagery grown out of the fecundity of the marshlands and fields.

On the other hand, temple artisans and construction workers would be more likely to have the Ptah-Sekhmet-Nefertum iconography functioning within their inner worlds. These are the patterns of the divine passion of the craftsman for the tools and the work, the joy of the hand's work.

None of these triads were fixed. The system was fluid enough to be universal yet applicable to each individual, not only in their individual differences but also through the changing experiences of each entire lifetime. I have not categorized trinities within my own work because of that very fluidity.

The ancient Egyptians believed in the fundamental constancy of objective reality, in *Ma'at.* They used this constancy as the ground of their own precepts of human reality. In the cyclical nature of the Nile's flood and retreat they saw a meditation on the timeless nature of the cycles in Nature, and the round of eternity that was imaged through them.

Their deepest meditations were on the divine and eternal nature of the human soul and of human consciousness, the eternal and unchanging center of the constantly changing action of the physical sphere. The unique nature of the individual experience of life was the counterpoint to the divine plane from which that life arose and to which it returned. The responsibility of that individual uniqueness is celebrated in change. The Egyptian culture changed so little precisely *because* they were living in a world-view of the unique individual placed in a universal, cosmic setting.

"I purify you.
My two hands are around you.
Your portion of the head is the gift of your ancestors.
Give me my voice.
I will speak with it.
I pilot my heart in its hour of fire and dark."

WHY THE CAT HAS NINE LIVES THE ESSENTIAL EGYPTIAN VIEW OF THE SELF

"I am the Cat who is splitting the *erika* tree, opened at its side in *Innu* centerpoint. It is that night of destroying the opponents of his Lord To The Limits in here. The cat is a child, and is Re himself. One calls him "Cat" because of the story of the sage about him: "Just like him," and because of what he has done while evolving his name, which is Cat."

"My *ib*-heart from my mother! My *ib-h*eart from my mother!
My *haty*-heart from evolving in spirit,
and from testimony about me,
from opposition against me from the Divine Precincts"

"My knowledge is in my heart,
and my spirit is in my attitude."

"My spirit is inside my *ka* when making love.
My person will not be imprisoned.
The stargates contained in the Hidden World are my flesh,
through which I enter in peace and emerge in peace."

The Nine Layers Of The Inner Landscape

The primary concepts of ancient Egyptian philosophy are expressed through a jargon of the soul. The terminology of these nine elements of the living human individual was known by every citizen of the ancient Nile culture, yet this knowledge survives in the modern world only in the form of the curious superstition of the cat's nine lives. (The Egyptian word for a simile, for something being "like" something else was a pun on the word for "cat," *miw.* Thus Re was the cat who climbed up the dawn tree. Re is "like" the Sun climbing through the trees. The Egyptian *khat*, the physical flesh which decays, comes down to us in "cattle" and "cat.")

Sigmund Freud divided the human psyche into three parts–*id, ego,* and *superego*–and this awareness revolutionized our modern view of being human. Carl Jung divided psyche into four parts–*ego, shadow, self,* and *anim*–taking that revolution immeasurably further. In ancient Egypt the psyche was divided into nine parts or layers of being–the *akh, sekhem, ib, khat, shuit, ren, ba, ka,* and *sahu.* It was a revolution of thought by which they built an empire out of the mud, using pen and paper, string, rocks, and conversation.

The goal of all these divisions of psyche–three, four, or nine–is self-awareness and natural self-control. The only significant difference between Egyptian psychological teaching and modern Western psychology is the place and function of the soul in the economy of the human psyche. The ancients did not question the existence of the divine soul; their entire civilization was built on belief in the soul's absolute reality and its absolute divinity. From ancient Egypt we learn that identity is the divinity of the soul.

1. *akh:* the divine substance of the human soul.
2. *sekhem:* the energy pattern of the divine spirit,
   the song of the soul.
3. *ib*: the life-force, territory of the heart.
4. *khat*: the soul's container, that which decays:
   "I stink, therefore I am."
5. *shuit*: the living shadow, proof of reality.
6. *ren*: the magic of your name, divine identity.
7. *ba*: the you whom only you can know, the inside of the mask.
8. *ka*: the you as others know you, the outside of the mask.
9. *sahu*: the natural boundary of the psychic self,
   horizon of the divine self.

These terms for the nine parts of being represent the key elements of ancient Egyptian philosophy. They are the definition of self that every child in the nation learned at its mother's knee, the beliefs that guided their lives. They are the primary vocabulary with which they talked about themselves. It is clear from the remarkably vast body of their writings that has survived millennia of destruction that they talked endlessly together about themselves, their world, their lives and their beliefs.

The experience of the immortal soul immersed in mortal existence is the central theme of all their stories and the foundation of their civilization, and they created an exquisite language for its intricate, detailed, and poetic discussion.

Akh:
Solid Light, Divine Substance Of The Human Soul

The Egyptians perceived the living soul, *AKH*, to be that most essential part of each person, the actual, transcendent substance at the center of being: a particle of the divine plane inserted by divine force into the reality of space/time through the doorway of birth. This divine soul is clothed in flesh by entry into life, and this garment is cast off again in death. (Their garment of flesh, *khat*, was to them a most beloved cloak, however mortal. *See below.*)

In the beliefs of the ancient world, the soul is that part of you that you can never lose nor abandon. Your soul is not just who you are. Your soul does not just belong to you–your soul *is* you. You can *never* lose your soul. The Devil cannot take it away from you, no matter what you sign. Your soul can *forget* all the names and experiences of your many-layered human life, but your soul will always be you, the sense within your flesh that feels like you. It is in the stories of Osiris that the soul's substance is explored.

The sacred nature of the act of love opens the soul door, giving entry to the divine substance of the living soul. In ancient Egypt, life was not seen as inherently sinful, and nowhere in their writings is the concept of "original sin." They wrote much about the sin involved in actions and intentions in life, but saw no sin in being born. There was no exile from the garden of paradise, because reality *was* paradise.

The hieroglyph determinative for *akh*, the soul, is a crowned stork or crane. These birds wading in the marshlands of the Nile stand as tall as a man, and they live at the interface of the worlds of land, water and air, symbolizing the soul's ability to span the planes of existence. This image survives today in the superstition of the stork as the carrier of newborn babies, because the entrance of the soul into its garment of flesh is the beginning of life.

"I am this:
I am a soul inside the light, appareled in flesh,
designed and created by divine forces."

Akh is still mistakenly translated as "spirit," since there is a current tendency to see the *ba* as representative of the soul. This comes out of modern confusion over the two concepts, soul and spirit, and the difficulty with *ba* and *ka*. (See below.)

Spirit is related to breath and the motion around a center, images related to the energy of the soul rather than its substance. *Akh* is the root of many Egyptian words, differing by the determinative symbol which indicates the specific nuance of soul-substance implied: It is, for example, at the root of the word *akht*, arable land, the bodily essence of Osiris that flooded the land with the black mud that was Egypt's life's-blood.

We find further that the *akht* or Uraeus serpents are the King Cobras of the Pharaoh's headpiece and adornment of the tomb, gestures of the energy.

Continuing in this way, we find:

Akht is the Eye of the Divine, the awakened soul oriented properly to both inner and outer reality.

Akht is flame, body of energy, substance of heat.

Akht is the horizon where the Sun rises and sets, that divine thresholds between dimensions of reality; the phrase "images of the horizon" is an idiom for "sacred images."

Akhty is the Horizon Dweller, another name for the Divine.

Akhu is the substance of the Sun, the sunlight itself.

Akh-akh is the verb "to grow green," which is the primary activity of Osiris, transforming the black river mud to green shoots of plant life.

Akh-akh are the stars in the sky, believed to be the purified being of past souls.

Akh-akh are the spars of a ship, that which hold the sail open on the mast to catch the breath of wind–and of life.

Sakh is the constellation Orion, which the ancient Egyptians believed to be the body of Osiris.

Sakh is the verb form of *akh*, translated as "spiritualize," and is the root of *skhm*, the spirit or energy of the soul.

Sakhu are the ritual recitations, the language of the soul.

Sak is "to pull together" and is used with the word "heart" to mean "self-possessed."

(The pronunciation is close to the American prounciation of "X." Consider the ways in which we use "X" today.)

Sekhem: Energy Pattern Of The Divine Spirit, The Song Of The Soul

SEKHEM is the energy of the soul, the divine spirit. It was recognized as a function of the soul's existence, separating substance and energy. The soul acquires its unique identity at the instant it separates from the divine plane; your soul is this particular bit of divine substance, placed into the reality of space/time at that specific here and now.

This unique identity has its own unique energy pattern, and this is translated to flesh via the DNA code that is the literal definition of the flesh's unique biological, living self. This divine energy dance is the *sekhem*, the spirit, and its harmonics define and sustain the soul through life.

The hieroglyph for the spirit is a musical instrument, the sistrum, used to create a droning vibration in ceremonies symbolizing the vibration of the spirit, the music of the soul.

This energy force is unique to the soul's existence; it is the source of energy from which the soul sustains its immortal life. Illustrations of sistrum, held by Lady Hathor, the divine mother, show the central portion of strings and rattling rings replaced by a soul-figure of the newborn individual emerging into reality.

IB:
LIFE-FORCE, TERRITORY OF THE HEART

IB is represented by a hieroglyph of the heart itself with the artery spouts attached. The symbol of the *ib* is not just the heart organ, but also the actual pathway of the energy flowing through the heart. The energy which the soul draws from the spirit is translated through the darkness of flesh as life--biological, biochemical life.

Ib is the force which informs life.

Ib is the awareness of flesh of itself and its duty and needs. *Ib* is the energy of the soul's dance translated through the flesh itself, experienced as the emotional, psychic world, the autonomic functioning of psyche that is outside conscious control; all those experiences of human life that we today still call "the territory of the heart," and to which we consign the mysteries of psychology, psychiatry, astrology, mythology, and so on.

The heart was the seat of the passions in ancient Egypt, just as it is today. *Ib* is feeling, passion, courage, and joy of life. The *ib*-heart harbors the compassion which can save the world from itself.

The Haty-Heart: The ancients also distinguished finer shades of meaning in the functions of the *ib*, naming both *ib* and *haty* when referring to feelings.

The *haty*-heart was represented by the foreparts of the lion, which was itself the symbol of Lady Sekhmet, goddess of fierce passion, linked with the *ib*-heart hieroglyph.

The lion hieroglyph also represented that which is in the front, in the lead. The *ib*-heart is the entire life-process of emotional energy, indicating the greater existence of such energy. The *haty*-heart is the attitude, the mood of the moment, the emotion experienced at this time, the feelings that are in front, leading life now.

These dual identities of the *ib*-heart have energy and power that function as integral parts of the personality throughout life, but the *haty*-heart experiences a variety of feelings over time. Attitudes in childhood are different from those in later life. Love, hate, fear, apathy–all can change the attitude of the heart completely. Attitudes change, but psychic energy, *ib*-heart energy, flows from birth to death.

"O my *ib*-heart which I had from my mother!
O my *haty*-heart of my different ages!"

Ib is also the Egyptian determinative for "imagination," and "to imagine," for other words relating to the expression of life through non-rational experience. "Sailing To Heart's Centerpoint" was a metaphor for the transition of death, and the soul itself is referred to as *The Great Thing Within The Heart's Centerpoint.*

KHAT: THE SOUL'S LIVING CONTAINER OF FLESH, "THAT WHICH DECAYS:"

I stink, therefore I am.

KHAT is translated as "that which decays," and is represented either by a mummy on its bier or by a stylized animal belly. *Khat* is the flesh we are born into, the flesh which clothes the divine soul. *Khat* is referred to as the garment of the soul, and the distinction between soul and flesh is clear. Living flesh is the doorway between the spirit dimension of the soul's source and the physical dimension of reality.

The reality of the Hidden Land, of the spiritual plane of the soul before birth and after death, was a powerful belief, and meditation on that belief was the science of those ages, accepted as logic and grounded in careful, empirical observations of nature, man, and life. These two utterly separate dimensions of reality are linked only by divine means, doorways, mystical passageways that communicate between the two dimensions. The immortal soul can pass through, but mortal flesh cannot.

The sacred nature of living flesh is in this paradox: that it can be both the absolute boundary between dimensions and also the only doorway capable of linking them. Flesh is both the key and the lock. The living body, activated by the male and produced by the female, is more than just the vessel of the soul. This divine power of the *khat* is represented in artwork and architecture by the "soul door," a false doorway carved or painted on the wall in both the birthing chamber and the tomb. The soul door marks out the sanctum where such divine doorways are opened. The Egyptian appreciation of the magical vessel of the body is very unlike the modern, Western view of the flesh. The goal of Egyptian spiritual training was to identify self with the soul within, and to respect and maintain the magical container which carries the soul through life, and to do so as elegantly and carefully as humanly possible. Their medical technology was more involved with daily care and comfort than with the wartime inspiration that has driven most medical research. The respect given to the miraculous potential of the body to house a divine soul reaches a pinnacle in mummification and the wealth of tomb objects. The body, as a reward for its service, is rendered inedible, safe from attack by the wild beasts that haunt graveyards and eat dead flesh. It is provided with every need, and allowed to rest, safe and secure, with all its favorite and lovely "toys" at hand. The soul has moved on to the other side of reality, where flesh cannot be, animated and energized by the host of images and memories of life. The body, left behind on this side of reality, can at last rest. "He who dies with the most toys wins" is a remarkably Egyptian sentiment, however modern the words.

This view point can be expressed in modern concepts through the language and metaphors of science and metaphysics. Life-force opens the gateway through which the energy of that invisible dimension pours into this visible dimension.

Consciousness is the form of that energy as it pours through the space/time dimension. Each gateway is a soul. The physical, living flesh is both the key and the lock to that gateway. Identity is the location of a specific gateway and a specific flow of this other-dimensional energy. Identity is the foundation of the soul, and consciousness is the experience of that invisible soul in the visible dimension.

Shuit: The Living Shadow, Link To Solid Reality

SHUIT, (also *KHAIBIT*), your shadow, (sometimes "shade") is proof that you are real; proof that you stand in the cold, white light of reality. The physical body, the *khat*, casts a shadow; unreal things do not. (For example, people and objects seen in dreams rarely cast shadows.) A shadow is proof of the solid reality of the thing which cast it, and shadow and object are intimately and uniquely related to each other. Whatever the physical meaning of the shadow, it was self-evident to the ancients that every man, child, and cat had one. The shadow faithfully duplicates every move and gesture. The shadow is a unique possession. It cannot be lost or separated from you. It is a lifelong companion. Whatever a person might lose in life, your shadow is proof that you cannot lose *yourself.*

Shadows are the footprints of the Sun. Daily time, in the experience of waking reality, is measured by the shadow's slow and stately dance with the Sun. Even solid, inanimate objects have animated shadows. Indeed, the measure of the great, round Earth was first taken by a shadow.

The shadow is the soul's marker in space and time, binding it to the Earth. It is as inescapable a metaphor in the inner world as is the Sun in the outer. The Egyptians did not limit their survey of the soul's dimension only to the soul itself; they were equally concerned with the place of the living soul together with other living souls in the world.

Ren: Divine Identity The Magic Of Your Name

"That face which is mine, my name for it will be known."

Identity was a crucial concept in the ancient world and a major focal point of Egyptian philosophy. Identity is the divinity of the soul. *Ren* is the social name you are given. That name is related to your absolute identity just as the face is related to the soul. The name you are known by is different from the DNA name which defines you as you. Just as the substance of the soul is defined separately from its energy, the absoluteness of identity is defined separately from the name. The face is the visual name of the flesh, and is often addressed as an individual in the texts. "Oh, face and head of the heart!"

Names were important in ancient Egypt, and everywhere the soul is referred to as "the designer of his name and designer of the name of his flesh." Naming is everywhere in their writing and art. Names are metaphors of identity, metaphors of social place, and landmarks of the soul's journey through life;. The texts are about the soul's journey through life to eternity.

The Pharaoh had five "great names," *rn-wr,* or "original names," a system that became more elaborated as the dynasties continued. These were: the Birth Name, also known as the Son Of Re name; the Throne Name, preceded by "he of the sedge and the bee," which is the title of the King Of Upper And Lower Egypt; The Horus Name, or the *Ka* name for formal ceremonials; the Two Ladies Name and the Golden Horus Name. The naming system is reminiscent of the Native American Navaho naming-system of clans, of being born to one clan and born for a different clan, an elaboration of family relationships that made it possible to keep village groups from intermarrying too closely.

The Egyptian naming system for non-royals was less complex but equally enthusiastic, and the elaboration of *titles* was wonderfully imaginative, with ones like "Pharaoh's Friend," and "Pharaoh's Breath," proudly displayed. "Earning a name for yourself" was more than just an expression.

Ba:
The Private Self, The Inside of Your Soul's Mask

BA is represented by a crowned head atop the body of a Horus-falcon or sometimes a kite, bird of the protecting spirits of Isis and Lady Of The House. The *ba* is sometimes shown fluttering over the tomb or with the mummy, and is present in many scenes of the tomb's art. The *ba* has been variously interpreted as the soul, or vital force, or as one of "multiple souls."

The *ba* is the private, inner experience of being within every person. *Ba* is the self, a composite entity created by a merger of archetype and individuation. The *ba* is the soul as it knows itself from within, from the inside of the mask. The *ba* is the symbol *par excellence* of the self, a living, conscious being. The *ba* is also the ultimate privacy, for it is that experience of being from within, which can be communicated, imaged and evaluated, but not shared.

No one can experience another's experience of being. *Ba* is the ultimate democracy and a paradox, for although each of us experiences reality uniquely, our unique experience is each unique in exactly the same, human way. I cannot know what you are feeling, but I can know that you feel to yourself as real as I feel to myself, and just as human. The bird's body represents the universal biological standard. In the head, however, the soul is unique, crowned by its individual identity.

The language of ancient Egypt does have generic terminology for such concepts as "humanity," "man," "woman," etc. However, when referring to the psychology of the soul's experience of life and death, the term for self is *ba*. This term implies a conscious, named entity; someone who could be known. As a symbol of the self, the *ba* is the sum total of an individual merged into a single focus. The *ba* is not consciousness in and of itself, but it is the only vehicle which will support consciousness. The *ba* is the dark magic of the flesh out of which consciousness is born like the Sun rising out of the night at dawn.

The *ba* is addressed often in tomb art, because the belief was that you would still be experiencing yourself *as yourself* even through the processes of the interface of realities. The focus of the rituals was to maintain the coherency of that self-experience despite the rending transition from time to eternity. Your flesh will be cut away, but you will still be you there within your soul. That coherency of *experience* is embodied in the *ba*.

There is a deeply moving piece of literature, "The Dialog Of A

Man And His *Ba*," in which a man talks himself out of suicide. That is a completely internal debate: a conversation with your own inner experience of your life, where no one else can stand.

The *ba* is shown with a human head and the body of a bird, because the inner self is always different from the outer self, freer and traveling on winged thought. No matter what attention and memory your *ka* is receiving from the living, you are the only one who will *experience* the transition to the next life entered through the tomb. Those haunting images of the *ba* fluttering alone over the coffin hint at the ultimate privacy of the experience.

It is too easy to attribute so much 'alienness' to their distant lives that their meanings become impossible, but they were the same kind of human beings that we are. Only the specifics of their environment and education differ from our own imagery.

The *ba* represents only a portion of the *ma'at* of consciousness, since the religion of ancient Egypt was also concerned with the place of the living soul within the reality of the outside world.

Ka: The Public Self, The Outside of Your Soul's Mask

The symbol of the *KA* is a pair of outstretched arms offering embrace. The *ka* is the essence of the "relatedness" of living beings meeting each other out in reality, where shadows entwine. The *ka* is the mask of the self that is seen by others on the outside. The *ka* is the person whom others see, the *ba* as seen by other *ba*. Each of us sees other people from his or her own point of view; no one can know the inner experience of someone else's soul. That is the ultimate privacy. The *ka* is the outside of the mask, and your soul can experience only the inside of your own mask.

The *ka* is a slippery concept for the modern mind to grasp. It is a concept we deal with in every moment of civilized life, yet we have been unable to describe it without using a confusing array of terms and conflicting ideas. Most Egyptologists dismiss the complexity of the *ka* in Egyptian writing and art by translating it as being one of "multiple souls," thus reducing this profoundly sophisticated religious philosophy to the level of pagan superstition.

It is no coincidence that *ka* is a pun on the Egyptian suffix for "you" in verbs, as in "you are doing this." The *ka* is the outside of the self, the outer mask whom only other people can see. The *ka* is shown in their art as a duplicate of the individual–there is you as you know yourself, and then there is the you whom others see, the outside of you. Others know you before you know yourself. Your survivors will remember you as your *ka* after you yourself have gone. Other people see your *ka* in the ceremonies and important moments of your life–but you cannot. You can only know yourself from the inside. You cannot know how others see you.

The truth is that each of us deals with the *ka* every day. It survives in modern words such as "character" and the Greek *charisma.* The portrait, family photo album, the public reputation, the public image, the boss, the celebrity, superstar, teen idol, cult figure, and friend–these are all forms of the *ka.*

The Egyptians describe the *ka* of each individual as being born before the child itself is born. This is because the parents and their friends know of the child's existence before its birth; others are aware of the reality of the soul clothed in infant flesh long before the soul is conscious of itself.

"You will see the face of everyone except
the face of your own flesh, while your father and your son
guard the face of their faces."

The *ka* lives on after death through the memories of the dead that the living keep alive in their own inner worlds. This principle has been practiced continuously for thousands of years, right into the present day. Many famous movie actors are now dead, yet each actor's *ka* on the screen "comes to life" whenever movies are watched by the living. The ghosts of the silver screen are, in a sense, the most distilled examples of the concept of the *ka.* The soul of Humphrey Bogart has passed on, but Bogart as "King Of The Silver Screen is alive (and still earning money for his estate!) That is the *ka* at work.

A person's *ka* can be shaped and its image changed. Your soul is yours and yours alone, but your *ka* can be stolen, ruined, humiliated, or changed, no matter how unchanged you are inside your mask. The *ka* can be deceitful and betray its owner. The *ka* can work for you or against you, even without your awareness of its working. The public image and the private self can diverge greatly. Much ancient and modern literature and art is based on the conflict and bond between the two. The *ka* is the central figure of ancient Egyptian morality, for the realm of the *ka* encompasses all aspects of human social and personal interaction. The mask of the *ka* that you show to the world marks you as a civilized person or a barbarian, friend or foe, acceptable or unacceptable, yet your *ba* can never see its own *ka* except in reflection (or, in modern times, recorded on film or video, but even then, you cannot know how others perceive you).

There is an entire class of ancient literature, called "Instructions," based on advice to the *ka* and how it is to behave in the presence of *ka* of various ranks, as peers, superiors, or workers.

It is all good advice, even today. There are careful, mature suggestions for polite and civilized behavior in the presence of a *ka* of greater rank, and for generous, caring behavior in the presence of those of lesser rank. These are public roles and public behavior.

The mind-games one can play of "It's not me–it's you!" come naturally to every child learning language, and are the birth of awareness of other people and their unique perspective.

The image is also profoundly condensed in the determinative for the *ka*: a pair of human arms stretching out, the reach of the human embrace, measuring out the distance from me to you. Even the ambiguity of the gesture is deliberate–are the arms reaching upward or outward? In the presence of *ka* of higher rank, the arms are stretched upward in the gesture of bowing or prostrating before them; in the presence of *ka* of equal or lesser rank the arms are stretched outward in embrace.

The nation along the Nile was humankind's first successful attempt at this kind of civilized cooperation on a multi-regional basis, and the careful rules of human interaction and individuation were the bedrock on which they built their unity. The mud of the Nile might wash away physical boundaries, but the cooperation of everyone kept personal territories respected and aligned.

Western culture has reverence for the *ka* of great individuals. We just do not have a word in English for the concept. Consider the wide range of festive events that took place around the world at the end of 2000 in "celebration" of John Lennon on the 20th anniversary of his death. John's body was cremated two decades ago; it is his *ka* which his fans revere to this day, the John who continues to exist in music, film, tape and writings, and in the memories of those who saw and knew him in the flesh. There is no shortage of people in the world who have wanted to *be* John Lennon, but none of us can ever really *become* another person. Even his closest friends and lovers have publicly acknowledged that no one really knew what John was going through inside of the Beatle image. One simply cannot. We can try to live the image vicariously, imagining the experience of his *ba*, of being the person inside a living myth, but only John Lennon could ever really know how it was to *be* John Lennon. Even he despaired of telling anyone what it was like.

SAHU: NATURAL BOUNDARY OF THE PSYCHIC SELF, THE SHAPE OF ETERNITY

A lifetime on top of the Earth is spent in adapting to reality and defining the boundaries of self and not-self. This sense of the shape and feel of the boundaries of being alive is the *SAHU.* The *sahu* is often represented as a mummy lying on a bier, because the awareness of the body's individual shape and function provides the soul with a sense of shape and boundary in the transition between the dimensions of this world and the next. The *sahu* is this self-defined psychic boundary.

(In recent years medical science has located the physical seat of the *sahu* in the human brain. The cerebellum has been found to maintain a constant electromagnetic replica of the body-self, a glowing self-image that is the true experience of feeling alive.)

The *sahu* is described as a being of glowing light. The stars in the night sky were thought to be the glowing souls of great beings shining from heaven. The *sahu* does not decay or die; it is as immortal as the immortal soul which it defines. This phantom body exists primarily to be activated in the next life as the identity of the soul in the spiritual dimension. The *sahu* is the immortal imprint of the mortal *khat* upon the soul. The process of evolving the unique identity of the soul has come full circle: the *khat* which is defined by the soul's energy defines the shape of the soul in the spiritual dimension to which it returns.

These nine parts are the shorthand terms for the fundamentals of this ancient philosophy stripped down to the dry, intellectual essentials of self. They represent the definition of self that all Egyptian children learned at their mother's knee. These are the beliefs that guided their lives and the primary vocabulary with which they talked about themselves. It is in the personification of these ideas as the living *Natur,* however, that the richness of their religion developed. The experience of the soul's immortality immersed in mortal existence is the central story of all their stories and the foundation of their civilization. No other civilization maintained its images and culture intact for as long as ancient Egypt did. There is much value to be found in their timeless philosophy. The *Natur,* or "gods" of ancient Egypt, developed as the Ennead, the "Greater and Lesser *Pot Natur* of The Divine," tell the stories of humanity, and the temples of their worship were dedicated to humankind's respect for itself.

OSIRIS, MYSTERY OF MYSTERIES: THE SOUL WITHIN

"That face which is mine, my name for it will be known. I will be taught what is their discipline by that which is inside the House Of Osiris and glitters in the eye when he is seen going around heaven with the flame of his mouth. I am just like the Hapy River, when he was seen. I am healthy on top of the Earth, possessing Re, and I am calmly moored in death possessing Osiris. Your sacrifices inside of me are for the faces of their lifetimes, the face which is what I am when in the company of the Lord To The Limits."

"I am Osiris, Lord Of The Mouth Of The Horizon,
a portion of Osiris immortalized as
that being on top of the steps.
I have entered at the desire of my *ib*-heart
through the Pool of Dual Flames:
I am quenched!

Orient your face, Lord of Radiance!
Facade Of The Original Home, and face of my head.
Darkness and twilights, I have gone carrying you, my soul."

Divine Bull Of The Goddess, Carrier Of An Ancient Message

In our modern era Osiris and Isis are among the most widely known names from the ancient Egyptian pantheon. They were popular deities to pharaohs and citizens alike from the very beginning of the civilization along the Nile.

The stories of Osiris and Isis evolved in complexity over the generations, especially in the civilization's later years, and their mythological iconography was borrowed by most religious movements following Egypt's decline. Their deeper spiritual values, however, as represented in the Egyptian mind, were eliminated by the onslaught of the Persian, Greek, Roman and Christian invaders who superimposed their own religious convictions upon the iconography of the ancient world.

The symbolism of Osiris arises from dreamlike roots deep in the Upper Paleolithic. Here is the sacred Moon Bull, whose body represents the ultimate mystery of the divine, incorruptible soul wrapped in corruptible flesh.

The great Bull, whose horns are the crescents of the new and old Moons, tilts his head, and one horn reaches down to touch the Earth, while the other horn reaches up to touch heaven, thus signifying the link between heaven and Earth represented by his biological existence.

An equivalent gesture is found in statues of the Goddess from thousands of years earlier: one hand resting upon her womb, the other reaching up to touch heaven. It survives in the Tarot (considered to be an inheritance of Egypt) as the gesture of the Magician, with one hand pointing up to the heaven, the other pointing down to the Earth. It is also the Earth-blessing posture of the Buddha. The sacrifice of the bull is the release of the inner divine energy from its magical container of flesh, whose death and dissolution releases the soul within to return to the celestial plane. This is the source of the Apis, Mnevis and other bull rituals.

The Moon Bull's sacrifice epitomizes the sacrifice of life to life, the continuing cycle of the divine soul, a being of light, entering and exiting reality through the magic gateway of its fleshly garment. The sacred bulls were living symbols of the mystery of the garment, the divine mystery of our living selves.

Mud And Blood Of The Nile, Dark Substance Of The Soul

Abydos (*Ibtu*) is the original home of *Khent Imenty*, the earliest Dynastic references to Osiris as "Foremost of the Westerners," referring to the dimension under the horizon to which the Sun goes, carrying with him the souls of the dead. *Khent Imenty* is associated with the jackals and hyenas that haunt the burial grounds.

Ibtu in Egyptian, "Heart's Town," or "Heart's Centerpoint," is known today as Abydos. It was the burial place of Osiris, and was considered a most sacred place from the time of the First Dynasty. Today Abydos is popularly known as the Valley Of The Kings. Finding peace in *Ibtu* was one of the goals of the funeral texts. It is another example of the dual-reality word-plays that appear so frequently in their writings: "Heart's Centerpoint" is both the physical locale of Abydos and the spiritual center of the soul, the "wheel turning out of its own center." (The hieroglyph of *Ibtu* is a heart and a circle with a cross in the center, marking the four quarters.)

Anubis*: Khent Imenty* is the divine plane to which the deceased soul returns. This is where Osiris acquired his association with the figure of a black jackal (or a wolf, in Ptolemaic times). This figure was carved on the divine standard that was carried at the head of ceremonial processions. The town later dedicated to this figure, *Asyut*, became Lycopolis in Greek. This is *Inpu*, Greek Anubis, patron of funerary rites.

These canine guides are the runners on the pathway of life, leading the soul through the maze of the journey between dimensions. The *Inpu* image reaches back into the Paleolithic past, when prehistoric canines forged their first alliances with humanity and became our companions, guides, and guards in a world full of dangerous animals and treacherous landscapes. *Inpu* is the "Caretaker Of The

Dead," guiding deceased souls through the processes of mummification and ensuring the success of the procedure.

Other ancient Egyptian divine *Natur* came from the same deep mythological strata as Osiris. From there evolved the vulture of *Mut,* the Uraeus Cobra of *Nekhbet,* the ostrich plume of *Ma'at,* and the Divine Cow of Hathor, the primary personification of Isis. The priestly tradition of the spotted leopardskin robe with the tail dangling hearkens back to the mythologies of the leopard-goddess shrines of the first villages. These leopard shrines themselves hearken further back to a time in the Sahara when Lord Death was a spotted cat who could reduce your beloved to meat draped across the branches of a tree.

The Great Bull, symbol of the power, might and miracle of living flesh, was the first carrier of the Osiris concept: the light of Divine, immortal energy captured in the physical plane by dark, mortal flesh.

Osiris's imagery arose with the first agricultural societies of humanity, a cultural gesture that contrasted with the earlier, Paleolithic mythic strata of the Animal Master who made a pact with humankind, agreeing to "recycle" the animals of the Great Hunt in return for the rituals of reverence that guide the animals' life-force back to the dimension of the Animal Spirit God. This is the Great Bull God we see depicted with breathtaking realism on the buried cave walls of humanity's earliest-known, magnificent works of sacred art.

The farming culture of the later Neolithic required a different sacrifice: the death of the Corn God, whose cut-up, buried body re-emerges as the agricultural bounty of Mother Earth. The great mystery of life demonstrated by the planting cycle is the necessity for the death of one generation in order to release the seeds of the next generation. This image is rooted in the depths of the human psyche; it appears not only on both sides of the Atlantic but also in the mythologies of Asia and the Pacific Rim. The figure of Osiris arises as the resolution of these two great mythological fields.

The mud which flowed down the river during the Nile's annual inundation was considered to be the decayed substance of Osiris' body, cut apart by Sut and thrown into the waters. His essence was thus the mud out of which Egypt grew, just as the soul is the undifferentiated divine substance out of which each individual grows.

As the living soul substance traveling between dimensions of eternity and reality, Osiris unifies the agricultural, flowering world of the harvest and the animal, carnal world of the hunter/herder. The pharaoh holds the flail, symbol of the agricultural world, separating grain from chaff, and the crook, the shepherd's tool for controlling his animals.

Throne Of The Eye And Seat Of The Action: Soul And Awareness

Human beings create mythologies for human purposes within the divine sphere. The function of a mythology, so aptly explained by Joseph Campbell in his many works, is to relate the individual psyche to itself, its environment, its social structure, and its spiritual values. Egyptian mythology relates the individual psyche to the divine soul within. The mystery of the nature of being is the core mystery in all their stories. At the core of the mystery of being, in Egyptian thought, is Osiris.

"Who is he? He is Osiris. Otherwise said: His name is Re."

The myths and mysteries of Osiris focus on the divine soul itself. Osiris is the actual substance and being of the soul, the ground of existence, while Re is the divine light by which the soul perceives reality, itself, and eternity. Osiris's hieroglyph and name mean "Seat And Throne Of The Eye." The "Eye" is Re, who is awareness, consciousness personified. The soul is the seat of perception, the centerpoint and throne of consciousness. The most important players in ancient Egyptian teaching, Osiris and Isis, primal elements of the soul, each have this "chair/seat/throne" hieroglyph in their names and as an essential element of their function.

The soul was represented as the central point at which existence exists, the "seat of action" from which perception is projected and to which it is aimed. Re sends out the Eye and it returns to him. This is the "still point" of Buddhist teaching, the central monad of being in which all archetypes are determined and out of which they are formed.

I like the essential practicality of the Egyptian image for this as "a chair, a seat." They were not quite as hallucinogenic in imagery as the Hindu, who constructed a more abstract personification of that monad. The Egyptians were *practical.* They were talking about everyday people in everyday life, the magnificent paradox of a divine being sitting down on an ordinary chair, in an ordinary room, and doing ordinary, human things. The "soul chair" as seat of the eye of consciousness is profoundly *accessible.*

The hieroglyph of the eye in Osiris' name can also be used as the determinative for the verb "to do, to make, to take action," implying that it is consciousness who acts out of the seat of the soul. Perception is required for the soul to function in reality. Even today, we have similar idioms, such as "I'll see to it," and "I'll see that it gets done."

Osiris is the uniqueness of each human soul, and universal because each soul is part of the same divine substance. One of Osiris's many names is *Wennefer*, which means Beautiful Being or Joy Of Existence.

"You are made living and green by the dual-worlds out of my immortality, embodied in the hand of the Lord To The Limits. He is led about by that which is not evolving in his name Earth Is Led About By The Face. He draws the dual-worlds together in his name that is Sokar. His power opens up much mightiness in his name that is Osiris. He has been on the two-fold path millions of years out of his name, Beautiful Being."

The most immediate clue to the meaning of Osiris's figure is the identification of the deceased with Osiris: "Now I am Osiris." Osiris is always depicted as a mummy because Osiris is that which survives death and the process of decay.

This is not to say that the Osiris figure is simply "King Of The Dead." That title is never actually used for him. He is "King of the Living," and "Lord of Persons" in the texts (among his many other titles). Osiris is the ground of being in which you are centered. Osiris is the totality of the divine plane of eternity to which the dead return from this plane of space/time reality. Osiris is the mystery of the divine soul within each of us and of the eternity from which it comes. To become Osiris is to be distilled to pure soul, ruler of the inner reality, the Hidden Land. The deceased is linked to the immortal continuity of humanity.

"I have come before you.
I am immersed in the soul.
I am distilled.
Give me my voice.
I will shape words with it.
I pilot my heart in its hour of fire and dark."

Osiris is the resolution of the paradox of soul and flesh. Osiris is the divine soul entering and exiting reality, wrapped in corruptible flesh. Osiris is the great mass of human souls who have gone before. Osiris is not wholly God, but, rather, the distilled essence of all that is Godlike in mankind. Osiris is the seed and centerpoint of divinity and is also the meat that rots and is eaten by the worm. Osiris is the paradox of the divine made manifest in the flesh.

In the religion of ancient Egypt, God did not send His son into the world to be sacrificed, but sacrifices Himself to the experience of being alive within reality, so that He can Himself be in love.

"He will have breathing breaths and making love, as he did on top of the Earth."

Land Under The Horizon, Inner Landscapes Of The Soul's Awakening

Another of Osiris' many names is The Bull of the Hidden Land, playing a double meaning on "bull," since the Egyptian word is pronounced *ka*, and punned with the meaning of the *ka*. The ultimate nature of the divine soul is unknowable. The metaphor of Osiris is, after all, only the outer mask which can be known and recognized. The actual experience of self is the ultimate privacy, known only to the inner soul and Eternity. The Bull Of The Hidden Land is the symbol of the substance of the soul, the mysterious substance that is soul. It is of the divine plane, but not fully God, divine and immortal yet, nevertheless, *human.*

As the mask of the Hidden Land, the *ka* of self, Osiris contains a territory, known as *duat*,. This is the personal territory of each individual soul: the private inner world that each of us inhabits. "This is Osiris. His circuit is the *duat.*" *Duat* is also the night sky blazing with stars, because each of us contains an inner world as vast as the Cosmos itself. The hieroglyph for *duat* is a five-pointed star inside a circle, and is the place through which Re travels in the sunboat. In its meaning as "morning" and "to awaken," *duat* represents the morning star, which "awakens" before the Sun. *Duat* is the psyche, defined as a place, manifest in the night sky of stars.

Duat is described as a narrow valley separated from the outer world by a high, curving mountain range. The mountains on one side divide the *duat* valley from heaven and on the other side from the Earth. Those curving mountain walls are walls of skull-bone, and the darkness of the *duat* is complete. The light of day can penetrate only through the eyes, an image intensified by the two staring eyes painted on the soul doors of tombs and birthing rooms.

A common symbol of Osiris is the hieroglyph of the box which contains the head and hair of Osiris. The box that contains Osiris is the skull, and the *duat* is the universe that Osiris is able to pack inside that small and fragile box of bone.

The meaning of the five-pointed star is worth noting. It is not the modern pentacle, but a circle (Re) surrounded by five looped rays, the stylized human limbs. Its meaning as the *sahu*-body within the protecting circle of the skull has come down to the present day in the concept of the pentacle's magical power to contain mystic beings and mystical powers, demons and devils.

The ancient, original meaning of the *duat*-star is one of awakening, of being aware of the landscape that lives inside the mind. Maps were drawn of the *duat*: elaborate, ornate, mystifying. Every room, pillar, threshold, herald, and doorway has its own name. The sunboat on its journey through the *duat* is a central mural of the tomb, because it represents the soul's voyage through life.

Ancient Egypt was dominated by the river imagery of their beloved Nile and these river-image metaphors appear quite naturally in all their inner design. A river divides the *duat*, and it is on this river of blood that Re sails in the sunboat. Itan is the Sun which sails in the blue sky, and is not to be confused with Re, who sails on the psychic waters of the Hidden Land inside the skull.

The ancient language itself elaborates the concepts of "inner self" and "outer self." Some time spent with a good hieroglyphic dictionary will provide valuable insight into their world-view. Use one that has the hieroglyphic spelling included, such as R. O. Faulkner's *A Concise Dictionary of Middle Egyptian.* (Griffith Institute 1962, 1981, 1986.)

Pages 18 through 22 of this invaluable dictionary list the words related to *Iman, Iman Ta* and *Imenty* beginning with the initial syllable *Im.* It is a most instructive list.

As in the name, *Immomet, im* is founded on the concept of immersion: of being within something in a three-dimensional sense. For example, *im* is "sea." *Im* is the first syllable on several words relating to boats and aquatic animals, that is, things which are immersed in water. *Imw* is "ship." There are also words about the position you hold within a given political group, your "fellowship." The word for "snake" is *Imyu*, with the hieroglyphs actually spelling out "those inside the Earth."

As a preposition it is "between, among, in the midst of."

We find cognates of *im* with the determinative of a tree, with the meanings "in a tree," "kind, gentle," "well-disposed," "to be delighted, charmed," "charm, kindliness, graciousness," and in plural, *impu*, "brilliance, splendor." This is particularly interesting; it points to the recognition that such human traits come from within.

Osiris, the substance of the soul, is the one who was "in a tree," bound in the coffin of Sut, with the *erica* tree grown around his coffin, while waiting for Isis to find him. Re is the one who "rises in the dawn-tree."

Imu with the determinative of an enclosure means "house," "home," "mansion," "place," "tent," "hut," "dwelling place."

This is followed by *imakh,* "spinal cord." One of Osiris' primary emblems is the *djed,* the column that is symbolic of the spine of Osiris and the divine energy channel it represents. In plural form, with determinative of the divine presence, it is "revered one of the blessed dead."

It is worth noting that these terms are cognates with *im akh* which means "within the soul, immersion of the soul."

Imn as a verb means "to create." With the divine determinative added, it is the name of Iman, creator of the universe, with both male and female variants on the name.

Imn with the determinative of a figure offering worship, is "secret, hidden." *Imnt* is "secret place, hidden land."

Imn, the hieroglyph of the west, means "right side," "starboard," "West." Since the Egyptians put south at the top of their maps, west was on the right-hand side. *Imnty* is the west wind. It is also a cognate for "daily offerings."

Imant ta is the Western horizon. Indeed, the modern, Latin-derived words "imminent" and "eminent" are not only cognates to these words, but also are indicative of the meaning which we are striving to define, since Osiris is the most "eminent" of beings and the very Imminence of Being.

Imkht is the netherworld of the tomb, with a wrapping twist of rope to make the *kht* sound.

Imsi, Isety is one of the four sons of Horus, components of his identity.

In, by contrast, is a preposition for "by," of agent. In verb form, with the determinative of legs walking beneath a vessel or jug, it means "bring, fetch, bring about."

It is the initial syllable of words relating to string, "cordage."

It is the cognate of "eyebrows," and *int,* with the mountain determinative, means "valley." (Compare *indus* in Sanskrit.) *inb* is walls, stockades, fences. *Inm* is the human skin.

Inkh is the verb "surround," "enclose," "include."

With a difference determinative, it is "unite," "collect," "gather together," and is part of the emblem of entwined lotus and papyrus plants that represents the union of the Two Kingdoms, the combined nation of Upper and Lower Egypt.

All of these meanings point to a concept *inside* something, but not immersed, a concept of two-dimensional linking. You are *inside* a circle. You are *immersed* in a sphere.

We are closing in on the definition of Osiris, who is *Khent Imentiu.* Just as the Sun rises from the East, emerging from its immersion in the Western horizon, Osiris emerges from his immersion in space/time, returning to the eternal plane.

DJED: BACKBONE OF OSIRIS, EMBLEM OF THE MYSTERY

One of the oldest symbols of Osiris is the *djed* column, Osiris' counterpart to the ankh figure associated with Isis. The *djed* figure was popular as an amulet and charm, and was one of the emblems placed within the wrappings of the mummy.

The drawings of the *djed* become quite imaginative at times, and these little figures become quite animated, shown with arms holding symbols of power and concentration. The *djed* is drawn as a banded column, tapering upwards, with four flat disks ringing it at the top. The colors it is painted in hint at its association with the tamarisk tree which grew around Osiris' coffin in the *Legend Of The Pillar Of Osiris.* The top is painted red or green, the bottom section in bands of black, white, yellow and red.

The rings at the top of the *djed* column have also been considered a stylized vertebra, since the *djed* is the backbone of Osiris. It was painted on the bottom of some coffins, placed where the mummy's spine would rest.

It was associated in later years with a bundle of wheat, since Osiris is manifest in the mystery of the seeded field. This is one of the fundamentals of the mystery cults of Greece and the Near East, in which the culminating ritual is the elevation of a stalk of wheat. This gesture survives today in the Catholic ceremony of the Elevation of the Host.

The *djed* is depicted sometimes with the Eyes of Re at the top, symbolizing the conscious perception that is rooted in, and the flowering of, the spinal column within the flesh. These figures became quite imaginative, with hands added as well.

The ancient Delta town of *Djedu* is the earliest source of the *djed* imagery. They considered themselves the birthplace of Osiris, and called their town *Per Usir* (Greek *Busiris*), "The Emergence Of Osiris."

Apep:
Serpentine Symbol Of The Living Nervous System

Thoth speaks:

"'To whom shall I announce you?'
'You will announce me to him whose roof is fire.
His house is of living *uraei*-serpents.
The floor of his house is the waters.'
Then who is it?
'He is Osiris.'

Studies of primate groups suggest that an utterance meaning "Snake!" as a warning could be one of the oldest "words" in the human vocabulary. There are some primate groups which announce snake sightings to one another, each using the same vocalization. Snake fear is very, very old.

This snake=fear reflex is a primal experience of the nervous system responding to the interface of self and environment. It is a reflex, hard-wired into our nervous system, which can also be triggered by art, just as a hawk-shaped shadow will alarm newly hatched chicks. This image of the serpent has represented the internal awareness of the human nervous system since the earliest days of religious art. The serpent image is universal, and appears with the oldest stories we have, representing the interface and link between mind and body, heaven and earth, spirit and flesh. Gilgamesh's serpent, the Rainbow Bridge, the Midgard Serpent, Quetzlcoatl in South America, the eagle and the snake in Mexico, the cloud dragons of China, the *kundalini* serpent of India–these are all the same serpent: the experience of the functioning of the human nervous system. Each image is symbolic of the emotional, psychological sphere of the cultural domain of its specific mythology. Egypt and India evolved the most profound and complex understandings of these private, internal perceptions–the universality of private nature.

There are many variations among the crew members on the sunboat in the company of Re, and many bizarre variations of the creatures pulling the sunboat along its way, but the towrope of the sunboat is always a snake. That snake is the serpent *Natur* APEP, a metaphor of the forces that move the sunboat.

More specifically, Apep represents the channel of the spinal column and the nervous system through which the life-force of nerve energy flows. Nerves burrow in the living flesh as snakes burrow in the living flesh of the Earth. The unblinking, lidless gaze of the snake is a metaphor of the ceaseless, unblinking protection of the autonomic nervous system. The cobra emblem of the pharaoh's crown stands for that protecting system. The minions of Sut, who is the force of habit, bear the snake on their staffs because habits are borne by the nervous system. Osiris is said to live in a mansion, the walls of which "are of the living serpents," in other words, housed in the flesh with its webbing of nerves.

Control of Apep is crucial to the success of the sunboat's journey, and Apep is constantly threatening to act up. Self-control is the goal of much of their religious training, and formulae for the control of Apep are everywhere. Self-control of Apep was taught as part of elaborate meditation training, known as The Pathway Of The Serpentine Embraced and Doing The Double Coil.

Most of the practical detail of this training has been lost, but poetic metaphors of the essentials abound. Learning to control the body is grounded in learning to control an image of oneself. The double coil of the serpent and its related meaning of healing survive today in the figure of the *caduceus*, which serves as the emblem of the medical profession.

This training was, no doubt, similar in nature to the meditation taught in Hinduism and Buddhism, which also focuses on the serpent metaphor of the spine and the nervous system. Chanting, directed attention, and forms of controlled self-hypnosis are hinted at everywhere. The images in the text of *The Seven Passageways Of The Pathway Of The Serpentine Embraced*, for example, are startlingly similar to the seven *chakra* of the spinal column in Buddhist training. Each portal has a threshold that must be named, and the right to cross that threshold must be earned. Each portal also has a complaint against it, which represents the changes of attitude needed to pass through to the next level.

"The Serpentine Embraced is he who has been cut from the template pattern of the holy standard. Take pleasure in the joy of Osiris, and rush to his standard."

The "holy standard" is that of Osiris, the divine soul, and the metaphor of the coiled serpent lies at the heart of the ancient religion and spiritual teaching of Egypt. Here, in this exotic imagery, is the sacrifice of the divinity to life for the sake of being alive. In the seventh and final portal, it is implied that the joy of having overcome the fear of death is so great that the complaint is about the need to refrain from tearing down the wall between this world and the next in order to experience its joy.

Satan Is Not A Serpent: Sut's Sacrifice Of Osiris

The image of serpent in the garden with the apple is a Biblical structure based on a remainder of the previous Mesopotamian World Mother Goddess religions. The Levant gave to the serpent the role of tempter in the process of reducing the matriarchal system to demonic content.

The serpent image began as the physical link between the living individual mind and the material body of the World Mother, the image it still carries in the *kundalini* system of India. The immortal serpent sheds its skin and is thus self-renewing. The snake burrows into the body of the eternal World Mother just as the nervous system burrows into the living flesh. Apep and its fellow serpent kind were of this category of image. The Egyptians did not separate Creator and creation as did the Levant, but lived within an order of divine reality. Dark and light were not opposing but interactive in a dynamic cycle that was the ongoing movement of existence.

The need for a disobedient, malevolent figure to counter the benevolent god is a structure which rises out of the separation of Creator and creation and is not present in the landscape of divine reality of the Egyptian system.

As soon as the image is created of "God, our Father up in Heaven, is all good, all-knowing and all-wise, and loves us, His children," the question follows: why do bad things happen to good people? A powerful counterpoint figure to the good power is necessary to maintain the purity of the divine image. It also helps to have someone from whom God must protect you.

From the earlier point of view of the universe as divine nature, the dark side is simply the natural balance to the light–it is amoral. "The impersonation of evil" is a Levantine image superimposed upon Apep and its struggle with Re, which I suggest was seen originally more as an internal personal struggle of the self to be in control of the living nervous system.

Within this system, the legend of Sut dicing up Osiris and scattering his parts is a mythological personification of the transition between planes of reality. Sut *must* dice Osiris up, otherwise Osiris cannot be released from the fleshly garment and vessel which has carried him through life "on top of the Earth."

The Egyptians clearly did not fear death, but they were none too happy about the *process* of dying. The belief in immortal continuity carries with it some heavy burdens of experience. If your experience of your self survives the death of your flesh, you must participate in its process of decay until release into the next plane. Think of Edgar Allan Poe's horror stories of being trapped within dead flesh. Thus Sut is playing the Dangerous Hero so that Isis can reassemble the identity of Osiris in the next life intact.

In the *Per Em Hru* (the Egyptian Book Of The Dead) texts that accompany the dead, the deceased is addressed *as* Osiris, so the understanding is that the Osiris within is released into the next plane by the processes of Sut and Isis. It would be more "evil" to stop Sut from cutting Osiris up, since that would force Osiris to remain trapped in "the cloak of the wearied one."

The Seven *Chakra* Of Osiris' Backbone: Egypt And India And The Serpent Within

"You have driven away all the sadness belonging to me, just like that which had been done by the Seven Divine States Of The Soul, those who are among the companions of their lord."

The faith of Egypt was in humanity. What it is to be human and how to be a civilized human are the central themes, and they studied the experiences of consciousness with respect, reverence, and in great detail. To the Egyptian mind, the evolution of civilized human beings in community is the purpose of the universe, and the central figure of divinity manifest in space/time is the immortal human soul within its container of mortal human flesh–True God and True Man, each of us. The interface of soul and flesh is in the nervous system, and the number seven has been associated in mythology with this interface for thousands of years, symbol of mystical awakening and rebirth into spiritual enlightenment. The serpent with seven coils or seven twists is a mythological symbol in many cultural systems around the world, which indicates the universal nature of the experience represented. The most poetically detailed and fancifully expressed explorations of the experiences of the human nervous system embodied in the seven-coiled serpent were developed in Egypt and greatly expanded upon later in India.

"In other words: Then these seven states of the soul are:

Tooth Tooth,
Mutilation And Slaughter,
His Fire Is Not Allowed To Blast The Dual Facade,
The Face Enters Into Its Past,
The Two Red Eyes,
That Torch Which Is Inside The House Of Bright Red-linen,

and
The Face Emerges As The Two Eyes Assume Their Station
When The Night Has Brought On The Day.

> Then Horus is upon the head of the divine precincts of that hall of his, orienting the face of his father. If it concerns that day that you must come here, it is Osiris saying to Re: "You must come here."

The number seven is determined by the organizational systems of the nerve bundle of the spinal column. The parasympathetic and sympathetic systems are grouped along the spine to the midbrain in seven major subsystems. The seven *chakra* of the Indian system and the seven portals of the Egyptian system–and, indeed, the presence of the number seven within any mystical system–relates to the internal, personal experience of the spontaneous functioning of these nerve systems and their connections to organs within the body. The imagery of the *chakra* are drawn directly out of the body's structure, and the training of that religious school is based on learning the greatest possible measure of conscious control over neural systems.

Coccygeal: at the root of the spine is the nerve grouping for the gonads and bladder.

Sacral: the next system as one moves up the spine is the lower digestive tract, the absorption and elimination of food.

Lumbar: third is the upper digestive tract, the stomach and its glands, input and breakdown of food.

Dorsal: fourth is the lungs.

Cervical: fifth is the heart.

Medullar: sixth is eyes, mouth, the glands of tears and spit.

Cerebral: the seventh at the top are the higher brain functions that relate these physical experiences into conscious experience.

The above is a somewhat simplified listing. These larger systems themselves include the many complexities of tissue and nerve involved in each process, but that is a matter of anatomical fact, not emotional experience. These mythological systems reflect the potential for spontaneous psychic expression of the functioning of the biological systems. The elaboration of imagery representing each level of awareness within this scheme comprise the ancient foundation of spiritual thought within the Egyptian and Oriental worlds. Egypt was an early source for this understanding, and her teaching spread for a thousand years and more, traded along with gold and grain.

This is the same serpent who taught Gilgamesh about immortality, the Midgard bridge in Celtic realms, the same serpent whom Adam and Eve encountered, the serpent whose teaching was denied them by their loyalty to Jehovah. It is worth noting that the Levant, confronted with this knowledge in their sojourn through ancient Egypt, rejected not only the World Mother Goddess but also the imagery of her serpent within our flesh.

The ancient Greeks, who gave greater emphasis to the fleshly container than to the soul within this container, also found little patience or capacity for this mystical study of human nature, and left the serpent of the Nile to be crushed beneath the heel. They were, nonetheless, obliged to pay tribute to it in the form of the caduceus emblem of the healing profession, the entwined serpents coiled around the staff of the spine. Ancient Egyptian medical technology was unmatched until modern times.

One of the most imaginative and personal treatments of the serpent is in the wonderful Egyptian fantasy tale, "The Shipwrecked Sailor." The descriptions of this magical beast, and the enchanted island where the sailor finds him give a charming glimpse into the Egyptian's magical, mystical world view. There is an excellent version of this story in Miriam Lichtheim's *Literature Of Ancient Egypt.*

The actual details of the physical training and self-discipline Egypt taught are, alas, lost, along with much of their written legacy, but there are surviving texts which offer revealing glimpses into the nature of that training. Just as the Indian *sutras* are condensed study guides for those involved in the deeper training, the religious texts of Egyptian tomb art are shorthand, almost mnemonic guides to this understanding as it was taught in life.

An interesting text, evocative of the Indian *chakra* and its related images, is *Spell 144* from the *Per Em Hru* (The Egyptian Book of The Dead). This spell is known by various names, including The Seven Portals and The Book Of Gates.

The Seven Portals Of The Coiling Pathway Of The Serpentine Embraced

The First Portal:

The name of its Doorkeeper is:
The Face Of Many Forms Turned Upside Down.
The name of its Guardian is: Affection Of The Flaming Eye.
The name of the complaint against it: Lowering Of The Voice.

Now, The Words of Osiris Immortalized, after things have arrived at the First Portal:

"I am the original *Natur* making his radiance. I have come because of you, Osiris, awakened purely to joy. Eyes Are Drawn To You is the name of the Mouth Of The Far Horizon for this. Orient your face, Osiris! I am raised up by you in Heart's Centerpoint, Osiris, because of your spiritual energy. You encircle heaven with your strengths in the Mouth Of The Far Horizon. You have sailed forth carrying Re. You have witnessed all of humanity."

Who is speaking the words of Osiris?

"I am a divine *sahu*-body, and Khepry does not hold back this face with his wall of charcoal, but opens the pathway out of the Mouth Of The Far Horizon, easing the sufferings of Osiris. The Serpentine Embraced is he who has been cut from the pattern of the holy standard in order to make his pathway through the valley, the Great Pathway of the radiance which is Osiris."

Gloss:

At the root of the spine is the coccygeal plexus nerve grouping, or ganglia, for the gonads and bladder.

This is the *chakra* of the opening of life and the entrance into existence, "awakened purely to joy." This is the beginning of awareness of self and the development of a mature human being. It is from the gonads that the "Affection Of The Flaming Eye" arises, and this guardian is the power of affection to create awareness within the individual. "Eyes Are Drawn To You is the name of the Mouth of The Far Horizon" represents the sexual potential now active in the individual. You now have, in other words, the power of reproduction, and are linked therefore to the mystery of the thresholds between realities.

Mouth Of The Far Horizon (or Mouth Of The Chambers)—*Rosetjau*—is the point on the horizon where the Sun disappears beyond perception, and is represented by the mouth of Nut swallowing the Sun in preparation for his journey through the *duat* to be born in the morning from the opposite horizon. It is the eternal mystery of mysteries to which the new human is joined, the unknown darkness before birth, from which you have come and to which you will return after death.

The wording of this passage suggests that this training did not necessarily begin in childhood but was more appropriate to adolescence. This is the beginning step of adult life. The Indian systems begin this with birth, and thus move the bottom *chakra* "down a rung," as it were, assigning to the dull pre-sentience of flesh itself

(Egyptian ankh) the role as foundation of this definition of being. The Egyptian perception of the fleshly garment, however, developed its own domain, since they focused on the joy of living, not the need for "release from *Maya*" that is the goal of Hinduism. Egyptians were content to dance with Black Time, and celebrated even the wearing-down of their dancing shoes. "Let's face the music and dance" is a modern expression of an ancient doctrine.

The Serpentine Embraced reflects the image of the coiling of the *kundalini* serpent of the Indian system, and images of Apep are similar metaphors of the energy of the nervous system and the mind/body interface. Control of this nerve network is the key to self-control, and losing the battle with Apep represents the dangers of angst, depression, anger, violence and insanity: all the raging dangers of a mind out of control, obeying only the unconscious powers within.

The initial paradox of Egyptian religion is that each unique individual is unique in exactly the same way. We each find our unique identity by fulfilling the patterns of a universal template. The Egyptian planned for the entire journey of life, as mindful of the inevitable end as of the moment at hand.

The desire for knowledge of the soul within emerges with this first awakening of the physical self, and the first step was gaining control of Apep, the serpent within. The goal was the "easing of the sufferings of Osiris," living with joy in a "world of sorrows" throughout life's journey.

The Second Portal:

The name of its Doorkeeper is: Opens The Attitude.
The name of its Guardian is: Jar Of The Face.
The name of the complaint against it is: Fighting The Sawblade.

"This is his youth of the face. The head must form even in the absence of the number two of Thoth. The proper stations of Thoth are with those weary of the Secret *Ma'aty*, those living with reality throughout their lifetimes. I am the weightiness of the hippopotamus going his way. You are undertaking the treading upon the pathway of the Serpentine Embraced.

Consider the Eye of Re: Who performs the offerings?"

Gloss:

The next system, as one moves up the spine, is the sacral plexus, governing the functions of the lower digestive tract, the absorption and elimination of food.

The opening of the attitude (the *haty*-heart) requires the acknowledgment that Consciousness, Re, at the top of the system, is the recipient of the energy absorbed by the body from food; in other words, the performer of the offering as well as the receiver of the sacrifice. "Consider the Eye of Re: Who performs the offerings?" The equivalent idea is represented in the teachings about Agni from early Hindu teaching, the acknowledgment that life is the fire that consumes the sacrifice of life in order to continue. You are the sacrifice. You are the one who makes the sacrifice, and the one to whom the sacrifice is made. That is how a "Jar Of The Face" is created and sustained, the identity of the living individual made possible by the mystery of the sacrifice within, the fires that consume matter and convert it to the energy of consciousness: the fire of the belly converted to the fire of the mind.

This is the realization of the mystery of existence, fueled by sacrifice and yet capable of the even greater mystery of supporting Re-consciousness. The Sawblade that must be fought is that of becoming merely the sacrificial meat and not a conscious entity in control of its being. The Egyptians did not fear death as much as dying, fearing the experience of the disintegration and dissolution of their beloved fleshly garment.

"The head must form even in the absence of Thoth" is a warning that without proper training the human being will grow up anyway and become dangerous. Those "weary of *ma'aty*" are, in other words, those who have been dealing with reality and are mature adults, and the goal is for "the youth of the face" to achieve these proper "stations of Thoth," or levels of understanding.

"The weightiness of the hippopotamus going his way" is an image of driving, unstoppable, natural power, since the hippopotamus coexists with humanity along the riverbank, but is irrevocably wild, powerful and deadly.

The hippopotamus is a creature of both the river and the land, and thus symbolizes the natural, uncivilized ground out of which Re's conscious, civilized riverboat journey has grown.

Treading the pathway of this knowledge follows a maze from the dark past into the bright future, your own future, now and for eternity, and controlling the animal that you are is as dangerous and powerful a task as controlling the mighty hippopotamus.

The Third Portal:

The name of its Doorkeeper is: Eating The Rot Of His Asshole.
The name of its Guardian is: Awaken The Face.
The name of the complaint against it is: The Stone Door.

"I am the secrets of the cloudburst, the judge of the Dual Companions, having come to hold back the sadness of the face of Osiris. I am his moment of emerging forth from cleansing. I have put things in order by means of Heart's Centerpoint, to open the pathway through the Mouth of the Far Horizon.

"Take pleasure in the joy of Osiris, and rush to his standard. I have made the pathway for his radiance through the Mouth of the Far Horizon."

Gloss:

The third *chakra* is the lumbar plexus, controlling the upper digestive tract, the stomach and glands; the breakdown of food.

The stomach does, indeed, eat what will become the rot of the lower intestines. The recognition of your biological, physical reality as being fully as mysterious and magical as "the secrets of the cloudburst," elevates these physical processes into the realm of mystic participation with the processes of nature and divine reality.

This acknowledgment of your essential humanity comes at this *chakra* of awareness, when the system is about to change from being merely learning and reactive, responding to stimulus, up into the higher levels of awareness in which one becomes an active participant in self-awareness and no longer merely reactive. It is an acceptance of the emotions of the flesh that impact the experience of Osiris, the soul. Rising above this *chakra* is the entrance into the more mature levels of spiritual attainment, and even the beginning of understanding is a pathway of radiance.

The Fourth Portal:

The name of its Doorkeeper is: Noisily Defending The Face.
The name of its Guardian is: Awakener Of Heads.
The name of the complaint against it is:
Holding Back Aggression.

Now The Words Of Osiris Immortalized:

"I am the physical *ka*, son of the kite-bird who is the Osiris in charge of you, witnessed by his father, Lord Of His Divine Charms. I have been cut from the pattern of the template, but there is wrongdoing. I have brought him life through his nostrils for eternity. I am the son of Osiris. I have made the pathway. I cross over on it as the *Natur* Under The Horizon."

Gloss:

Fourth is the lungs, the dorsal plexus.

The training of breath control in the Indian system is perhaps its most popularly known element, since the control of this vital system is the beginning of establishing conscious control over specific hormonal and enzymatic responses within the body.

"I have brought him life through his nostrils for eternity." Just as breath quickens in anger, learning to hold back aggression has elements of breath control intimately involved. The Awakening Of The Head that such breath control creates is an important goal in both systems, Egyptian and Hindu, and the individual who has reached this level is, indeed, able to defend the soul's unique identity with the considered words of a maturing human as well as with the gusto of living breath, "Noisily Defending The Face."

The Fifth Portal:

The name of the Doorkeeper is: He Lives Out Of The Nerves.
The name of the Guardian is: Hot Meals.
The name of the complaint against it is:
Portions of Your Face Are Lower Than Before.

Now The Words Of Osiris, Immortalized:

"I have brought the two jawbones into the Mouth Of The Far Horizon. I have brought you the radiance within Inner centerpoint. Unify his fragments there! I hold back Apep for you. I have exposed the wounds. Make the pathway inside you! I am an old man among the *Natur.* I make the purification of Osiris, oriented by him out of immortality."

"Unify his bones. Pull his limbs together."

Gloss:

Fifth is the heart, the cervical plexus.

This is the *chakra* of spiritual awakening, often represented as the spiritual birth or virgin birth. The nervous system is now the control panel for the soul's navigation, no longer responding just to the prompting of the flesh. "Make the pathway inside you!"

This has been the goal of all these meditations, and the goal is in sight because understanding is achieved. Now the individual is ready to: "Unify his bones. Pull his limbs together." The training led to awareness of the transfer of self-identity to the Next Life.

The Sixth Portal:

The name of the Doorkeeper is:
Your Shout Of Acclaim Offering Lowers The Voice.

The name of the Guardian is: Gift Of The Face.
The name of the complaint against it is:
Cutting Anger of The Divine Face of The Pool.

Now The Words of Osiris:
"I have come here twice now. I have made the pathway, my movements created by *Inpu.* I am Lord Of The Serpent Crown. In the absence of magical words to orient reality, I have oriented his eye, and I have filled Osiris by means of it. Making the pathway and Osiris ..... and walking it together with you from ..."

Gloss:
The sixth *chakra* is at the medullar plexus, and involves the eyes and mouth, the glands of tears and spit.
This "Gift Of The Face" is the prize of self-identity, the individualized soul who has faced the meaning of his life and accepted it.
The spirit guide, *Inpu*, who runs the paths of the Westering Sun and the long shadows of the graveyards, is no longer feared. He is the guide now, preparing the pathways of Osiris to eternity.
All life now is oriented, with or without the "magical words." The silence is now filled.

The Seventh Portal:

The name of its Doorkeeper is:
Spirit Energy Through Their Killing Knives.
The name of its Guardian is: The Mightiness Of Immortality.
The name of the complaint against it is:
Refraining From Tearing Down The Wall.

Now The Words Of Osiris:
"I have come concerning you, Osiris, purified of bodily fluids. You go around heaven. You see Re seeing humanity. You were alone in the Evening Boat, and You go around the horizon which is heaven. I speak of my love for his *sahu*-body. His strength evolves just as he said. You restrain his face. You have made for me all the pathways of beauty before you."

Gloss:
The seventh *chakra* at the top of the spine symbolizes the higher brain functions that relate these purely physical experiences into the realm of conscious experience.
An important step in accepting the reality of death within the Egyptian system is the process of releasing the soul from its magi-

cal, animated container once it is dead. The profound mystery of the flesh is its power to anchor soul-stuff within space/time, and even modern minds have expressed fear of being trapped within dead and decaying flesh, unable to escape to the next dimension. (Compare Edgar Allan Poe's evocative horror stories of this fear.)

Texts dealing with this fear represent the process of release in scenarios of intense violence, butchery described in vivid and luxurious detail, dwelling on the fragmentation to such a degree that the final release of the soul is a frantic explosion out of this reality and into the next.

The attachment to the container, the body you have ridden in for a lifetime, is the final barrier the soul must encounter in order to safely cross into eternity. "I speak of my love for his *sahu*." The *sahu*, the reality of the soul's identity shaped by the processes of integration throughout the lifetime, carries the soul past this barrier. The Mightiness Of Immortality guards the soul through this rending transition.

Once the realization of the training is accomplished, the wall between the two realities is the barrier, separating you from the eternal joys of the Next Life, "all the pathways of beauty before you." Thus, the realization of this knowledge is such that one must, indeed, "Refrain From Tearing Down The Wall" between the two worlds and making an early exit from this life, out of yearning for the joys and peace of the next.

The many serpents who writhe and swarm through the illustrations are the representatives of the network of nerves that permeate the human body, carrying the messages of the soul to the darkness of flesh. The Uraeus Crown and the many variations of serpent crowns are the symbols of personal victory over these inner powers: graduate degrees in the school of life.

RE, THE SUN IN YOUR MIND
THE LIGHT OF CONSCIOUSNESS

"Who then is this?
    It is Re, the designer of the name of his flesh.
    Existence is evolved by the *Natur* in the Company of Re.

I am without denial in the *Natur.*

Who then is this? It is Atum inside his globe.
In other words:
    It is Re while he rises in the eastern horizon
    which is in heaven.

I am yesterday. I have known awakening."

Osiris And Re: Soul And Awareness

Spelled "Ra" in older textbooks.

(The actual pronunciation of the vowel sounds of the ancient Egyptian language cannot be resolved, and this is the subject of serious, ongoing debate among experts. In the latter half of the Twentieth Century there was a move to change the spelling from "Ra" to "Re." I have adopted this modern spelling throughout, to match up with the most recent translations. The pronunciation, as closely as it can be discovered, is somewhat like trying to say the English words "rise" and "raise" at the same time, without voicing the "s." For simplification, it can be pronounced as the English word "Ray," rather than the "Rah" pronunciation we grew accustomed to from its use in the movies.)

Ancient Egypt was dominated by the river imagery of their beloved Nile (named *Hap* in their language) and these river-image metaphors appear quite naturally in their inner design. A river divides the *duat*, and it is on this river of blood that Re sails in the sunboat pulled along by Apep. Itan is the Sun which sails in the blue sky above, and is not to be confused with Re, who sails on the psychic waters of the Hidden Land inside the skull.

"Then who is he? It is Osiris. In other words: his name is Re."

The separation of Osiris and Re into two *Natur* demonstrates the subtleties of meaning which the Egyptians gave both to being and to awareness, and indicates the intensity with which they studied consciousness. Osiris, the soul, is immortal and of divine stuff, and can exist without awareness of itself; therefore, Re is separately defined. Re is the soul's experience of awareness and of itself. Re is the divine light by which the soul perceives. Put another way: Osiris is being; Re is the *perception* of being.

Due to the conventions of ancient Egyptian artistic style, their drawings of Osiris and Re, the soul and its awareness, are more like diagrams and maps than photographic representations. For example, one particular stylistic convention governs the hidden contents of containers: the contents are shown above the container. Thus a box would be drawn in side view, with the items inside the box drawn above it: *this* is the box, and *this* is what is *inside* the box.

Like the computer programmers of today, the ancient artists needed to get universally accessible information packed into a small space. Their art had a job to do. This diagrammatic depiction of containers and their contents is used for the globe of Re floating over the head. Re is the light contained inside the skull. Re is symbolized by the Sun because the light of awareness is a natural, divine light. The actual Sun in the sky, Itan, was vital and divine, but the ancient Egyptians were far more fascinated by the Sun in their minds.

Re is an energy force in the inner world, just as the Sun is an energy force in the outer world on top of the Earth. Like light, Re appears and disappears. Light does not have substance, yet it is the stuff of vision. Light is the symbol of the carrier of consciousness: it functions in the outer world, yet it is light and light alone that can cross the mysterious boundary of flesh separating the outer and inner worlds. The photon is the carrier of the message. Light was visible magic to the ancient world. The images and poetry of light abound in their literature and art. In that desert place light is inescapable, and its impact is utterly real: sunlight in the desert can, and does, kill.

The image of the masculine Sun, enfolded by, created by and supported by the feminine space/time continuum represents an even balance of elements. Space/time provides the body of our lives; the Sun provides the steady run of energy.

The masculine/feminine dichotomy of the Sun exists everywhere. In Germany, for example, maintaining the Teutonic *gestalt,* says *"Die Sonne, Der Mond."* The French, based on the Latin *gestalt,* has the opposite. The masculine Sun is birthed in and supported by the feminine principle of the Cosmos, the space/time continuum itself pouring energy into the world.

The image of the masculine Moon is a survivor of Paleolithic culture, when the Great Moon Bull, whose horns are the two crescents of the Moon, was the Consort of the Great World Mother

Goddess who was the universe itself. His cycle of life and death, pouring her energy into the world and cycling in and out of it, are represented in many forms, ultimately given profound expression in Osiris, Bull Of His Mother, the divine soul entering flesh to experience reality and returning to the divine plane in death.

The Sun, as a major deity, arrives fairly late in the ancient pantheon, since he only became important in village life with the birth of farming. In the nomadic lifestyles of earlier cultures, the cycles of the Sun are more related to physical changes in the seasons. A fixed horizon is needed to record the Sun's cycles. The Moon, however, presents a changing face to the entire world, always the same, no matter where we wander. The mythologies of the Sun are more recent constructs, based more on the concept of leaving reality entirely, finding a "final exit" so that you can escape reality and the rounds of existence. This is the "Door In The Sun" of Tibetan religion.

The Circle Of Perception: Symbol Of Re

The hieroglyph for Re is a circle with a single point in the center and a line underneath. The circle and dot are symbols of the range of perception, since light expands in a circle. The dot indicates the centerpoint of perception, that which is contained within awareness. The straight line beneath the circle indicates that the hieroglyph represents a thing, in this case, a thing of light.

From this ancient name, via Latin, we ultimately derive many of our modern terms related to light, such as "ray, radiant, radiation, radius, radial, radio," etc.

The circle and dot hieroglyph is also used as a determinative for words related to time, such as "day" and "hour," since consciousness is the perceiver of time. "I am he who made the hours, thus the days were born."

The cobra-Uraeus coiled around the disk of Re links consciousness, the light of Re, to the living nervous system. Consciousness is bounded by and carried by the serpentine nerves of our flesh. Most often written with two mono-consonantal hieroglyphs, r and ^ (short "a" sound) indicating the stress placed on the vowel sound. This relates it in pronunciation as well as meaning to the concepts "to rise and shine" as the light of dawn rises, swelling in brightness. This survives today in the words "to rise" as well as the words listed above. In the same way, consciousness "rises and shines" through the nervous system as light rises in the day.

The Legend Of Re And Isis
Threats To Identity

"The book of the divine *Natur* who evolved himself, forming heaven and earth through the breath of life and fire of the Divine, humanity, cattle, reptiles, birds and fish, divine king of humanity and the *Natur,* of one form, whose one-hundred-twenty years are as single years, whose names by reason of their multitude are unknowable, the *Naturu* know them not.

Isis was a woman who had knowledge of words, and despair turned her heart from millions of humanity. She chose the millions of the Divine instead, and she opened the millions of divine souls."

Isis realizes that if she learns the secret name of Re, then she and her son Horus would rank next to Re at the head of the *Pot Natur.* She takes a droplet of Re's saliva, spilled as he travels the pathway, and mixes it with dust. She uses her magic to create from it a living serpent, which she places at a crossroads. This serpent bites Re as he walks past. A raging furnace of pain fills Re, and he calls out to the *Pot Natur,*, "You *Natur* who originated in me!" They rush to him. They cannot help him. They mourn his weakness and vulnerability. Isis knows the cure, but she must have Re's secret name, his true name, if she is to heal him. Re stalls by identifying himself with the universal consciousness from which creation has sprung:

"Creator of the heaven and the earth, molder of the mountains, creator of the water for the Great Flood (Hathor), maker of the bull for the cow in order to bring sexual pleasure into being, controller of the inundation, Khepry in the morning, Re at noon, Atum in the evening."

These are the attributes of the powers of universal consciousness and not of the individual identity. "...My father and my mother hid my name in my flesh as I was born." This is the name which Isis must have. Re makes her promise that Horus will never reveal it to anyone, then he reveals to her his secret name.

Lady Isis, the great magician, is addressed here as Re's daughter, with "knowledge of words," because here she represents the enlightenment of the *Naturit* as a function of deliberate, conscious study of the spiritual life. Her unifying power is therefore the product of awareness and not just its source.

Re in his most profound form represents the Universal consciousness of divine reality born at the birth of reality. Isis is "daughter" or a function of that power. "She chose the millions of the Divine instead, and opened the millions of divine souls."

Lady Isis is the source of the divine bonding, the energy of coherence that sustains individual identity through all the tribulations and dangers of existence that threaten to dissolve it back into undifferentiated mud. The fear of that dissolution is the poison that fills Re's being, the confrontation with mortality that is the "serpent in the path" bringing to full awareness the realization of the reality of flesh's mortal limitation. All the greatness of Re's divine source, part of the forces which built the mountains and the world, cannot sustain the transition of dimensions from reality to eternity without the coherency of identity.

"For he who is able to pronounce his name lives."

This is the name that, together with the *ka*, was formed at birth. "My father and my mother hid my name in my flesh as I was born." Scholars have expressed regret that the name was not in the text, but the story is not about a remote deity. It's about you. This identity is beyond names, beyond pictures. It can only be known by you yourself within the depths of your own soul. This pursuit of yourself is the course of Lady Isis' teaching, and part of that teaching is the distinction of the universal aspects of your being from that which is distinctly you. This process can take a lifetime, as the text says, "one whose one-hundred-twenty years is as one year."

That is the power of your name, that is, of your unique identity. Your identity will carry you intact through the dangerous transitions of darkness. Not just your name as others call you, or that name you have acquired through your actions in life; not the name which is painted on your coffin. It is the identity that is painted on your soul, painted *by* your soul, the unique absoluteness of your own existence, secret from everyone except you and your awareness of yourself.

The more completely you know your own self, the more of your own secret name is revealed to you, then the greater the strength your conscious self is able to draw from the spiritual wellsprings of your soul. Self-creation is the ultimate magic and the most enduring, because it is that secret self who goes into eternity, into "the millions of years" as "That Great Thing Under The Horizon." In other words, as *you* experiencing eternity.

Re consciousness is dependent upon the physical body which houses it, however unfailing the Sun. Emotional pain can threaten the strength and focus of consciousness, leaving it as weak as Re, dribbling on the pathway. Unless the individual is aware, while alive and conscious, of the relationship between the Re of being and the Osiris of being, that is, aware of awareness, there is the danger that Re will die with the flesh, unable to separate the experience of dying from the reality of dying, unable to separate flesh from perception.

The coherency of being which Isis represents transcends consciousness, which is the reason that Re must ask her for her magical support in order to sustain himself.

MENDET AND SEKTET: THE MORNING AND EVENING BOATS OF RE

The sunboat which Horus pilots for Re changes over the course of the day. Re rises in the *mendet* sunboat, the Morning Boat, and rides it for the first part of the day. Re changes over to the *siktet* sunboat, the Evening Boat, once he begins to tire, sailing in it at night. The two boats are similar in appearance, because they are, in fact, the same. The Morning Boat is the body when fresh, newly rested. The Evening Boat is the same body at day's end, tired and ready to rest. The body is the same body despite the wide differences in perception of self. Re is dependent on the physical vehicle which carries it, no matter how divine the source of Re's energy.

This difference in self-perception is marked enough an experience to warrant the metaphor of the two boats. It is a fair warning: things *will* look better from the Morning Boat.

THE EYES OF HORUS AND RE: THE SOUL'S MEMORY

The Right Eye Of Re Horus is the Sun and the Left Eye is the Moon. One of the most familiar and widely known images from ancient Egyptian religious art is this carefully outlined and ornamented Eye Of re Horus, separated from the face and made into a single icon. The *Wadjet* Eye is the vision of consciousness, the organ of awareness just as the eye of the *khat*-body perceives light. The *Wadjet* Eyes, left and right, fly along beside Re and Horus to guide their journey as they rides in the sunboat.

The ancient spelling is, approximately, *wadj*t,* punning with "Watch It." Puns were used often in their language, and this pun defines the divine eye too effectively to ignore.

The *Wadjet* Eye icon was much loved in ancient Egypt, and

appears everywhere. It was worn as jewelry, carved in every material, painted on everything. It is the constant reminder to pay attention to life.

The *Wadjet* Eyes are memory, the vision of the soul within. The photon is the carrier of the message. The Eye Of Re represents detached perception, pure perception focused by reality but not by a specific individual; it is the vision by which all souls perceive, yet is not attached to any particular soul. The Eye Of Horus, however, is the perception of an individual, personal point of view: the perception focused by the living soul behind the face.

Khepriy: Light Dawns, Enlightenment, The Gesture Of Maturity, The Egyptian Scarab

"Khepry is face and heart of his sacred sunboat and is Re himself."

KHEPRY is the rising Sun, the light of dawn on the horizon. He is Re at the moment of awakening, at the moment of enlightenment out of darkness. He represents the miracle of consciousness rising out of the darkness of flesh, sleep, and death. In his most profound form he represents the moment of enlightenment in which creation arose from the darkness of nonexistence.

The well-known hieroglyph for Khepry is the scarab beetle. The living scarab beetle places its eggs into balls of dung and rolls the balls into a nest in the sand. Once the larva hatch, they eat their way out. The beetle itself has shiny green wings, like green plant shoots in black river mud, and green stone of various kinds were favored in carving them.

Khepry is the creative potential of black mud and the darkness of the soul. The scarab symbolizes the rolling movement of the beetle's process, a metaphor of transformation, of growth, the physical process of evolution, and the mystical experience of maturity. The rising Sun and the emerging beetle together are the images of the evolution of opposites out of each other. Shiny bug rolls into a ball of dung, and the ball of dung rolls out into a shiny bug. Day rolls into night, and night rolls into day. Each of us experiences a round of waking out of sleeping, sleeping out of waking, life out of death, death out of life.

In the human mind, enlightenment, the light of understanding, is as profound and transforming as the birth of the world and consciousness itself. Khepry, then, represents a class of experiences woven together by light.

Atum: The Night Sun, Unfailing Time

"Lord Atum, I am Atum in the beginning.
I am one. I am evolved in Nu.
I am Re in his rising in the beginning, this prince of his."

ATUM is the night Sun, the security of the Sun's unfailing momentum. *Atum* is the security of the pathway, guarantee that life and reality will continue.

The hieroglyph of Atum is a sleigh, the sleigh on which the image of a *Natur* was carried during ceremonial travels. It indicates the sense of momentum, of being pulled along. Atum was always popular in ancient Egypt because this *Natur* is the essence of reassurance: no matter how dark the night, the Sun will rise tomorrow.

The sleigh on which our modern figure of Santa Claus travels is a dim, surviving echo of the ancient meaning of Atum, carrying the gifts of light that are the preparation for the birth of the new Sun; in other words, the rising of consciousness.

Atum has the role at the initiation of creation as the first principle which stirred in the primeval void, creating the primordial mound and revealing the solid ground of reality.

Time is the modern concept of Atum. Time is the force which guarantees that life and reality will continue. Time is unstoppable.

"Father Time" is also a modern echo of Atum, demonstrating that the human impulse to personalize abstract concepts thrives now as it did then.

"Childhood is the union of the seat and throne of Osiris.

Having built your house, Atum measures out the foundation of your House Of The *Natur* Of The Twin Lions (Yesterday and Tomorrow) accomplished by mortaring the reeds of Horus, dual *Natur* who is Sut, and the other way around. He has come into this world. He has tread upon it with his two feet."

HORUS AND SUT: HEROES OF IDENTITY THOSE TWO COMPANIONS THE ORIGINAL JEKYLL AND HYDE

"In other words:

> It is Horus. He will be in the dual head, and will be the one possessed of reality, the other possessed of wrongs. He must give wrongs for the wrong-doer, and things of reality for the company of my possessions.

In other words:

> It is the mighty Horus Facade Of The Holy Place Of Spirit. It is Thoth. The Provider is the calm of Atum, halting the things of opposition contained in the Lord To The Limits. You assume your role."

HORUS:
THE FACE OF THE HORIZON, HERO OF IDENTITY

HORUS is one of the oldest *Natur* of ancient Egypt and the falcon one of the earliest symbols of kingship and divinity. His name translates as The Face, referred to as The Face of Heaven.

He is the *Natur* of identity: the archetype of the universality of uniqueness, the individual face which identifies the individual soul. Horus embodies the paradox that each unique soul is unique in exactly the same way. He is that set of all sets which can contain only one member, the generalized rule which defines the specific, just as every unique name is spelled out by a universal alphabet.

The symbol of Horus is the falcon, a prized hunting bird of the Nile Delta. The falcon soars almost invisibly at great heights, dropping down to strike with such remarkable swiftness that it seems to appear out of the air itself. The Egyptian verb for this diving flight, translated simply as "to swoop," is the same as the word for the soul. The soul is that which "swoops" into reality from out of eternity. The falcon also has the inner value of being a sky-denizen who can be made to obey the hand and the will of man.

Just as Re personifies the soul's awareness, Horus personifies the soul's identity. Horus is each and every living human being, and each human is a Horus.

Osiris is universality; Horus is uniqueness. Identity is the divinity of the soul. Osiris is the substance of being. Re is the perception of being. Horus is the identity of being.

"The Divine Precincts Of The Great Thing Within *Jadjad*
Centerpoint are Osiris, and Isis, and Lady Of The House,
and Horus Who Orients His Face . . ."

Naming was important in ancient Egypt. There was a "Horus-name" for every town and village. The Horus-name of the pharaoh was the one of the royal names, along with a golden Horus-name, the Re-name and the Golden Name Of The Two Ladies, and the Throne Name. The presence of Horus in the earliest art of the Nile is an indication of the importance of identity and self in the creation of civilized life. Horus and the Greater *Pot* evolved steadily throughout the course of Egypt's five thousand years into a complex and vital system of spiritual teaching.

The now-familiar *Wadjet* icon of the Horus Eye was used to represent the common fractions. Horus was the *Natur* of the integrity of unique identity, the whole that is the sum of its parts; therefore each section of the Eye, or "fraction" of the whole, was a symbol for a particular fraction. This was known as "Counting the parts of the *Wadjet* Eye." It was even celebrated with its own festival day, January 30. (*See above.*)

"The *Pot Naturu* are in adoration when they see the Eye Of Horus The Elder in its place. It is perfect in all its parts, 1/2, 1/4, 1/8, 1/16, 1/32, 1/64 in the counting for its master."

Horus is sometimes shown crowned with the Re-crown of the Sun, and is depicted as a composite *Natur*, "Re Horus," the symbol of the ego of the fully conscious adult. Horus is the pilot of the boat of Re in the stories and images which symbolize the daily journey of the soul through life. Re, consciousness itself, sits unmoving in the sunboat, ever the detached observer, while Horus performs the actions of living.

He is Re Horus, however, only when he *knows* that he is himself. Our Newtonian presumption of the Absolute Witness, Divinity On High, removed and instantaneously observing every jot of reality, is sharply at odds with the ancient Egyptian point of view. Perception implies one who perceives; perception *demands* one who perceives. For example, without the presence of a living eye to focus a single binocular point of view into an image, a mirror reflects all light equally. There is no one image; there are all possible angles of reflection, all possible angles of perception. An image requires a single living point of view. That is Horus. Compare the Book Of The Dead texts which ask at every turn, "Who is it who speaks?" "Then who is this?"

Horus is intimately related to the visible horizon. His name and qualities are now considered the root origin of the word "horizon," via the Greek. Indeed, Horus is the horizon of identity. One of the observational "miraculous properties" of the horizon is its intangibility: You can "close your horizon in" with four walls (round walls, in ancient times) but you cannot pass beyond it. It "travels" with you. You can change places, but the limit of your horizon travels with you. You can change the territory your horizon encompasses along with you, but you cannot escape it.

The Sun can.

Horus, in his Solar aspects, is that which penetrates that horizon line, like the falcon diving out of sight behind the hills.

Akht, the word for that place on the horizon where the Sun rises and sets, is a cognate for the word *akh*, which represents both the substance of the soul, and the arable land created by the Nile's annual inundation. Horus' name of *Horemakhty*, "Horus Of The Two Horizons," is a wordplay on these two cognates. Horus is the "Face Of The Two Horizons," as well as the living face of the soul's substance. Thus he is all the aspects of identity (of "face") that function both within the perceptual sphere and beyond it or "under" it, depending on perspective.

North American Plains Indians have some fascinating observations to make about this phenomenon of the "hoop of the horizon." This is another of those metaphors of daily life that have been removed from the daily life of modern man. Like the stars lost in city-light haze, we travel too fast to be amazed by the blur of the horizon rushing along with us.

The flesh is the ultimate "horizon line" of the territory that exists inside each living being. Horus, as the face of that flesh, is the identity of the horizon that encompasses each of us. It is a function of the observer.

In Egypt, the observer was the focal point, and was important. In the Levant it is only what is observed that counts because there is only one Divine Eye permitted, only one Divine Vision. Re Horus carries the perception of consciousness below the perceivable horizon into unconscious territory. Identity is the horizon which is your boundary, "king of all you survey." Alone in the broad desert, your personal horizon reaches the sky. In closer quarters of human community, that horizon may encompass no more than four walls—or the confines of your skin.

The two eyes of Horus are sometimes symbolized as Sun and Moon. This imagery corresponds to the tale of Odin hanging for nine days on the World Tree in order to sacrifice one eye for the power of prophecy. The association of Sut, who took Horus's eye, and the World Tree on which Odin was hung, is through Apep, the serpentine symbol of the human nervous system.

These images belong to the systems by which spiritual energy is channeled into the physical reality of living flesh, the interdimensional link between heaven and earth, divine and mundane, thought and flesh.)

The sacrificed eye represents vision into the Other Dimension, into the divine realm of the soul within. The sacrificed eye of Horus is the same image as Odin's. Having wrestled with his own shadow, with Sut, Horus has come to terms with the dark side of himself. The self-identity that Horus stands for has one eye cast to the internal dimension of the soul, represented by the Moon's reflection of solar light. The other, Solar Eye, is cast to the light of daily reality. Such living men can, indeed, understand human nature and the nature of reality well enough to know what to expect of people, and of Nature. Isn't that the birth of wisdom? It seems to be "prophecy" only to those who have not yet grown up as much. But many such individuals have had to cut away parts of their youthful selves to learn the lesson.

Re Horus was the form in which Horus is most often encountered, especially as the nation grew up. Re Horus not only knows, he knows that he knows. He has experienced Sut, and understands why the light of the Sun creates shadow. He also knows that he does not know.

The religious art of ancient Egypt is full of representations of Horus in each of the three stages of life. He may be depicted as a child at his mother's breast, known as "Child Horus;" as an adult, fully active in life, known as "Re Horus Of The Two Horizons," and as an old man, leaning upon a walking stick, "Horus The Elder."

The life of Horus is the life of each human being, and the stories of Horus are about the trials, tribulations, and triumphs of life among the living.

Sut: Dark Reflection Of Horus, Divine Force Of Habit, Protector Of The Sunboat's Journey

"Horus, dual *Natur* who is Sut, and the other way around."

Also spelled Seth, Set, Sutekh, or Sutek in various modern texts.

In the last hour of the night before dawn, when Re consciousness is dissolved in sleep in the House Of Osiris, it is SUT who rises first and bids Re "rise and shine." On the soul's journey through the process of death, referred to as The Great Road, Sut guards the doorway to the Innermost Chamber Of Dual Reality, the first confrontation with the divine, using a door called Blocker Of Light.

Sut is the dark and inescapable reality of the corruptible flesh which houses the incorruptible soul.

Horus is the pilot of the vessel of the body, the sunboat of Re, but the fact is the vessel can and does pilot itself. Controlling the sunboat's self-navigation is, in fact, Horus's primary duty. The human body can do a great deal without being told. Re Horus is conscious control. Sut is not. They are, however, partners: "When he stands up, he is Horus. When he relaxes, he is Sut."

The neural systems of the body that automatically learn good habits will learn bad habits just as automatically. Habits must be consciously cultivated and moderated or else they will rule life. Sut is the protector of the sunboat. Proper habits can save lives. Society grows more dependent on the proper habits of its citizens as civilization becomes more complex. Egypt knew this, and respected Sut for it, and they died rather than surrender to the desert.

Sut is discipline, the training that keeps the sunboat safely on course through the daily journey. It is an uneasy alliance. Discipline and habit do not have the flexibility of conscious control. Sut is sometimes referred to as the burning heat of the desert Sun, because the soul does have the power to discipline the flesh to death. Sut must be balanced by consciousness; the guard must have a guard.

Sut and Horus are constantly wrestling with each other for the control of the sunboat, and the stories of their struggles are morality tales, learning how to behave not just as a human being, but as a civilized, conscious adult.

The conquering of Sut is shown in images reminiscent of St. George and the dragon: Horus is shown standing triumphant upon Sut, who is represented by a slain hippopotamus, an animal which was then, and still is, the single most deadly wild animal on Earth. The conquering of this mighty monster is an image of power, and the conquering of oneself is no less difficult.

Horus and Sut are the original *Jekyll and Hyde:* two opposite kinds of behavior struggling for the control of the same human being. This composite or dual *Natur* Horus-Sut is known simply as "Those Two, The Rivals," or "The Two Companions," and is represented by a two-headed figure, one head that of a man and the other the dark silhouette of an animal, a jackal. It is the difference only of the same face seen in the light and then in shadow.

The ancient Egyptians saw life as the interface and balance of opposing tensions at the nexus-point of reality. The stories of Those Two represent the divine role of each human being in that balancing act. "Loosen the bonds of Sut, who is guardian of my mouth."

The Hyksos, who were the first foreign invaders to capture the kingship of ancient Egypt, took Sut as their main emblem, using a Sut name rather than a Horus name. They believed that faith in their desert-bred discipline had led them to victory; indeed, it was most often the disciplined ruthlessness of the desert invaders that ultimately overwhelmed the gentle nature of The Land of Love.

The Pharaoh
Role Model Of The Inner Man

We humans see ourselves as Man The Tool User, but it has been demonstrated that not only do our Chimpanzee cousins use a variety of tools but also that there are many in animalkind who use objects selected from their environment as tools. There is even the clever Honey-Finder bird of Africa who has learned to use humans beings as a tool, by leading humans to beehives so that they will open the dangerous beehive and expose the precious honeycomb for the bird to reach. Apparently the instinct to use objects as tools is part of our animal inheritance. Indeed, our oldest myth-stories are the legends of the animals who taught humans how to survive. In these legends even fire, considered wholly of our domain, is brought to us by an animal. This would seem to be tacit acknowledgment of humankind's relationship with the natural environment from which we have emerged. Curiosity and learning were our newest, greatest gifts, and we used them to explore and imitate all the fascinating beings around us. Monkey see. Monkey do. And in so doing we redesigned ourselves into civilized beings.

Humankind does have the profound capacity to improve vastly upon the nature and use of tools, but the basic ability of tool-use is not really one to which we can make a unique claim. The arts of weaving baskets learned from nest-building is only the most obvious tool-working technique which we borrowed from our animal relatives. Nest-building, however, inspired humankind to invent a class of tool that does *not* exist in the animal kingdom. Carrying stolen eggs home in their nest gets you more eggs than you can carry in your two hands while climbing down safely from the tree. A container that carries tools, yet frees the hands, is the one class of tool to which humankind *can* make unique claim. Other animals make tools and use them, and some even carry tools for a short time, but only humans make a toolkit to carry more than one tool and to free the hands for tool use. We are actually not so much The Animal Who Uses Tools as The Animal Who Carries A Purse. (Gentleman, for your sakes: The Animal Who Carries A Toolkit.)

Basket-weaving is one of the oldest arts of humankind, with many examples surviving from the early Neolithic era, and hints of their use into the Paleolithic. Every available form of plant fiber is used for basket-weaving, and Egyptian basketwork demonstrates a solid tradition and extensive development of the technique.

I point this out because one of the oldest recorded hieroglyphs is *nb*, translated as "lord, sire, sir, prince, nobleman, master," etc., terms of nobility and respect. The hieroglyph is of a basket. The image is of nobility being symbolized as that which contains us as a basket contains loose objects. This is a marvelous demonstration of the Egyptian concept of the responsibilities pertaining to the role of the nobility. This appreciation of leadership is far more sophisticated than the warrior-leader image that comes to us from other quarters of that ancient world, the Assyrians, from whom we get the related but distinctly different concept of "aristocracy." The nobility unified the group and contained the disparate elements of the group. Their persons and their roles were the "emotional baskets" which carried the emotional and cultural strengths of the varied individuals of their households, villages and territories.

The basket which contains all the baskets, of course, is the house. These images and concepts evolved in the African environment where house-building and basket-weaving are closely related technologies. This concept of the greater unity containing all the pieces of the nation is behind the Pharaoh's name, image and responsibility to his people. The word Pharaoh is a corruption of *Per-Aah (pr-aa)* meaning "Great House." The Pharaoh was the Great House which contained all the individual baskets of nobility, as well as all that they carried and protected.

In later generations, when the nation faced political pressure and serious threats and invasions by the chariot-driving barbarians out of the desert and the east, this leadership became dominated by the military-styled role that we assign to it through our modern eyes. The Pharaoh was, first and last, symbol of the *civilized* unity of the Egyptian people, the ultimate cultural expression of their unique identity and ancient traditions.

The best definition of the Pharaoh is in the gestures of being civilized, with every nuance of art, humanity, compassion, technology and power implied in that term. The Pharaoh was the representative, *par excellence,* of the Civilized Human Being.

Iman Re, who is the conscious awareness of the organizing principles of the Cosmos, of the World and of Life, was the spiritual father of the Pharaoh's role. Every member of his court was a further extension of this uniquely human perspective on life: being civilized. More than any other peoples of their time, the ancient Egyptians enjoyed all the pleasures of a remarkably *civilized* life. Even their medical care was the best available until modern times.

The Egyptians lived with their "hearts on their sleeves," as it were, with a fine appreciation of a rich inner life expressed in every aspect of their outer lives. Egypt was in their hearts. They carried her with them no matter what foreign lands they traveled.

The Pharaoh's role as spiritual role model extended beyond this life into the next. "Ruling as Pharaoh" is one of the attributes of the soul who has successfully crossed the boundary between the dimensions of reality and eternity. It is more than a wish for luxurious surroundings. It is an acknowledgement of self-control and self-possession, an active image of a soul at peace with itself and its experience of life.

The word *pr* in Pharaoh is used in a number of words, including the original title of the Book Of The Dead. *(Pr Im Hrw)* The concept behind all of them is "emergence," as a person emerges from a house, as islands of land emerge from the floodwaters of the Nile, as fruit emerges from the plant. The hieroglyph is a rectangle with an opening in one side. This concept of inner and outer is very important in Egyptian belief. Osiris, substance of the divine soul, is the ultimate "inside" from which our outer lives emerge.

The elaborate religious rituals of the Egyptians revolve around this relationship of inner and outer, and around the dynamics of the flow of life energy through that relationship. Horus, symbol of unique identity, represents the actualization and experience of that dynamic, and Pharaoh's role as the avatar of Horus was the nation's role model for each individual's experience of themselves as the Horus of their own, inner Osiris.

Confronted with the statement by a modern person that what is in the imagination is "not real," an ancient Egyptian would ask, "What do you mean by real?" We are obsessed with physical reality in our modern minds, and we have no formal training in the reality of our own inner reality. "It's just in your mind," is a dismissal, a denial. To the Egyptian, it is a statement of a different order of reality, the order of reality from which we have each come and to which we each return. They knew perfectly well that the "realities" of that inner world could manifest themselves with harsh impact on the outer reality of other's lives. They understood the concept of "personal space," something which modern psychology has only begun to address.

This respect for the value of an individual's inner thoughts and feelings is the primary gesture of civilized life, and the ancient

Egyptians expressed this respect in every aspect their lives. The elaboration of this civilized gesture is the manifestation in outer reality of the inner realities of the human mind and spirit. The greater the civilization, the greater the freedom for individual expression of those inner realities, and the more profound the need for individual training in understanding the symbols of that expression. The elaboration of the Pharaoh's role as such a symbol went hand in hand with the expansion of the nation, both economically and politically. This is the logic behind the religious ceremonies which began as public processionals through the temple courtyard, but continued on with the Pharaoh going in alone to the "holy of holies" in the innermost sanctum of the temple. As role model for the individual's "procession" through life, there are public dances and public expressions, shared by all. The confrontation between self and soul, between Horus and Osiris, is a private one that must take place within the innermost sanctum of the individual's mind and soul. The glowing, sunstruck interiors of those sacred spaces glimpsed, then shut behind golden doors, became the imagery and décor of each person's imagination and inner world.

You followed along with the Pharaoh behind those closed doors in your imagination, which is precisely where that inner sanctum and its meaning, import and value belong. Pharaoh had led you inside yourself where your divinities, divine images and divine nature dwell. As Pharaoh went into that inner world to confront the ultimate divine in privacy even though in the midst of a public event, surrounded by the gathered peoples and the temple, so each of his people could "go inward" to their private, inner sanctums, secure in that inner privacy despite the most public of occasions.

This balanced dynamic of inner and outer is the foundation of self-control, of joy, of peace both within and with those around you. It was a solid cornerstone of ancient Egypt's longevity and supported the complex evolution of their culture and mythology.

During the five thousand years of the nation's history, they had every kind of pharaoh, from every major pattern of human nature. Pharaohs were long-lived, short-lived, healthy, weak, physical, intellectual, poetic, warlike, trusted, hated, accepted, respected, rebelled against, genius, ingenious, mediocre, neurotic, heroic and genuinely insane. They had one pharaoh who outlived almost everyone in the country, and ones who ruled as children and died before puberty. The pharaohs loved Egypt, hated her, cared for her, neglected her, led Egypt astray or to glory, but every single one left a record of pride of place, patriotism and the absolute conviction in the eternal values of Egyptian civilization.

The Riddle Of The Sphinx: Better To Be A Child Than A Barbarian

The riddle of the Sphinx, which comes down to us through the story of Oedipus on the road to Colonus, retains the echo of its ancient Egyptian roots.

"What goes on four legs in the morning, two legs at noon, and three legs in the evening?"

It is a riddle about the nature of Horus, *Natur* of identity; a riddle of the kind which the Egyptian children learned in play, the stories of the *Natur* that would guide and shape their adult lives.

The Egyptian child would have quickly guessed that these are the three faces of Horus: Horus The Child, Horus Of The Two Horizons, And Horus The Elder.

This was too sophisticated a concept for Athens and Rome. Oedipus suffers because he is ignorant of his true identity. His parents suffer because they deny their child's true identity. This ancient, peculiarly Egyptian morality tale has evolved over the centuries into a dry, enigmatic parable on oracular prophecy. For the Egyptian, the moral core of the story focuses on the tragedy of lost identity and the revenge of the *ka*. The core of the Greek moral interpretation, on the other hand, focuses on the tragedy of denying prophecy and the revenge of the gods.

Confronted by the complex philosophies of the Egyptian civilization they had conquered, the Greeks created their own *Natur*, which they called Serapis. Serapis is a hybrid *Natur* synthesized from Osiris and Apis, who is the actual, living bull was regularly sacrificed to Osiris in holy ceremonies. The Greeks were able to worship only the fleshly container of the divine soul, apparently unwilling to compromise the image of the gray, lonely next life which their own culture supported.

The Divinity represented by the Great Sphinx of the Pyramid Complex at Giza was known to the builders as Re Horus Of The Two Horizons. The Sphinx was a monument to the nation's pride in their own civilization. Re Horus Of The Two Horizons is the personification of the mature, civilized conscious adult in full possession of all his awesome power. "All men fear Time, but Time fears the pyramids." The Egyptian mind and hand designed and built the pyramids, and to the Egyptian mind nothing was more powerful–not even Time itself.

THOTH, DIVINE THOUGHT THE MIND OF THE SOUL

"Thoth and *Ma'at* record your moments every day. "

Thoth, Djehuty: The Counter Of The Moon And Of The Days

"Thoth makes Re calm."

THOTH's name in Egyptian derives from *t*kh,* which is the plumb in the balance, the weight in the scales. Thoth is the Measurer. The *ib*-heart is also part of his hieroglyphic spelling, indicating that he is the measurer inside the mind. From his name and his meaning come "thought, technology, technicians," and the "tick-tock" of time. Thoth is thought. He is reason. He is the archetype of the human intellect, of mind, logic and rationale. Thoth is the source and the repository of learning, knowledge and training. Thoth is science. Thoth is the genius of the *Pot Natur.* He is the mind of the soul.

His hieroglyph is the ibis-bird and he is the ibis-headed *Natur,* perhaps because the gesture of the ibis-bird searching for food in the river mud is the same gesture of the wrist and hand made by scribes while writing and drawing. Thoth is the scribe of the *Natur* and the *Natur* of scribes. As the scribe of the *Natur,* pen, paper, and ink are the tools of Thoth.

Ancient Egypt built the first civilized society out of river mud and the inhospitable desert with little more than paper and ink. The intellect of the nation was respectable indeed.

"I am your writing tablet," was a prayer to Thoth. "I bring you your ink." The territory of Thoth is the *tabula rasa* of the brain waiting to be written upon. "I am an ape of gold," is another phrase from a prayer to Thoth.

Because of our minds, we are more than animals.

Thoth is credited with the composition of the text of the Book Of The Dead, which comprises a portion of the murals of every tomb and is the substance of spiritual training. "Thoth wrote this with his own fingers." is inscribed at the beginning of the *Book of the Dead*, the actual title of which is *Per Em Hru*, "Emerging Awake." The emergence is into the next life of eternity, and this vital spiritual training was considered to be in the mind, in thought, in learning. The premises were considered to be logical thought. It is not Osiris, the so-called king of the dead, who writes the instructions on dying correctly.

Thoth wears many crowns, but his primary crown is the globe of the full Moon framed by the two crescents. The association of Thoth with the Moon dates back to Neolithic times. The Measurer of the Moon and the Moon's phases was the first scientist of humankind and seeded the beginnings of astronomy, astrology, science, and mathematics. The study of the Moon's phases and cycle date from the days of caves and stone knives, charting the Moon's phases on antlers and thigh-bones. The Moon symbolism shows that the ibis-headed *Natur* Thoth has roots more ancient even than the black vulture of Mut. The nomadic and semi-nomadic lifestyles of early man obscured the daily and seasonal fluctuations of the Sun's path because the Sun's changes are horizon-related. For the nomad the horizon travels along beside him unfixed, un-measurable, altered by every change in geography, a curiously personal possession of the individual viewer, yet the possessor of all. The Sun's impact is marked by the seasons and changes of the Earth and stars, but not by the daytime sky. The cycles of the Moon's changes, however, are everywhere visible, and everywhere the same. The regular marking of the Moon's changes predates the establishment of the first villages, but, once people settled into villages, they began to mark, year after year, the cycles of the Sun's patterns on the now fixed horizon.

The deeper value of the association of Thoth with the Moon is, as with Khonsu dream-consciousness, in the image of Sunlight reflected. Intellect and dreaming are both forms of perception, but they are not consciousness. The thinker can be conscious of thinking, but there are also unconscious thoughts. Who is it who is thinking? That is why Thoth is only the scribe of the *Natur.* Knowledge can be put on paper, but consciousness cannot. Consciousness is the perception of the soul and all the *Natur* are but categories of image. This is also why Thoth is the navigator of the sunboat but not its captain. Who is it who chooses where the boat is going?

Lady *Ma'at* is at Thoth's side in the daily journey of the sunboat, because reality must be the guide of thought, and thought is the guide for a rational, civilized life.

Re Horus is Captain; consciousness is king and decides the course.

DIVINE THOUGHT, HUMAN MIND, INTELLECT AND SCRIBE OF THE GODS

Humans are thinking animals, and this was also believed in ancient Egypt. The familiar of Thoth is an ape, named *Ain*. Thoth and Ain are the original "brains and brawn" team. Ain carries the ink block and paper for Thoth, and he is Thoth's assistant.

The body does function as the "ape" for the brain: a pair of hands to do the bidding of the mind. Today we recognize the reality of the ape "secretary" who sends neural data to the mind as the sensory basis for thought, for knowing.

This ape, *Ain,* sits atop the balance bar of the scales that weigh the soul at death, and Ain calls the measure on the scales to Thoth for his judgment.

Thoth is the judge of the soul, weighing its worth for the next life. Thoth is the judge of what you think of yourself, sometimes the most harsh judge of all. Thoth is the "Great Judge," the judge of the *Pot Natur* themselves. Thoth is the arbiter of Those Two, the Two Rivals, Horus and Sut, and all the *Natur* bow to the judgment of Thoth, of thought.

The ancient Egyptians accorded great honor to the intellect, believing that the powers of the mind were gifts as great as the powers of the heart. Indeed, the gift of the mind was considered the greater, since it is Thoth–thought–which will pass judgment on you in the end. What you think of yourself–truly think of yourself–will determine what you take with you into eternity, into "the millions of years."

The Egyptian word for "scribe" is *sesh*, and the word for "magic" is *heka*, source of the Roman Hecate and the modern word "hex." It means, in Egyptian, the power of speech, the magic in words and names–but also the power of chanting.

Magicians were popular heroes in their stories, and one word for magician is *hekay*. Magicians were temple-trained, and the ability to read and write would have been a first requirement. Allchemist is the modern term for "magician, sorcerer, philosopher" that is derived directly from the original name of ancient Egypt.

SASHETA, LADY OF THE HOUSE OF BOOKS
SAINT OF THE SOFTWARE

Thoth has no wife, not officially.

Lady *Ma'at,* although closely associated with Thoth, is not his feminine form. *Ma'at* represents the field of logic within which the mind functions.

Thoth's feminine counterpart is Sasheta, and she has been called upon since earliest times.

Sasheta wears a panther skin dress, with the tail and paws at the hem, linking her back to the most ancient priestesses and their responsibilities as archivists and guardians of knowledge. Lineage was traced through the mother and, even today, women are most often the keepers of genealogies and family histories,.

When the foundations of a building were measured out by the string-stretchers, the record of the measure was kept by Sasheta. She was called upon to keep the measure true. Sasheta holds the notched palm stalk that symbolizes the counting of days and months. She also carries the tools of a scribe, as the historian. She is sometimes shown holding a cartouche, recording the names of the pharaoh. She is the keeper of the divine databank, and keeper of the calendar count. In her profoundest form, she is the continuity of civilization. Her recorded knowledge provides the database of the new generations.

Her crown is a seven-pointed flower on a long stem, sometimes mistakenly called a seven-rayed star. This mistaken association has led to the current belief that she represents the seven stars of the Pleiades, but in ancient days, the skies were dark enough that ten of the stars in the Pleiades constellation were visible to the naked eye.

Seven, however, is associated with seven *chakra* of the spinal column. Over this seven-petal flower standard, Sasheta wears a pair of inverted bull horns, an enigmatic and ancient emblem. In later dynasties, she is shown with seven horns, and is known as the Lady Of The Seven Horns. She is also known as *Sefkhet Abut,* relating her name to the word for "seven." Thus Sasheta also represents the brain's ability to record the events of life and to memorize and learn the measure of things. She is a patron of mathematicians.

The popularity of Sasheta is on the rise once more. Nice images of her can be found in basic clip art collections. She is called upon in secret by many computer programmers, praying that their databases will remain uncorrupted and incorruptible.

Sasheta has become the Saint Of The Hard Drive, Recorder Of The Magnetic Moment.

The Egyptian Book Of The Dead —*Per Em Hru:* "Emerging While Awake"

"The Beginning Words For Emerging While Awake,
Praises And Spiritualizing Emerging And Entering
As *Natur* Ruling Under The Horizon,
A Soul Distilled Within The Beautiful Western Horizon!"

"The Great Road" was a familiar euphemism for death. The Great Road begins in *Rosetjau,* "The Mouth of the Far Horizon," where Nut the Sky swallows the setting Sun. It is is often translated simply as "the necropolis." The Great Road was the journey through the body of Nut, to be born in the East of the Next World and rise there, just as the Sun rises on top of the Earth. Their belief in the two dimensions of reality was strong, and their language reflects it. Where we would say "while alive" or "in this life," they used the phrase *em tep ta,* "on top of the Earth," counterpoint to referring to the deceased as *ntr-xert,* "*Natur* Under The Horizon."

The *Per Em Hru* is a collection of instructions on the course of the journey, the vehicle of the journey, the progressive stages of the journey, the elements of your self which are your companions on the journey, the dangers and obstacles to be met on the journey, and the goal of the journey. The prayers and magical spells are for your protection and reassurance along the way.

Your primary goal throughout the journey is to remain firmly centered in your own identity. Re Horus must ride calmly in the boat, because the only real danger faced throughout the journey is the dissolution of self-identity into non-differentiated soul stuff, to return to the mud of primal existence with identity, memory, and love all lost.

The progress of the text is loosely structured, since each is a personal encounter. Parts of the text are based around seven passageways, (which are the seven *chakra* of the spinal column) and others around twenty-one gates and fourteen mounds. These comprise the landscape and course of the journey. At the heart of the journey is the Egyptian image of the coiled serpent, just as in the *Tibetan Book of the Dead.* The meaning of the image is the same as in India's yoga tradition, in which the *kundalini* serpent represents the pathway of spirit energy flowing from the dimension of the divine into the physical world. That pathway of energy is the central coil around which flesh is formed. It is the dynamic link between outer, physical self and the inner soul.

The Great Road Of Death is the journey of that soul energy back along the same pathway, returning to its source. This is the journey which is described in the *Per Em Hru*. Unlike the Tibetan book, however, the intention is to remain identified as your own, named, remembered self. Isis struggles to reassemble the scattered being of Osiris so that he can recover his imperishable identity, his "Horus of Gold," for all eternity. In contrast, the Buddhist tradition is based on an intentional erasure of identity, a deliberate dissolving of the individualized self into non-differentiated consciousness, like an ice-cube dissolving in water.

Even though the basic premises of the two have the same regard for the divine nature of the ground of being, their intentions for that soul stuff are poles apart. Buddhists say that all life is sorrowful; they desire not only to escape life, but also yearn to be released from the bondage of individual identity. The Egyptian goal was not to erase self but to define self, and to embrace the greater value that joy is given when experienced in a world full of sorrow. Their joy in their riverside life was so great that they wanted the memories engraved on their very souls, memories to be cherished and relived for eternity. The elements of your identity serve as your companions in the Sun boat, accompanying your soul on the journey. Identity is the emphasis throughout the journey. The name of everything you encounter must be known–the threshold of each portal, the door, the guard, the oars, everything. These things are all manifestations of your own identity. By focusing on their meaning you remain focused on your own cohesion.

There are images of sailing a lake of flame, navigating through the union of opposites. The choice is given of sailing as cargo or captain: trusting to the natural forces of Osiris, or experiencing the journey awake.

The Egyptians did not fear death, only the act of dying. Some wished to fall asleep and wake up in the lovely Marshlands of the Afterlife. Others wished to remain awake and see the scenery along the way. The story of walking the maze to the underworld is a world-wide and time-honored story in the mythologies of humanity. The ancient Egyptians based the journey of the *Per Em Hru* on an ancient roadmap. The leopardskin robe worn by the Egyptian priest is a million-year old echo of human awe from a time when Lord Death was a wild cat on the African veldt who could reduce your beloved to meat draped across a branch.

The many wonderful variations and descriptions of this maze map, the *Per Em Hru*, are a testament to the strong and happy imagination of the Egyptian citizen, celebrating the terrible joys and delicious fears of this last, most important transition through dimensions. Changing the maze's run to a riverboat journey shows how thoroughly the story was integrated into their daily lives. Life itself was the Maze, and they sailed it with delight.

The "Negative Confessions" is not a text like the Bible. It was intended as a teaching, as the starting point for a meditation. The "lesson" is the realization that you take *all* your deeds with you when you cross over to the Next Life. The Great Judge at the Weighing of the Heart is Thoth, who represents the thoughts, training and intelligence of the conscious mind, *your* thoughts. The final judge whom you must confront in the passage to the next life is yourself, with all pretense stripped away, all excuses silenced. You and your deeds will be part of you for eternity–and eternity, you remember, is all time and beyond time. It is more than forever.

The "Negative Confessions," like the "Weighing of the Heart," is about the recognition that for every deed you do in life you must ask yourself, as part of the decision-making process. can I live with this deed for eternity? Can I live with the guilt of consequences for every instant of forever? There is no "father forgive me," no erasure of the deed–in order to cross over into Eternity as yourself, with your identity and memories intact, you must also take with you the guilt of what you have done in your life. The weighing of the heart is not the weighing of "sin," because the Egyptian concept of sin was so different, but the weighing of pain, sorrow and guilt. If your heart, at that confrontation of the Next Life, is too "weighted" with sorrow, with guilt or shame or some other emotional pain too heavy to endure, then *Immomet*, "The Eater," swallows you. Now, the name *Immomet* is translated as "The Eater," but it would be more correct to translate it "She Who Internalizes," since the image is of immersion, dissolving. In other words, she is the ultimate mercy–If your life was too sorrowful for eternity, then *Immomet* dissolves your divine and eternal identity back into the plane of divinity itself, so that you erase the identity–and the sorrow that goes with it–and start the cycle again.

This is a profound, self-directed morality. It leads to good behavior, neither from of fear of punishment nor from desire for reward, but as a recognition of that eternal aspect of behavior. *You have to live with yourself;* that is the bottom line.

They loved their life by the River so much that they thought very hard about what an eternity of life would be like. So many other religions are grown out of a distaste for life, disapproval of the world. There was no Fall, no Original Sin in the ancient religion, and their joy in life, their joy in the world around them, is clear in their art and writings.

IMAN AND PTAH: ORGANIZING FORCE OF PHARAOH, GOD AND MAN

Iman:
Divinely Organized,
The Secret Contract Of The Civilized Soul

Also spelled "Amun" or "Amon."

IMAN's name means "the hidden, the secret, the invisible." Iman is always depicted as a human being, a man crowned with the various attributes of his power. Iman's primary crown and emblem is a pair of stone writing tablets, since the written word is the primary vehicle of civilization. His symbol is the source of the image of the stone tablets bearing the Ten Commandments, for Iman is the original social contract between eternity and the soul. His name survives in the "amen" at the end of Christian prayer. Iman is the archetype of the contract itself, of the civilized honor of agreements between souls maintained out here on top of the Earth.

Iman is the invisible, hidden force of civilization, the magical power of organized effort among human beings, the whole that is greater than the sum of its parts. Iman is the first truly human human, because it is the soul's ability to civilize itself that sets humanity apart from other species.

The earliest demonstrations of Iman's enormous power were in the network of irrigated fields that fed the growing nation. This immense, organized effort turned the natural disadvantage of the Nile's flooding into the agricultural bounty of an empire. Over the course of the generations of that empire, the most stable culture humanity has ever created, the civilizing power of Iman was recognized as the greatest gift of divine Nature. The hymns to Iman reached profound depth and scope, poetic expression of the citizen's gratitude for the benefits and joys of civilized life.

As the pharaoh assumed ever greater importance as the central figure of civilized organization, his figure progressively took on the attributes of Iman. The crown and attributes of Re were added to Iman as their society became more aware of being civilized, and Iman Re was a powerful *Natur.*

Iman Re is the civilized man who knows that he is civilized and who feels the pride and honor of citizenship.

PTAH: THE SOUL OF THE PROFESSIONAL, HAPPY AT WORK IN REALITY

PTAH is the *Natur* of work, the archetype of the professional. The hieroglyphs of his name comprise a wonderful emblem of visual puns:

- **P** is a woven mat, or carpet, representing the skill of weaving;
- **T** is a loaf of bread, the magic of baking and pottery, relating back to the *Pot Natur* itself;
- **A** is the hand and arm, which is Ptah's primary tool;
- **H** is a coil of rope, which symbolizes the early string and fiber technology that predates recorded history.

(Rope was used on the boats and sails used for sailing the river and the marshes. "String stretching" was the surveying tool used to re-establish the territorial boundaries of property after each annual flood of the Nile and to outline the foundations of temples. It was the forerunner of geometry.)

Thus Ptah embodies the works of the human hand. Ptah is known to us primarily as the potter who shapes human beings on his potter's wheel. God as The Professional was highly revered. Ptah represents all the potential for crafts and technology in the human hand, the magic which can be created only by the human hand. Indeed, ancient Egypt's splendor was built *entirely* by hand, so they had good reason to respect and revere the reality of Ptah.

Ptah was eventually mated to Lady Sekhmet, lioness *Natur* of the fierce, driving passions of the soul. The acknowledgment of the passion of the artists and craftsmen who built their civilized world shows the deep respect that was given them. It is possible to see Egypt perhaps as the first nation to be led by artists–certainly every communication between the government and the people was translated through the hand of an artist. Ptah is different from, but related to, Iman. Even the finest workman has a plan from which to work. Iman is that invisible plan. Ptah is the skill which translates that invisible plan into actual work: the invisible made real.

PTAH-SOKAR: SILENCE RULES

Ptah was closely associated with the ancient *Natur* SOKAR (also spelled Sekher) who is Silence. Sokar is embodied in the Boat Of Silence, the sleigh which carried the coffin on its final journey to the tomb. This sleigh was pulled by hand, and such sleighs were lovingly crafted. Sokar's sleighs are masterpieces of graphic and technical skill, incorporating the primeval imagery of their predynastic roots into a transcendent purity of design. This hand work came under the domain of Ptah.

Sokar is a mystical, poetic conception born of the first spiritual awakenings of ancient Egypt. Silence is a legacy of the desert that can teach profound spiritual values. In silence you are alone with your soul. Silence is the eternal answer from the next life, the spiritual continuum to which all souls return. The sleigh carrying the mummy bears of the ultimate silence–the silence of the grave–and the expression of Sokar is an example of the studied sophistication of ancient thought.

The culture of ancient Egypt was the most logical and practical to arise in the entire Bronze Age, and the mysticism that is its legend and legacy is nonetheless founded on a profoundly logical set of premises, worked out for generation upon generation and thoroughly tested for millennia. The ancient Egyptians worked outward from the essential premise of the soul's absolute and divine existence; being of divine stuff, the soul is immortal, and eternity is the true goal of mortal life. The workings of their great civilization began and ended with this belief. The longevity of their culture and of its legacy are proof of the depth and soundness of their faith.

Their religion was based upon meditations, in silence and in conversation, on the realities implied by this belief, unfettered by the concept of original sin, in an environment whose very existence was the living expression of the divine. Their belief in the absolute reality of the next-life dimension, the Hidden Land under the horizon, was complete. The next life was the spiritual counterpoint to, and centerpoint of, physical reality. The reality of the spiritual plane of existence was as unquestioned as the reality of this life on top of the Earth. In fact, reality itself was considered the proof of the existence of the spirit plane.

The absolute separation of these two dimensions was also reality. This world and the next are as utterly divided as the two banks of the river, as life and death. Travel between these worlds is possible, but the journey is never easy. The doorway between them can be opened only by divine action. The doorway opens once to put the divine soul inside the flesh at birth, and once again at death to allow the soul to exit.

The soul door in the front parlor of every ancient Egyptian home is visible evidence of this belief. The soul door is part of the birthing chamber, serving as invitation to the new soul to cross the threshold of that chamber and be born among the living. The same door is added to the tomb so that there might be no hindrance to the soul's exit. The opening of this spiritual doorway is a divine event, for only the soul has the power to link these two absolutely separate dimensions.

Light is divine substance and the stuff of which souls are made. Souls in heaven are referred to as "beings of light." Light is everywhere in ancient Egyptian thinking and art. Light is the only carrier of information between the outer world of reality and the inner world of perception. In this way, light is the only carrier of information between this life and the next. The divine light of the next world is the actual light of The Divine Being and Presence.

This divine light spills over the threshold of the soul door when it opens, just as light from a house spills out into the night, just as a flash of lightning reveals a hidden landscape. This divine flash illuminates everything in the tomb chamber like a spiritual x-ray, and the touch of this illumination is the touch of eternity, imprinting the images in the tomb onto the fabric of the soul as it crosses that dimensional threshold. The information stored in the tomb art is carried across that absolute boundary, imprinted on the soul itself. Ptah-Sokar, then, came to represent the power of the hand and mind which could create a message to be carried through absolute silence and through absolute darkness into absolute light. Ptah-Sokar is the assurance that the soul will not lose the precious images and memories of life, of identity, of love gathered over a lifetime, beloved enough to endure for "the millions of years."

It is in the contemplation of Ptah Sokar that the truly civilized adult is born.

Khnum: The Solar Ram, Handles Of The Mind, The Bulls And The Rams Of A Different Sport

(Also Khnoumos) Northeast African cave art from as early as 7,000 BC shows images of Khnum, the Solar Ram, with the radiant Sun shining from his brow and, most noteworthy, with a collar around his neck to show that he obeys the hand of man. Sheep and goats are among the earliest of domesticates, although they appear long after the dog who guarded them.

The image of the civilized man in control of his own flesh is an ancient concept in Egyptian culture and is at the core of their millennia of civilized, cultural continuity.

The great bull who is the symbol of the substance and flesh of Osiris, the sacred soul within, is an even yet more ancient image of the potential of the soul's living container, an image rising from our Paleolithic past. The identification of the horns of this bull with the crescents of the waning and waxing Moon link him to some of the earliest art of humankind, deeply conceived images of the eternal, divine force, represented by light, that alternately clothes itself in flesh and then sheds this garment again in an endless, reliable round.

The Bull's consort is no less than the World Mother Herself, the physical space/time reality that creates the bull-flesh around the energy of His light. This image is seen in every quarter of that cultural stratum, and the stories that survive of this Moon Bull are some of the most profound echoes of humanity's earliest days.

The great bull, however, like a man who cannot control himself, is a semi-wild animal, a powerful, dangerous creature who must be corralled, around whom you must always be on guard. The fabulous bull dancers of the Minoan/Mycenaean world are an example of the delightful ways that this power was assimilated in the ancient world, but there is always an element of danger around these creatures that is unsettling in the daily round of civilized life. From the same strata as the Bull Dancers comes the Minotaur, that dangerous creature raging deep within.

The sacred Apis Bull was symbol of each succeeding generation's living flesh of Osiris, body of the soul. Egyptians named themselves often as the sacred "Cattle of Re." The names of the Solar herd were used as mnemonics of the self.

These images of the Great Bull remained dear to the hearts and minds of Egypt from beginning to end, but the happy, more personal symbol of the Khnum Ram was widely popular as well. Sheep, although stubborn creatures, are small enough that they fall under the command of the hand. A ram can be effectively controlled by a firm grip on its horns, and the natural products of this useful creature easily obtained. It is not necessary to kill sheep or goats to benefit from their flesh. These useful herd animals were part of the village household compound, and were gentle enough to participate in the daily play of life yet just "wild" enough to represent a mischievous spirit sharing the unchanging round of time.

Combined with the other elements of the soul's evolution through life, the Solar Ram, Khnum, "Flesh of Re" is charmingly Egyptian. It is a personal symbol of the profound potential of the man who knows himself, knows his body, knows his own powers–and his own limitations. Such a personality has the "horns of his mind" firmly gripped in his own hand. He can share his natural energy and productivity with his community, just as the gentle sheep do who sleep outside his door and gambol with his children.

As the nation evolved, the populace become more aware of their civilized benefits in comparison to the barbarian world beyond the Red Desert. Their appreciation of their own self-control was demonstrated by their growing admiration of this image, and by the assimilation of the Khnum Ram into the Iman-Re complex.

Khnum was associated with Ptah and the power of the hand to shape reality, becoming the spiritual archetype of the flesh's mystical power to shape itself into a human animal. This image is embodied in the art and stories of Khnum as the Potter, who, like Ptah, shapes humanity on his wheel.

All the conscious powers of Re and the educated strength of Iman cannot digest the food in the stomach, grow hair, or mature the body from infancy to adult power. These things are the province of the flesh's space/time reality, and represent a level of "cellular consciousness" which must simply be trusted, because even Re cannot see them happening. Re can know they have happened, can experience their functioning; but they exist beyond the realm of conscious perception. They exist in the changing half-light of the Moon. This awe and respect for the miracle of biological existence did not survive the fall of Egypt, and has arisen again only in the most recent years of our own civilization.

To the Western mind, the flesh is perceived as "the scourge of the soul" and nature as something which must be risen above. Our Greek heritage has given us a powerful sense of identification with our bodies, to the extent that the soul has been almost eliminated from modern consideration, consigned to a once-a-week exposure in Church or the occasional confrontation in crisis. The Egyptian concept of the beloved garment that carries the soul through life is therefore a difficult image to comprehend today.

Egypt's perception of the soul's reality, however, was so all-pervading that a most careful distinction between soul and container was at the center of their world view. This most precious vessel of flesh was not something to be scourged and denied, but recognized more on the scale of a dearly beloved and most magical pet who must be carefully trained, groomed, loved and maintained–and for which you, and you alone, are responsible.

The deeper meaning of the Ram of Re's flesh is in the image of the sacrifice. Despite the love and care given the body's container, the body must be sacrificed at the end of life so that the soul can be released, so that it can return to the spiritual plane from which it came. The ram who can be led by its horns to sacrifice is the civilized, educated person who can willingly submit to the progression of time and decay, enjoying the falling-away of the body in anticipation of release into the next life, "ruling as the *Natur* Under The Horizon."

Just as Ptah shapes the vessels of clay on top of the Earth, the images of the body that are represented by Khnum shape the images of your self that you carry into eternity.

It is not a random shaping, however. You *do* have the power to participate in the creation of yourself.

LADY ISIS: DIVINE LOVE, POWER OF THE SOUL'S SELF-BONDING FORCE

"Come to me!
I am Isis, divine *Natur,* and Lady of Magic Spells of the Soul,
hearing truthful words from every mouth which can bite."

Lady Isis: The Throne Of Egypt

Comparative mythologist Joseph Campbell has pointed out that our dreams are our private myths, born out of imagery belonging solely to the dreamer, while myths are public dreams, born out of imagery belonging to everyone, universal in their metaphysical symbolism. The mythology of the ancient Egyptian goddess Isis grew out of mankind's earliest communities in Africa, the Near East and Asia, and within her images are preserved elements of the most ancient philosophical thoughts of our race, our deepest dreams carried by universal images tens of thousands of years old.

The symbol of loyalty and devotion in ancient Egypt was not the faithful dog, but Isis the loyal partner. In Egypt, man's best friend was his wife.

The primary hieroglyph for Isis' name is the same as that for Osiris, the identification of the soul as the throne or seat of being. Osiris' name in hieroglyphs has the eye-hieroglyph added, but Isis is the throne alone, without the eye, since love is a natural function of the soul's dark and mysterious substance. Love can live in the dark. Isis is the wife and female counterpart of Osiris but most specifically Isis is the soul in love, representing every level, state, form and experience of love of which the human soul is capable.

Osiris' role as the carrier of the soul image is explored more fully in the chapter above. It is important to explain his role in the context of Isis as well, not only because Isis is so intimately linked to him, but also because Osiris represents the masculine counterpart of the form that was, in earlier stages of human development, given pre-eminent expression in the symbolism and iconography of the Great *Naturit.*

The most important players in Egyptian teaching, Osiris and Isis, who are the primal elements of the soul, each have this "chair/seat/throne" hieroglyph in their names as an essential element of their function. The soul is that central point at which existence exists, the "seat of action" from which perception is projected and to which it is aimed. Re sends out the Eye and it returns to him: This is the seat of being.

The definition of Isis is as misty, mystic and elusive as all definitions of love must be and have always been. The grandeur and passion of her imagery bear witness to the Egyptians' fascination with the power of love and the mystery of a woman's soul.

Isis is the throne which is the power unifying the land of Egypt. Isis is wife, lover, mother, temptress, witch, bitch, guide, protector, nurse, sister, companion and always, above all, the loyal power *beside* the throne. In the ancient view, we are met out here on top of the Earth for the sake of being together.

LADY ISIS: THE SOUL IN LOVE

It is only on the facades of their public temples that pharaohs stand alone. Wherever else they are represented Pharaoh's Beloved stands close beside him, her hand on his arm. In hunting scenes and in triumph, his comrades are around him. In many scenes, husbands and wives and their children are seen touching in close groups in the eternal sitting-room of their tombs. The loneliness of death is countered with images of hands touching. Nut bends close over your face in your coffin so that you and the night sky can whisper together. Conversation, friendship, and the coherency of the personal group are everywhere in Egyptian art. Their literature is filled with dialogue; the notes of their conversations abound. They wrote letters. Snippets of dialog are painted into tomb art so that talking together goes on uninterrupted by death. Even divine beings talk eagerly with your soul, in the lush poetic language of the tomb texts and in the images emblazoned in magnificent art over every wall and surface of the temples. This art of dialogue, of conversation among friends about the great issues of life, is the hallmark of Egyptian daily life.

Isis represents all the forms of bonding that friendship, love and sex create between people. She is the electricity, chemistry, and magic of that bond—and its dangers. The many temples dedicated to Lady Isis and her many aspects were more than just ceremonial buildings. They were schools and counseling centers for women, sources of learning for the many duties, responsibilities and needs of women. Her priestesses were teachers, guides, therapists and midwives as well as entertainers and professional mourners.

Isis was not just the power beside the throne. As *Natur* of the divine nature of love, she ruled in every heart along the Nile. Love is that force of bonding; not only the bonding of soul to soul but also of the soul to itself. Love is the soul's ability to bind, the very essence of integrity, the personal experience of the divine coherency of the *Pot Natur.* The experience of love is the direct participation in the energy of the spiritual plane from which the soul emerged, the participation in the coherency of being, which is and will always be the prime mystery.

Isis *is* love. She is the spiritual equivalent of the physical forces of space/time that bind atoms together and fire the hearts of suns. Her story and her love for Osiris are the most powerful elements of Egyptian religion, representing the process of the soul's journey into and out of the physical plane.

Lady Isis Of The Many Names: Channels Of Divine Experience

The Number of the Great Goddess is nine because she is that bonding force joining eternity and reality, represented by the four cardinal points of heaven and the four cardinal points of space/time. These eight are linked by the ninth that is the life-column of the Goddess, the link between heaven and Earth that each living soul embodies. She is the Tree of Life that supports the world, joining the two separated dimensions of eternity and reality, the Sacred Sycamore of Hathor. She is the serpent of the spine through which the energies of eternity pour into reality. She is the column that holds up the sky. She is the sky and the Earth, and our living beings are formed around her energies pouring into reality from the divine dimension.

Modern biology has reinforced this image in discovering that the ancestor of land animals began as "a tube within a tube." The life energy represented by the Hindu god Agni is seen in the process of oxidation, which sustains cellular life on Earth as we know it. The biological form in which we began is a physical reflection of the Goddess' image as the channel between heaven and Earth, the "tube" through which life-force flows. In other words, the primal image of life force is contained in the Isis story.

These are among the most ancient of the principles which lie at the foundation of later Egyptian philosophy. The overlay of the bright, hard-edged masculine culture of the chariot warriors placed these images of the Goddess into a different relationship with the Egyptian world, but the syncretic flexibility of the Egyptian mind kept her mystery teaching intact in the lyrical and lovely figure of Isis in her many forms.

Isis, as the power of love, embodies the coherency of each soul's unique identity, a coherency which can survive even the dissolution of death. This binding force of the soul is, in fact, the ultimate *source* of identity, which is why Isis is the Mother of Horus. Identity is the divinity of the soul.

The egg is a very old symbol of the mystery of the Goddess' creative power, and the hieroglyph of the egg is the feminine determinative in the Egyptian written language. Woman's motherhood is locked up within her as the bird is locked up within the egg.

The ancient Egyptian divine *Natur* came from a deep mythological strata. From there evolved the vulture of Mut, the Uraeus Cobra of Nekhbet, the ostrich plume of *Ma'at*, and the Divine Cow of Hathor, primary personification of Isis.

The priestly tradition of the spotted leopard skin robe, with the tail dangling, hearkens back to the mythologies of the leopard-goddess shrines of the first villages like *Catal Huyuk* and *Hacilar.*

The Great Bull, symbol of the power and might and miracle of living flesh, was the first carrier of the Osiris concept: the light of divine, immortal energy captured in the physical plane by dark and mortal flesh. From these ancient human roots come the legends, faith and hope of Isis, counterpart to Osiris, mysterious, celestial Queen, coherence and energy of Osiris' transcendent substance.

Isis is depicted most often in the context of her family. The Egyptian family was a strong unit. The devotion shown in their tomb art, their literature and the gentle arts of their daily lives show clearly that family was the centerpoint and heartbeat of Egyptian life. Isis' role as Hathor The Divine Mother evoked some of Egypt's most lyrical, graceful and lovely art.

The primary function of Isis in many of the myths and rituals is the conception, bringing forth, and education of Horus, child of Osiris. The power of her image and symbolism long outlived even Egypt itself. The role of Isis as bonding force of the soul is demonstrated in the symbolism of her child, Horus.

The Greeks identified the Egyptian Isis with their Greek goddesses. As provider of the grain, she was identified with Demeter; as goddess of love, with Aphrodite. As wife of "the king of the gods" she is likened to Hera. With her power as "a magician great of words," she is Hecate, the Greek goddess of magic, who is herself derived from the Egyptian for "magical words" or "words of power," *heka*. As the prototype of the human woman, she was identified with Io, who was loved by Zeus and changed by him into a cow, that is to say, Hathor, transformed back to human on the banks of the Nile. Behind her many faces and names is the one divine Unknown, the same mystery of the coherence of being.

There was an entire vocabulary of religious symbols in the faith of Isis, a vocabulary drawn from the life-experiences of humanity. Life's journey was a pilgrimage along the river, or even a sea voyage. The dangers of the world were seen as the dark sea, and faith in Isis was the ship and haven. Isis herself was mast and sail of the soul's journey through life. Her priests were the fishermen who rescued the souls from the sea, from the confusions, sorrows and evils of the world. These priests were also seen as bird catchers who caught the souls (birds or butterflies) with their lime twigs and nets: images that carry Isis back to the earliest art works of village life. The fervor of her mystics made them into soldiers on holy military service for Isis. Gentler believers saw themselves as gardeners who laboriously cultivated the garden of their souls.

The Isis priests were philosophers who devoted their lives to the attainment of an emotional and immediate perception of divinity.

In Ptolemaic times the community itself was called *Ecclesia*, an organizational structure adopted by the Greek general assembly and later by the Christian Church. By that time, of course, only the outer forms were preserved. The true meaning of the Lady was buried under the patriarchal layers of Christian interpretation.

Ankh: Life Force, Anchor Of The Soul

The ANKH is a familiar symbol from ancient Egypt, and one that is seeing a revival in use as a religious icon. Many theories have been put forth to explain its distinctive shape. The evidence that it is a sandal-strap fits in best with the Egyptian meaning of the symbol: life force. The ankh symbolizes the divine gift of living breath.

The sandal-strap is related to the footprints of Buddha painted in the center of Buddhist mandala art. To understand the strap metaphor of ankh, you have to focus on the central point of Egyptian religion, and that is the absolute and divine nature of the substance of the soul, personified in Osiris. The flesh which is the container of that substance is itself magical, and divinely formed, but it is not the same as the soul. Flesh is the mortal "net" that catches the soul, the "anchor" that holds the soul in place in physical reality. It is not a coincidence that this ancient mariner's term has "ankh" in its name: compare the ankh and anchor shapes.

Walk in a pair of real leather sandals for even a short distance, and the impression of your individual foot will be permanently pressed into the leather. A pair of sandals is as much a "signature" of the owner as is the body, as recognizable as a face or hand. It is a splendid metaphor for the "impression" of your self that your soul makes upon reality through your fleshly container. As a metaphor of the soul contained by the flesh and shaping it, the sandal is a most ancient and concise one–as old as shoes. Ankh is the magical ability of life to be that anchor for the soul.

Life force is the magically divine force represented by the sandal strap of ankh. Life force is that force which binds your soul to your flesh just as the strap binds the sandal to your foot. Perhaps this is why our words for the sole of a shoe and the soul of a human are cognates? It is not the sandal and it is not the foot. It is the binding of them together by the strap that is life, and that is why the strap became stylized into a body-graphic as well as the knot.

The ankh is presented to the soul as the final gesture of divine action–soul and identity bonded permanently. Your soul puts on and takes off the body the way you put on and take off shoes, and you can only judge another's decisions after walking a mile in theirs. Now think about all the many fancy walking-and-running-shoe commercials you have seen, and consider the passionate art and high finance involved in their creation. That is a modern metaphor of ankh.

Lady Isis And Sirius, Activator Of The Inundation

A major feature of Egyptian spiritual thought, often misinterpreted by modern minds, is the awesome majesty of the night sky over Egypt. Today we have so drenched our skies in city lights that few people experience, on a nightly basis, the pageantry of glowing stars, each utterly and hopelessly mysterious, unreachable, untouchable yet completely reliable, arriving in the sky each night with stately, silent regularity. This sky was the shared, common experience of pharaoh and citizen. Clearly, this magnificent celestial display was the backdrop of their religious imagination. This heavenly spectacle was believed to be the actual body of the divine World Mother, the ultimate prototype for Isis. She is Nut, the spangled goddess bending over the Earth to kiss the horizon and give birth to the Sun. The stars overhead were perceived to be the souls of the departed, shining from heaven. Osiris, divine source of the soul's immortal being, was envisioned in the constellation of Orion.

Following him always is his loyal partner, Isis, as the "Dog Star," Sirius, *Sopdut* in Egyptian, the brightest star in this sky. Observations of the dance of Sirius with the Sun around the cycle of the year are indicated from earliest times in that region. This dance was associated with the movements of Isis. From earliest Dynastic times Isis was associated with Sirius and with the heliacal rising of the star which announced the start of the inundation of the Nile. This was the beginning of the New Year in Egypt.

Isis is shown as the Hathor cow with a star between her horns in her aspect as Sirius, opener of the Nile flood. The black, fertile silt carried by the inundation of the Nile was considered to be the decayed juices of Osiris' divine corpse. Isis' role as the assembler of his corpse made this rich potential for agricultural bounty possible each year. The wealth and security of the entire nation depended utterly on the inundation and its burden of fertile soil, so the rising of Sothis was an important event.

Sirius's cycle is the closest to the solar year, but it is only one of several calendars that the Egyptians used. The Sothic Cycle was the sacred year, relating to the course of the Nile's rising and falling, but there was also a civil calendar based on the reign of the current pharaoh.

The Legends Of Isis And Osiris: The Egyptian Family Saga

The mystery of the nature of being is the core mystery in all ancient Egyptian stories. At the core of the mystery of being, in Egyptian thought, are Isis and Osiris.

An Eighteenth Dynasty stela, that of an official named *Amenmose* (*Louvre C 286*), contains the fullest account of this legend known in native Egyptian. The traditional versions most familiar to modern readers are most familiar were derived from the Greek retelling. This account appears as part of "The Great Hymn To Osiris."

As with all powerful mythological formats, the story is not meant for a simplistic theatrical "plot," but, rather, an experience

The king makes a gift of the pillar to Isis. She places the coffin upon a barge on the river to return to Egypt. While the barge is floating upon the river, Isis removes the lid and uses her magic spells to conceive a child from the dead Osiris. That is how Horus the child of Isis and Osiris was conceived. With the help of her friend and sister, *Nobt Hut*, Isis hides with the coffin in the swamp, and there she bears the child Horus.

This is a story of the divine innocence of childhood and of Egyptian sensibilities about the adult responsibility to shield that innocence for as long as possible. Indeed, the childhood years of the average Egyptian were delightful, carefree, and well protected.

Joseph Campbell in his lecture "Love and The Goddess," called the spiritual life of man the bouquet, the glorious flowering of the natural, biological life, not a supernatural state imposed upon it from without. The flowering of this purity is represented in the lotus Isis holds, or those of a child holding a lotus in its hand and sniffing the "odor of sanctity" in the blossom. Indeed, the innocence of childhood has served since ancient times as a symbol of the purity of the spiritual plane. Pluto, lord of the underworld, of the spirit dimension, was *puer eternitas*, the Eternal Youth, as well as an aged man. "As a child we come to the Kingdom of Heaven."

In studying the lyrical tale of Isis and the Pillar of Osiris, we realize that this spiritual instinct arises in our earliest moments, a life-long echo of the divine resonance from the eternal plane out of which the newborn soul has come. This is rapture of the infant, the passion of the dream.

Sut is jealous of Osiris and *Nobt Hut* for having had a child together, the boy *Inpu*. The Greeks assumed it was sexual jealousy, but it is actually a much more subtle story. The rule which Sut represents is the rule of the flesh over the soul; the rule of instinct and emotion over civilized, conscious self-control; the rule of the physical world over the world of the soul. Every human life, at every moment, is a struggle for this self-control. Sut, the natural instincts and powers of your human body, its learned habits and natural reactions, is constantly ready to control the decisions and actions of your life that are not consciously made. Once awareness of the soul has awakened, represented by the conception and birth of *Inpu*, Sut no longer has absolute rule of the body.

The victory of Horus is the that of self-control, of conscious decisions: the victory of yourself over yourself.

One of the truths of reality, of *ma'at*, is that to be born is to begin dying. At the moment you were born the measure of your coffin was made. The end of your journey is marked by your first step. The first breath at birth is exhaled as the last breath in death. Human beings are the only animals who know they are going to die. Awareness of this is one of the great mysteries of the human experience and provokes a powerful psychological confrontation. The full emotional realization and acknowledgment of our own mortality comes differently to each of us, and at different times in the course of our development. An acceptance of that mortality and of the burden of spiritual awareness it imposes, are the first awakenings of adult consciousness. That awakening is the birth of the unique identity, the birth of the Horus of our souls.

The celebration to which Sut brings the beautiful coffin is the celebration of life, the birth of a new soul. The physical realities of the flesh represented by Sut have given birth, via the natural instincts and potentials of the child's parents, to a new soul, a new person. The flesh has "betrayed" the soul by ensnaring it in the physical world, just as Sut betrayed Osiris by creating the coffin. The seventy-two minions of Sut who put Osiris into the coffin are the seventy-two years of life–a generous average–and the many events that move your life along its course. The number seventy-two was chosen because of its significance to the World Mother. Seventy-two is significant of this both because it is four times eighteen, and because the two digits themselves, seven and two, add up to nine. (*Note: see the chapter above, on the ancient Egyptian calendar, for further material on the number 72 and its function in this story.*)

These numbers are related to the number of the World Mother, which is nine. Not only is eighteen twice nine, but its digits add up to nine. These are then multiplied by the four cardinal points, as many Egyptian rituals were repeated at each of the four directions, four being the number of the field of space/time in which the World Mother's creations are active.

The tree which grows around the coffin of Osiris is the eternal Tree of Life, the living pillar at the center of the universe that is the axis of the world, and the centerpoint that is everywhere at once. It is indicative of the age of this portion of the Isis legend that the tree which grows around the coffin is located in Syria. Some of the oldest centers of the World Mother worship are in that region.

Just as in the fairy tales of Europe, every child is "a royal child, a prince within its own household." Hidden in the pillar of this homey palace, Osiris is already present in infancy, manifest as the infant's soul.

In other words, the soul is already a presence at birth, functioning in the living being. Osiris is, indeed, the pillar and support of the child's environment, and the centerpoint of its being. Osiris, the soul, is hidden and as yet unperceived, present as an "odor of sanctity" that enchants all.

Isis is found beside a well, because the energies of the spiritual plane which she represents pour into the world from out of our greatest depths. It is as if the natural instinct for spiritual survival arises out of the moist depths of the Earth itself, out of the deep oceans of the inner landscape. It is the mystery of the source of our own being.

This experience of the eternal plane lingering in the infant mind is symbolized in the burning-away of his mortal parts in the flames of Isis. The infant still dwells in the glory of that immortal dimension from which it has come.

This was said in modern times by the English poet William Wordsworth in his poem, "Ode: Intimations of Immortality from Recollections of Early Childhood" (lines 58-76)*

"Our birth is but a sleep and a forgetting:
The Soul that rises with us, our life's Star,
Hath had elsewhere its setting,
And cometh from afar:
Not in entire forgetfulness,
And not in utter nakedness,
But trailing clouds of glory do we come
From God, who is our home:
Heaven lies about us in our infancy!
Shades of the prison-house begin to close
Upon the growing Boy,
But he beholds the light, and whence it flows,
He sees it in his joy;
The Youth, who daily farther from the east
Must travel, still is Nature's Priest,
And by the vision splendid
Is on his way attended;
At length the Man perceives it die away,
And fade into the light of common day."

**Together with the editors, the Department of English (University of Toronto), and the University of Toronto Press, the following individuals share copyright for the work that went into this edition: Screen Design (Electronic Edition) Sian Meikle (University of Toronto Library) Scanning: Sharine Leung (Centre for Computing in the Humanities)*

Just as the mother's panic in this story is the event which reveals the magical experience of the infant suspended in Isis' magical flames, it is the mother who brings the emotional awareness of life to her child. The father, in calming everyone and agreeing to give the pillar with the coffin of Osiris to Isis, demonstrates the father's role as the provider and role model of rational judgment in life.

The journey of human life in Egypt was most often symbolized by sailing on the river Nile, life's blood of Egypt. The river journey of Isis on the barge with the coffin of Osiris is symbolic of the beginning of the life's journey of a child.

Horus, the child's unique *identity*, is "conceived" during the early years of infancy and childhood, and the experiences and training of this time in life shape the adult personality. "The child is father to the man."

The birth of spiritual understanding comes with the realization that, from the very beginning of your life, your coffin awaits you.

Isis' instinct to life powers the river journey, and her power of coherency is the guide and magical strength of each of us. And, as always, the assistance of friendship, loyalty and family love, represented by *Nobt Hut*, (Nepthys) are the support and comfort of each us along the way as we grow up.

The primary function of Egyptian religion and training was to make possible the best, smoothest and most successful transition through the stages of life: to grow up healthy, sane and happy, but, most important, to grow up. Adult maturity marks every gesture of ancient Egyptian art, literature and lifestyle. These were not the childish, adolescent reactions and desires of a barbarian people, but the mature, studied work of a truly civilized, grown-up nation.

In this story of Isis and Osiris and Horus we see the way Egyptians began this process of growing up. Step one was to look at your own coffin without fear.

In the next story fragment, Sut finds and dismembers the body of Osiris, scattering the pieces throughout the land of Egypt.Here we see Isis bringing this sense of dynamic unity to the abstract creation of the nation of Egypt itself, binding the people and land together in the symbolism of reunifying the slain Osiris.

There is a mythological process of land-claiming called *"land namen,"* known in early cultures. People link their own geography to mythological scenarios by ritually enacting the stories of their gods along a specific pathway of the rite, thus gathering in the boundaries of their territory to the interior landscapes of mythology. This is a universal process, older than Egypt and world-wide. Isis must gather up each and every piece, or else this or that nome will be left out of the ritual assemblage. She is the force of bonding, and she bonded the nation as securely as she held Osiris together.

The Magic Of Lady Isis

There has always been a hunger in the world for great magicians. There are magicians everywhere around us but we have been given the wrong names for them and cannot easily identify them. Our century has seen the rise of many great magicians: D.W. Griffith, Hitler, Elvis, John Kennedy, John Lennon, Martin Luther King, Gene Roddenberry, Mother Teresa, Princess Diana, Bill Clinton, so many others. There is no explanation for the power and impact of these people. There is no logic in the fanatical faith of their followers. It is not about logic. It is about magic.

Both science and mythology struggle to find the proper alignment of self and reality. Do you see the wind as the manifestation of an invisible presence, or as the manifestation of invisible force? Is it magic or magnetics? Absolute angles or absolute Angels?

The members of an African tribe were told that germs were tiny, invisible creatures, too small to be seen, that got inside them and made them sick. They replied politely that the missionary had taught them not to believe in invisible demons anymore. The difference between mythology and science is often only in the spelling of the terms. They just have a different word for everything.

Reality remains unaltered by vocabulary.

Magic, "true magic," is wholly a function of will power and *only* of will power. The cause and effect of magic are not tied to physical law. Levitation differs from flying only in the source of lift energy. Flight can be examined, explained and duplicated. Levitation cannot. Anyone can make a machine or an engine. The instructions for these are simple and direct. How do you make a leader? An artist? A kind person? A psychotic? How do you make someone love you? How do you make someone *vote*? Getting people to *agree* with each other is the most powerful magic we have and the most difficult to use

Technology uses physical law to make the tools that shape and change reality. Magic is the power to change people's behavior, beliefs, hopes or fears, to make people *do* something that will change reality, and to motivate them *only* by means of will power.

Stage magicians who use sleight-of-hand trickery, and con men who use outright fraud, have always been pointing to the truth. Their *real* magic lies in their ability to make us believe that we have witnessed physical law overcome by will power.

The dismissal of this kind of magic as "merely psychological" is an attempt to defuse its awesome power. We are afraid of its reality, yet in the same response we yearn to control it. We do not elect leaders. Rather, we elect the magicians who made us believe that they can overcome physical reality with political will power. We do not choose our entertainment, rather we rejoice in the will-o'-the-wisp phantasm that catches our delight, leading us beyond mundane thought.

Being fully civilized requires the use of *both* technology and magic. Medicine has been the first science to acknowledge that some degree of magic is needed to make the technology work. Magic and technology are as different, and as much alike, as differing orders of infinity. Technology is really very simple. Magic is so profoundly complex that often those who use it best have the least understanding of the tool they have.

True magic can turn back on the user and undo them. Black magicians are as common as any other. They can and often do masquerade as white, and vice versa. It is as subtle and as powerful as the difference between mind control and thought control, between self control and mob control. The magic of will power is a most difficult force to master. Once under control it is the single most powerful force on Earth. It is the highest magic. Even global famine created by the realities of physical law can be averted by the magic of human cooperation.

With human cooperation, we could survive even the death of the Sun itself, but only if a powerful enough a magician can make us want to cooperate. Science and technology are needed to measure the reality of these changes, but only magic will make the better angels of our nature reach for the stars.

This is the magic which Isis, Magician "Great of Words" brings to the human community. It is within the light of her spiritual understanding that the magic of human cooperation is worked. Our understanding of our own humanity, accepted in all its smelly detail through the love of the divine Lady Isis, will guide us to our best possible human destiny.

THE LAMENT OF LADY ISIS

"I am Isis!
I have emerged from that place
into which my brother had placed me.
Behold! Ancient Thoth has spoken to me,
face and head of *ma'at* in heaven and earth."

"Come, Isis! *Natur* of beauty, you who are that obedience of one life leading forth another. Conceal her carrying of the son, and the child will come forth, his limbs growing. He is strengthened while he rests in peace. Face of the throne of his father, he is oriented as the ruling prince of the two worlds."

"I emerged, the face in the season of darkness when the maateet emerge, carrying my beginning. They endured in me, the arm of *Tofun* and *Bofun* behind me, She Is Born and He Is Born carrying my *ma'aty* place, and *Poteet*, and *Thoteet*, and *Maateet*." The face showed me the way.

"I chanted to them, loudly, loudly. My spell went into their living ears, by learning and listening. They sing praises to the red color of the standard of the son, and have the wisdom to humble their faces while carrying the face along my pathway. Wandering did bring me to the marshes of *Suey* (Crocodile Town), town of the two sandals of the *Natur*, at the beginning of the marsh processional to the *Dob* Town.

"I was liked in the women's quarters by the concubines of the husbands I was witnessed by the chief wife while on the path, and she closed her doors to my face. She was angry of face and heart at those two who prayed together with me in front of her.

"We placed their poison on the face and top of the sting of *Tofun*, and I became a young woman of her entourage, going into her house. Tiny *Tofun* crept under the door panels of the servant's passage, and she bit the baby son of the first wife. Then did a conflagration break out among the chambers of the first wife! Nothing could quench it, and the sky did not let fall her water among the chambers of the first wife, not even in the season for it. She will have closed up, but I will have opened the doors of her heart to sadness, not knowing if he is alive. She went round her town among those who cry inside. Nothing will come of her inquiries. My heart is saddened by her child. Her face vitalizes the breath inside his weak body. I cried out to her face:

"Come to me! Come to me! I am the mouth carrying life,
I am the daughter of learning inside her center,

driving out the serpent demons inside her head.
I am the star-child of my father because of learning.
I am his daughter."

Words concerning the illness of his flesh, and Isis laying her two hands on the face of the child and healing that which was inside closing the throat:

"Poison of *Tofun*, come out!
Emerging Face of the Dual World,
without saturating him, without poison entering.
Come out! Emerging Face of the Dual World.
I am Isis, *Natur*, and Lady of Magic Spells of the Soul,
hearing truthful words of every mouth which can bite.
Overcome the poison of She is Born!
Do not bring forth the poison of He is Born!
Untie the knot of the poison of *Poteet* and *Thoteet*
without entering!
Conquer *Ma'ateet*!"

She has given Geb his divine soul in order to expel the semen, because her divine spirit moves through the semen as it rises.

The word of Re On Course, Egg of the Semen Goose emerging out of the dawn tree:

"You are in charge of chanting her words at twilight. I am talking to you of that Lady *Natur* Isis while she was alone and in great sorrow because of those of you throughout the counties, because the lovers of *Kemmet* who cease to seek for and to look to the chief women in their places, or to the face of Isis while the face is carried along the pathway, to be hidden in *Chob* Town."

"Hey! Life and the Child!
Death and Semen! Life and Re!
Death and Semen! Yes! Health!
Horus and his mother, Isis, yes!

Health to the two who are under the blade,
just as the flame should be peacefully quenched by the sky."

Face and head of Isis, Lady *Natur* and First Wife, she had to carry her things, (i.e., was homeless) and she lacked a place for the conception, for the *ka*, for the fetus.

Isis speaks now:

"Either I shall have opened her doors (of her heart) or first wife, facing pain and sorrow on one night, she will swallow her words. I can poison her son. She brings her affairs to skin and bone because she closed up to what I am."

"Hey! Life and the Child!
Death and Semen, yes!
Horus and his mother Isis, yes!

Health for all those who are under the blade,
just as it is bread because of the barley."

He expels semen, and it comes. It is the burning organ and flesh of Isis, of Isis! The arrival of Horus and knowledge of her mouth, the arrival of the daughter.

"Oh! it is the Lady *Natur* when she is in love,
just like those whom *Tchart* has penetrated,
and *Maateet* has pierced,
and the *int*-fish has led astray."

It is the emergence of Isis from the penetration of her private parts, and she spreads wide her two arms:

"I am!
I am the child of my soul,
before the evolving of anything evil from you
or from the essence within you!"

FORMS OF THE LADY: THE MANY FACES OF LOVE

THE MANY FACES OF LOVE: MASKS OF THE DIVINE LADY

Isis is shown as womanhood in all aspects, roles and stages of life. Womanhood was so greatly revered and studied that the many faces of Isis were eventually personified into a variety of seemingly separate *Natur*, each identified by different crowns and headdress combinations. Every masculine *Natur* has a feminine counterpart in acknowledgment of the universal duality of nature. The many aspects of Isis, identified by her crowns and various attributes, represent the many faces of love experienced in the human world.

MUT: DIVINE MOTHERHOOD, MOTHER OF NATURU AND KINGS

The ancient, pre-historic roots of Isis survive in the ancient Near Eastern vulture figure of Mut. As Mut, Isis is the primeval mother, "Mother of Mothers, and Mother of the *Natur*." Mut is the looming, dark-winged power of motherhood itself, the impersonal nature of creation that devours its own offspring. She is the death aspect of the ancient Mother Goddess, symbolizing the eternal round of life out of death, and death out of life.

The hieroglyph for Mut is the black vulture, a huge, impressive bird with shiny black plumage and a wrinkled neck. The image of this black vulture is among the most ancient of that region of the world, painted on wall murals in villages as early as 8,000 BC. Mut is the mystery and paradox of the warm tenderness of love, and the coldness of death, that is the equal potential of all flesh.

Mut was seen as bisexual, transcending the duality of space/time, demonstrating the profound reach of her imagery. She was called "The Great Sorceress, Mistress of Heaven, and Eye of Re." She was in later years generally seen as a woman, sometimes with a vulture's body as her head, sometimes only with the vulture crown.

Over the generations Mut evolved along with the other *Natur* of Egypt. Her imagery, even though grown lyrical in the forms of Isis and Hathor, never lost the shadowy brush of dark wings in the background. Mut is the mighty and divine mother, represented on the Pharaoh's crown in the vulture head beside the Uraeus serpent, merged with *Nek-hebet.*

In the Theban Triad of Iman Mut, and Khons, Mut is seen as the mother of the Moon. The Moon was the pre-eminent symbol of the Goddess, Queen of the Night Sky, originally an aspect of the Mother Goddess' Moon Bull consort. It was the counting of the Moon's cycles that led to the Neolithic development of the calendar, astronomy, mathematics and the metaphysics of the sky.

Thoth, also associated with the Moon, took over these intellectual aspects of the mythology as the Ennead became dominated by male forms in the later Bronze Age. The careful conservatism and syncretic tolerance of Egyptian philosophy, however, maintained their reverence for the black-winged eater of death.

Having arisen in the southern Ancient Near East and the Saharan regions of Africa, the desert was always implied in the imagery of Mut, just as the fertile fields of the Black Land are symbolized by the cattle imagery of Hathor. In the Eighteenth Dynasty, therefore, when desert tribes were much more a part of the environment of Egypt, Mut rose with the Iman cult in Thebes as Lady *Asheru,* wife of Iman. She is identified here with one of the four cosmic, demiurge-couples at the creation of the universe, Iman and *Imaunet,* partly restoring her to her position of World Mother from millenia before.

The marriage of Mut and Iman was a great annual celebration during the New Kingdom, the *Opet* Feast, or "Feast Of The Harem." The company of Iman would bear his statue from his temple at Karnak on the Nile to visit Mut at her temple at Luxor, uniting these two potentially rival city states with loving celebration. This ceremony and procession was occasion for oracular pronouncements by Iman Re and most popular. It was the first national celebration reinstated by Pharaoh Tutankhamun when he ascended the throne.

Het Heru, Lady Hathor: Home Of Horus, Your Mother

The milk-giving cow, gentle counterpart to the wild bull of Osiris, has been a sacred symbol in Africa, Asia and the Near East since earliest times, represented in the oldest cave and village art throughout the region. She is the universal Mother, she from whom the world flowed forth, as milk flows from the cow. She is the starry heavens and the bright day-sky, one divine hoof planted at each quarter of the world. These are the beginnings of Hathor's place in the pantheon. Although she was assimilated into the later, patriarchal structures, she never lost her resonance as the Mother Of The World.

Hathor is mother of Horus, and her hieroglyph is a very literal visual and verbal pun. She even wears her name in her crown, which is the hieroglyph for "home" with the Horus falcon inside. (The name, "Hathor" is the Hellenized pronunciation of *Het Heru*, which means, literally, "Home of Horus.") Hathor is *your* mother.

Hathor is the warm, nurturing comfort of the daylight. Hathor is the romance of caresses in the moonlight. Hathor is Isis at her most graceful and lyrical. It is Hathor whom we honor on Mother's Day. Hathor is music and art, dance and romance. She is the *Natur* of affection, and the bright, warm memories and experiences of mother and child, and she governs the attitudes these create in the adult personality. Hathor is the entire role that a woman plays in creating the environment of the ego, and the shaping of the child who shapes the adult. Hathor is the *Natur* of nature and nurture.

Even though in later years Khnum and Ptah took over the role of shaping the human body on the divine potter's wheel, nonetheless, the touch of Hathor's ankh was needed to initiate life in the newborn. This divine energy dance is the *sekhem*, the spirit, and its divine harmonics define and sustain the soul through life. The hieroglyph for the spirit is a musical instrument, one that was used to create a droning vibration in ceremonies symbolizing the vibration of the spirit, the music of the soul. This energy force is unique to the soul's existence; it is the source of energy from which the soul sustains its immortal life. Illustrations of this musical instrument, held by Hathor, the Divine Mother, show the central portion of strings and rattling rings replaced by a soul figure of the newborn individual, emerging into reality.

"The Golden One" is a favored name of Hathor, and the beautiful love poems in which she is evoked show the depth and emotional sophistication of the Egyptian heart. She is the giver of the inspiration of love, demonstrating the joyous participation of the Divine in the experience of love "on top of the Earth."

It is in the form of Hathor that Isis is most frequently encountered. Hathor's crown is the familiar quail wing helmet and towering horns, linking Hathor to her even more ancient form as the encircling horizon who is Consort of the Moon Bull. The Bull is the being of divine light who is born in the new Moon, King in the full Moon, and who dies in the dark of the Moon, only to be reborn again in the next new Moon. This round of resurrection is a spiritual image reaching down from the Neolithic, stories from nomadic shadows out of which those first Bronze Age civilizations grew. Hathor is implied in the four horned symbolism of the "Utterance of Unas," an ancient text on a northern wall of the tomb of Unas, last pharaoh of the Fifth Dynasty. She is the divine being whose one horn touches the Earth and her other horn reaches to heaven.

In India, her figure survives in the Cosmic Cow who stands with a leg at each of the quarters of heaven. Hathor's horns represent the horns of the crescent Moon, but also they link her imagery back to the Neolithic burst of mythological development of the Near East and Saharan regions. She is the cow-faced divinity who bears the new Sun, the beautiful calf who runs before the Moonlight. She is the loving coherency from which the world is born.

On the Narmer Palette, oldest surviving iconography of Egyptian kingship, a pair of Hathor-faces with horns adorn the top edge. The pharaoh has the bull face on his belt and a bull's tail. He is the Moon Bull Consort of the Celestial Cow, she from whom all reality has come. In the beautiful Dendarah Temple to Isis, the full face of Hathor is beautifully rendered everywhere.

There are the Seven Hathors who attend the birth of each child, usually represented as a group of young women, wearing the disk and horns of Hathor, and playing musical instruments. They represent the newborn's arrival into the physical world of the Goddess, and later they became the fate, good fortune or bad, of the child.

These are the forms of the Isis associated with the Sycamore tree, surviving symbol of the great World Tree that stands as the axis of reality and eternity. In Ptolemaic times these Seven Hathors were associated with the seven stars of the Pleiades.

The physical innocence of biological virginity became a symbol of spiritual purity with the rise of Christianity. In the World Mother mythological systems, female sexuality was differently beheld. The virginity of the Goddess was a symbol of the soul's emergence into the larger world of evolved consciousness and spiritual awareness.

This is the birth at the heart-*chakra* of the *kundalini* system, and the birth of Buddha from his mother's side, (or in the charming Chinese version, discreetly sliding from his mother's silken sleeve.) It is Dionysius growing in his father's thigh.

It is a virgin birth only in that it is not the *biological* emergence and separation from the mother, but the psychological and emotional birth of true self-identity. It is a separation not from the mother's body, but from her *identity.* You are born now as yourself, no longer just your mother's child. That is the role of Hathor, as

"Home of Horus," the bonding force of the soul successfully shaping a new, unique individual from the universal stuff of reality.

That is the virgin birth.

NOBT-HUT, NEPHTHYS: "LADY OF THE HOUSE," ARCHETYPE OF LOYALTY AND MARRIAGE, SISTER OF ISIS

Just as Lady Isis's title as "Home of Horus" became the name Hathor, the name of Nephthys comes from her title of Lady of The House, *Nobt Hut.* (Hellenized later into Nephthys) Her crown plays a similar role as visual and verbal pun: the hieroglyph for "home" is drawn standing on its end, with the hieroglyph for "lady" on top. Drawn this way, the hieroglyph for Isis is hidden inside, showing that a home is shaped by souls in love. Lady of The House, however, is more than a soul in love, more than potential motherhood. She represents loyalty, commitment, and partnership. Lady of The House is marriage. Lady of The House is separate from Hathor, because there can be love without marriage, and marriage without love. She represents a commitment that is higher than law, because it is an action of the divine soul. There were no civil or formal wedding ceremonies in ancient Egyptian society, because marriage was seen as a private contract between equal souls. Although, it was an excuse to throw a party. Egyptians loved to party. Women had a more nearly equal place in ancient Egyptian society, quite unlike her counterparts in other societies of that time.

The hieroglyph for "Lady" in Nepthys' name (the same as "Lord" with the feminine "t" ending) is a basket, pronounced *nob,* and symbolizes the Egyptian concept of "nobility"–a word which we have ultimately inherited from them. The nobleman and noblewoman were the unifying "containers" of their group, not only in the image of the many individual reed strands woven together to make a solid whole, but also in the image of the container which gathers loose, disparate pieces into a single, central place, that is, as organizers. These woven baskets were of the same technology as the reed boats that were the primary means of transportation in the Delta, and they represented sophisticated technique and patient craftsmanship. These are indicators of the truly noble nature, and this basket symbol reflects the Egyptians use of images from the living world around them for meditation upon the nature of life and reality. This nobility of the female heart lives in the character of Lady of the House, Nephthys, in her ability to contain all the household within her being.

Isis, as Lady of The House, is wife of Sut because the discipline and habits of married life must be learned. Horus does not officially have a wife, but as Horus and Sut were understood to be dual aspects of the same being, the wife of Sut must then also be the wife of Horus, and also of Osiris, because, at bottom, it is all soul. This does not mean, however, that Horus was sleeping with his mother. The *Natur* are roles, role models and idealized forms, and they tell stories of the relationships and relatedness of living souls. Each of us plays many roles in life, as called upon by family and fate.

As lover to both Osiris and Re, Lady of The House represents the romance of the soul and the awareness of love. As lover to Osiris, she conceives Anubis, the jackal-headed *Natur* who is the spiritual guide running ahead of the soul, leading the way to the next life. Anubis has the same animal head as Sut joined with Horus as "Those Two," thus symbolizing the instinctive nature of spiritual understanding.

Anubis is the "Typhonic animal" whose territory is the graveyard, with the dead his food. He represents the natural instinct of the flesh to seek the light of the spirit, the instinct born of the soul. Lady of The House is the source of this, because, in her role as wife and mother within the daily household, she is teacher, role model, confidant and guide. The ancient Egyptian child learned the first "Sunday school lessons" at mother's knee. Lady of The House teaches the first habits of religion and ritual, the spritual training that guides one through the changes of life and death.

As the sister of Isis, Lady of The House gives aid and comfort to Isis in her grief and helps in the search for the parts of the slain Osiris. Lady of The House stands beside Isis in the funeral ceremonies and they ride behind Re in the sunboat, one on either hand. Their love for each other and their friendship in the stories show the close ties between women in ancient Egypt. The mythological tales of the brothers are stories of rivalry, betrayal, and murder, but, most often, the women work together.

In the ancient "Land of Love," a man's wife and his concubine could be best friends, comfortable with sharing the duties and pleasures of his household. Isis and Lady of The House are the archetypal examples of sisterly loyalty, love and cooperation. They guard your precious moments.

Lady of The House was identified with *Anuket* (Greek Anukis), wearing a crown of red parrot feathers. Her name means "embrace," and *Anuket* was the consort of Khnum in the Elephantine Triad, representing female physical lust, one of the great joys provided by the commitment of marriage.

Marriage

Let me say first that there was no ceremony–civil or religious– that corresponds to the wedding ceremonies of today. The majority of the ritual, ceremony and intention of the our modern concept of marriage is based on medieval patterns established in the Byzantine courts of Christian emperors. The exchange of rings was a "bonding ritual" of Celtic Europe for millennia, used to symbolize soul bonding for *any* close relationship, not just for the marriage vow.

Marriage contracts between man and woman were common in ancient Egypt, and they even had *written* marriage contracts, common with families wealthy enough to afford a scribe. These were similar to modern pre-nuptial contracts, and often covered the distribution of property in the case of divorce. The parties to the contract were only family, the parents and witnesses, not priests or government officials.

Divorce was as simple a matter as moving out. Women kept their own property in divorce, and had as much right to be the one "moving out" as the man.

There would have been, of course, a wedding party. They enjoyed their lives very much. The community of human beings gathered together for conversation and companionship was central to their civilization. The couple who was setting up a household together would certainly invite all their family and friends, who would bring gifts and food, and there would be musicians, singers, dancers, acrobats and animals, and flowers, all the flowers they could get, as well as incense and lots of food, wine and beer.

The Egyptian woman was not seen as the property of her husband in the way of our Western world. The wife, referred to as the Lady of The House, is the loyal partner standing not behind but *beside* her man, arm in arm.

Love was the central mystery and guiding force of the Egyptian civilization, and they had a much more open attitude toward sexuality than you find in much of the Western world. An Egyptian man could, and often did, take more than one wife. There were concubines as well, women whose primary role was motherhood. Concubines were more likely to be occupied with wet-nursing, child care and education, so that Egyptian children always had many loving women surrounding and caring for them, women who could afford to devote their full attention to the children. These women were less involved in the running of the household estate.

Management of the household was most often was in the hands of the first wife. This was a powerful position, ruling the lives of family, servants and retainers. I get the distinct impression of a tightly-knit group of women sharing the responsibilities and work of their household, without the kind of automatic sexual jealousy that we have been raised to expect in ourselves.

They experienced, of course, the jealousy and fighting that is natural to human nature. Their attitude about its place in society was different. Fidelity was expected, but the reality of the briefness of life was the ruling passion, and love was considered a treasure too dear to deny.

There is a wonderful volume, recently published, of translations of some of the best of their love poetry, *Love Songs Of The New Kingdom,* by John L. Foster, I highly recommend it. You can order it easily from Amazon.com or Barnes and Noble. There is more of the living heart of Egypt to be found in these charming, passionate songs than in the mysterious matter of tombs and temples. These works are so masterfully written and so intuitively translated that even the most tongue-tied male will find his secret longings revealed and therefore easier to convey.

A marriage was decided between two souls, the man and the woman involved. The rest of the community respected their decision without the interference or sanction of any "higher authority." There was, in the Egyptian world view, no "higher authority" than that of the divine, immortal human soul, and marriage was seen as a decision between two such souls. What right had the rest of the universe to intrude upon such a private decision? The community was a gathering of such souls, and they worked together to celebrate the mystery of Reality, of *ma'at,* but the privacy of the soul's moments was sacred. Even your beloved had to acknowledge the secret moments of your soul, as you must in return.

There is nothing in this Egyptian doctrine of the "possession" status of Western wives, nor of the "obedience" demanded by the Roman/Victorian world we have inherited.

The stories that have survived are of men and women standing equally against the wild realities of the universe, glad to have these moments to be together, to know their own spirit, and to have a constant, loyal best friend with whom to share these moments, someone to trust.

As for royal weddings, although there is quite a lot of tomb and temple art surviving that portrays the loving dedication of pharaohs for their wives, it is always about the marriage, about the relationship and not the wedding. That is, of course, the clue: the ancient Egyptians understood human nature so well that they knew that a marriage really exists only in the relationship, private and personal, between two people, and has nothing to do with the public, the government, or the gods. A marriage is a partnership of two souls in life "on top of the Earth," two people sharing companionship on the daily voyage through time toward the inevitable conclusion of eternity. Divine "weddings" were regular ceremonies, during which the statues of the divine couple were brought together to celebrate their mattiage, but here again the emphasis is on the active energy of the relationship.

The most famous ceremonial ritual recorded is from the tomb of Tutankhamun. He and his young bride put locks of hair, bound in jeweled clips, together in an ivory box that was included in his tomb possessions. I think the image that has come down to us of the braided lock of the lover's hair is from this ancient Egyptian tradition, and perhaps there is something in this that inspires. Rings of your beloved's braided hair pre-date the engagement ring in pre-Roman Europe. If you are going to use Egyptian artwork in your wedding theme, I would recommend the tomb sculptures of Tutankhamun. There are some alabaster lamps that are worthy, on their own, of the profound emotions of a new marriage.

Lady Net: Divine Weaver, Threads Of Destiny

(Neith in the Greek version.) Lady Net is an interesting figure from the broader prehistoric background of Saharan Africa. Her primary attributes are the bow with crossed arrows, and the weaving shuttle. Her name and figure come from predynastic times and survived to the end, relating to words for yarn and the name of the workroom, hall or house where weaving was done. It may have been a sailor's job to make the heavy cordage used in Egyptian boats and sailing, but the wicks, nets, knots, knitting and woven cloth of the household technology were the domain of Lady Net.

Fiber technology in Africa goes back to the Stone Age, but it reached its zenith in Egypt, not just in boat-building and sailing, but in every aspect of their daily lives and in every field of activity. "String-stretching" was the predecessor of surveying, used to reestablish boundaries buried under the annual inundation of the Nile. The fundamentals of geometry inherited by the Greeks also arose from this ancient study. String was used to measure out the foundations of sacred buildings, tombs, palaces and homes, and to create the clean, even lines and measured proportions of their wall paintings and carvings. The Pyramids were measured out by string, and its stone blocks were dragged into place with handmade rope.

Weaving was practiced from earliest times in many cultures.

Knitting, however, is an Egyptian invention. Three- thousand year-old knitted woolen baby socks have been found. Egypt was noted in Roman writing for producing the finest linen, strong but so sheer as to be transparent. These skills, although not exclusively within the sphere of woman's work, were most often associated with the women in the household. Lady Net was patron of their activity. Lady Net was called upon for guidance while making the magic knots in amulets, and she was associated also with the divinities who prepare and weave the threads of individual fate. Her shrines stood in every town.

Ancient petroglyphs of Saharan women, carrying bows and crossed arrows, and running with fine, long legs can still be seen in deep places in Africa. The image of the independent, strong woman remains vital in African cultures, even those in America. This spirit of the desert-bred huntress survived in Egypt as Lady Net, wearing the Red Crown of the North and holding her bow and arrows. The symbol of arrows crossed upon a shield represented her everywhere in the empire.

Just as the huntress of the predynastic time became the civilized housekeeper of the First Dynasty onward, Lady Net transformed her skill at fiber technology from that of stringing bows to the needs of the household. Making a good bowstring requires knowledge of fiber technology in general as well as experience with the tools, materials and material sources. You must know which plants or animal products to choose, as well as when and how to harvest and prepare them. This knowledge is easily adapted to the demands of weaving and knitting as well as net- and rope-making, so women who were skilled in the one were also skilled in the other. Stringing a bow and stringing a loom differ only in degree, and both can be applied toward getting you something to wear.

The festivals, rituals and ceremonies in which Lady Net is featured demonstrate the Egyptian's reverence for these vital tasks. The production and maintenance of lamp wicks was another responsibility of her devotees, and there festivals of lights associated with her. The ritual of lighting lamps was dedicated to her, on *Altar Offerings Day, Famenoth* 5, (December 28 in the modern calendar.)

Oil lamps are older than villages, as old as art itself. There are stone and clay bowls with animal-fat and plant-fiber wicks found at the sites of the great cave painting cathedrals dating back 30,000 years. This ancient duty of Lady Net carries the continuity of the cultural strata underlying dynastic Egypt well into the Paleolithic.

The role of Lady Net is not the same as Hathor's role in motherhood, nor even that of Lady Of The House in her estate-management responsibilities. Lady Net provided the equally necessary role model for unattached maidens and women without children, women who have time, energy, skills and intelligence to offer. The social equality and personal freedom which the Egyptian woman enjoyed was reflected in the sincerity with which she devoted her energies to her family and friends, and to her duties to community and nation.

Lady Net's primary center was in Sais (*Saut*), the capital city of the fifth nome of Lower Egypt. Lengthy texts surviving from this site place her at the creation of the world, naming her as the Mother Of Re and Mother Of The *Naturu*.

In her profoundest form, Lady Net is the "weaving" of atoms into molecules and of cells into tissue.

Lady Net is with us still today. Modern fiber technology has gone so far beyond sinew, hemp and flax as to seem utterly unrelated to them, but our technological marvels are as strung together with fibers and cables now as when the Pyramids were built. We do not use these fibers and cables for sheer brute strength (except, perhaps, in bridges and parachutes.) We use fibers to communicate and to link us together into a single society. Every time you make a phone call to network with colleagues or friends, every time you use the Internet, you are relying upon the skills, technology and experience that began with Lady Net's patient handiwork in ancient gardens and fields.

SOLQET: THE POISONS OF PASSION

SOLQET is the scorpion-form of Lady Isis and she wears a golden scorpion as her crown. Lady Isis, the soul in love, suffers the pains of love as well as the joys. Lady Isis has a darker side and the blessed poison in the flesh that is passion can sting and even kill. Hatred is the opposite face of love, a relationship driven by a force equally powerful, but turned backwards and upside down, and wrong. Jealousy is the most common motive for murder in the world, and loneliness is fiercer when lonely for the beloved.

Solqet is the chemistry of love fermented by pain and anger. The bite of the desert scorpion of Africa is highly poisonous but not necessarily fatal. Its toxin is painful and feels like dying, as do the pains of love. This chemistry of poisoned passion and its impact on the experience of consciousness are the territory of Isis as Selqet.

Love comes from the soul. So does heartache.

Isis shows her more deadly, primeval face as Solqet. Solqet is one of the guardians of the sarcophagus in the tomb because belief in the reality of the next life was so carefully elaborated that they knew the pain of wounded love could accompany the soul into eternity, a heartache that might go on for "the millions of years." They were not afraid to look evil in the face and give it a name, because they knew that knowledge of a thing was power over it.

Lady Isis is sometimes accompanied by her faithful but deadly mascots, her seven scorpions, who travel as her protecting guard. "*Tofun* and *Bofun* before me, *Mestet* and *Mestetaf* beside me, and *Potet, Thotet*, and *Ma'atet* behind me." These seven scorpions survive today only as echoes in the seven deadly sins, and the poison-dipped arrows of cherubs. This image of the "stings and arrows of love" was reduced by the conquering Greeks, male-oriented thinkers, to the impotent figure of Cupid randomly flicking poisoned arrows at hapless lovers. Love in ancient Egypt, however, was a powerful figure, and Isis ruled in every home and temple and palace.

Bastet:
The Soul In Love With Life Itself

BASTET, the cat-headed *Natur,* presents a charming and personal glimpse into the warm heart of ancient Egypt. Bast was the original "party animal" and her religious ceremonies were riverside festivals of wine, women, song and flowers, many kinds of flowers, lots of flowers, for she is the ephemeral joys of being. Bastet is Isis in the sheer delight of being alive, the soul in love with life itself.

The cat, mascot of Bastet, has always been a symbol of sensuality, sometimes revered for that, sometimes reviled. Her name survives in our concept of "the beast." Bastet is associated with Re, as wife or lover, and she is also one of the *Wadjet* Eyes of Re, representing the sensory nature of perception and conscious awareness of sensuality. Bastet is one of the mothers of the moon, demonstrating their awareness of the sensory nature of the source of dreams.

The "home town" of Bastet is Bubastis in the Nile Delta, and recent archeological evidence, together with genetic studies, have suggested that the temple grounds there are the site of the origin of the domestic cat in this region, from a deliberate interbreeding of two types of small wildcats.

The Cat: Mascot Of The Nile

An excellent resource is a book by Jaromir Malek, *The Cat In Ancient Egypt*, which I have found to be not only a detailed study of the subject but also quite entertaining. The illustrations of ancient

Egyptian "cat and mouse" cartoons will delight everyone.

The cat itself has proven to be a pure descendant of ancient Egypt, and earns the right to be the mascot of the Nile. Recent archeological digs in the Delta region have located a temple, dedicated to Bastet, which may well be the actual breeding ground where the cat was domesticated, around 3,000 BC.

The domestic relationship of human and cat was important to the Egyptians. Their household cats were not "fed at the table" the way our modern pets are. Cats had to work for a living, as farm cats do today. They lived on vermin: mice, rats, snakes and bugs. I had a cat who spent her entire day hunting and eating bugs in our backyard, and the vet reprted that to be quite normal. My cat even brought down and consumed a four-inch long locust. We never had to worry about flies or moths in the house. If you think about the problems the ancients would have had with no screens, a cat who would chase down that annoying bug in your bedroom would be important. Snakes were a constant threat in their homes, thus a cat could literally be a lifesaver. The cat was a household guardian, and would have been revered on those grounds.

The only dogs were large animals, worlf, mastiff and greyhound prototypes, and expensive to keep and maintain since a dog that big is not as self-supporting as a cat. Small dogs as pets were still hundreds of years in the future.

Monkeys were kept as pets by the wealthy, but they were as expensive to keep and maintain as child, and more demanding. So the Egyptians, who were a deeply affectionate and sensual people, appreciated the unique value of the cat's independent nature.

The Egyptians were remarkably family oriented, and cats were valued and beloved members of the household. I think that had more to do with the ban on killing them than any other factor; it would have been similar to killing a child, in their point of view.

The number of different animal mummies found demonstrates the reverence with which animals were held. It also suggests, however, that mummification was too important a craft to allow novices to get their first practice on human bodies. Practicing on animals was logical, and served emotional as well as practical ends.

SEKHMET: HOT BLOODED LIONESS, A RAGE TO LIVE

(Also *Sakhmit* and *Sakhmis.*) Bastet has another side, with another face–the shadow of a kitten cast lion-sized against a wall. As Bast, she dresses in green like the new Spring, and she is adorned with flowers. As SEKHMET, the lioness, she dresses in red–her face has turned green, and she drinks blood.

Sekhmet is passion run to its extremes: love into hate, fear into hysteria, pain into rage, greed into war, passion into obsession. Sekhmet is the gentle, domesticated cat grown suddenly to the wild, savage strength of the lioness. "Hell hath no fury like a woman scorned," and Sekhmet is the original fury, the archetype out of which every harpy was born.

Sekhmet is hunger, wild savage hunger beyond the simple appetite-for-life of the cat. The green face of Sekhmet is the origin of the images of "green with envy," and "the green-eyed monster" of jealousy. The name Sekhmet is derived from *sekhem*, the spirit energy of the soul, the divine energy which drives life and fills the heart. When the soul expresses itself through the flesh, *sekhem* is the energy, the *ib* behind that expression. When that expression boils over into high emotion, Sekhmet earns her name of Mighty Lady Of Flame, the passion of the soul blazing in the flesh.

The ancient Egyptians knew the ways of lions and lion prides, and even though the great solar lion has been given the respect of being "king of the beasts," the Egyptians knew it was the *lioness* who does the work, and who is the active participant in the round of life and death. Like Re, the lion waits for life to flow through him. He does not chase the gazelle; he receives the tribute of his active counterpart. Thus Sekhmet, the popular lioness form of Isis, represents the active force of the soul's energy and place in life.

The control of high passion was seen to require love and clear thinking. In "The Destruction of Humanity," Sekhmet is driven by rage and disgust to destroy the world. Humanity is saved only by the quick thinking of Re and Isis, who mix beer with the blood Sekhmet drinks. She is tranquilized into sleep and recovers from her fury so that humanity is spared. (Beer and wine were brewed first in ancient Egypt, and they were proud of their brew.)

Just as Bastet is the joy of being alive, her passionate counterpart is Sekhmet's raging will to live. Sekhmet is the fire that burns in the center of every cell. The greatest ills of the flesh can be burned away in Sekhmet's passion for life. This spirit of Sekhmet was the guide and inspiration for the physicians of ancient Egypt, who were second to none for technique, technology, and note-taking. Healers to this very day are able to work realistically from the collected medical writings of the nation's many physicians. Their medical profession was well organized and represented the highest of Bronze Age technology, working together with the finest psychological training and spiritual guidance ever formulated.

The Sekhmet cult of healers continues strong even today, proving themselves to be useful practitioners in our modern age struggling to understand holistic medicine and to incorporate it, as the ancient civilization did, with the empirical understanding of technological advances.

The ancient Egyptians were a passionate people, both in their private and their public lives. Sekhmet, for all the dangers of surging emotion she represented, was dear to the Egyptian heart, and a healthy respect was given to her value in their lives. Sekhmet's place and power grew steadily in the nation. Her primary center was in Memphis, first capitol city of Upper and Lower Egypt united, where she was a member of the popular "Memphis Triad." She was established there as the wife of Ptah, linking the magical potential of the skill in the human hand with the driving passion of the soul's emotion. (*See above:* Ptah.)

The third member of the triad, Nefertum, was called the child of Ptah and Sekhmet. Nefertum is a form of Atum, *Natur* of the steady movement of time, and his name translates to Beautiful Time. He represents the satisfaction of the soul that comes from working with the hands, drawing from the passion that Sekhmet brings to the task. The man who is truly in love with his work is, indeed, having a Beautiful Time.

The ancient Egyptians created an incredible amount of superb, highly crafted work of every kind, with a quality of skill and technical proficiency unparalleled in her time, and unmatched even today. Few people in the modern world can afford to pay artists to turn out the volume and quality of artwork produced daily by the Egyptian artisans and craftsmen. Such passion of the soul translated by hand is beyond price now, and can only be done for the sake of the task.

Tasurt: The Oldest Woman In The World, Archetype Of Female Wisdom

TASURT (*Toeris* in Greek) means, literally, "Oldest Woman of the World," or 'The Original Woman Of The World," and she is the *Natur* of feminine experience and wisdom. Tasurt is a jolly, grandmotherly figure, more accessible than formidable Mut. She is Hathor grown old and wise. Tasurt is Isis as Grandmother, no longer young and beautiful as Hathor but as much beloved.

Tasurt's image is of a hippopotamus/lion-woman with huge, pendulous breasts and a royal crown. The hippopotamus is the most dangerous animal in the world, and Tasurt has the power of that huge animal.

Images similar to this, with the exaggerated female characteristics, have been found in Africa and surrounding geographical regions, in cultures that date back well before 10,000 BC. The suggestion has been made that these were used as aids in pregnancy, both in teaching young women what to expect, and as talismans and holy objects for the protection of women in childbirth. Tasurt is the guardian of childbirth, *Natur* of the midwife. Although as cuddly as a teddy bear, Tasurt brings the power of the mighty hippopotamus to the protection of those who call upon her.

She has many assistants as outlandishly cartoonlike and bizarre as she is. The dwarf-figured Bes is the best known. The Egyptians understood that humor is useful in stressful times, and Tasurt and her entourage demonstrate the earthiness of their humor.

SKY AND EARTH, BREATH, LIFE AND CREATION

"The plants will fall down in their season; I have initiated the process inside her. I emerged as the plants and all creeping things, and all the evolution inside them."

Nut:
The Star-Spangled Sky,
Body Of The Divine Plane

NUT, the sky, is shown in the elongated, stylized body of a woman arched over the world. She was a much loved figure, and one who was a daily experience of the divine. The skies above Egypt are wide and hot during the day, and profoundly spectacular at night. In a modern world of electric-light-washed skies, it is difficult to imagine the reigning majesty of such a nightly sky overhead. The comfort of the sky and the delight in its presence is a strong image everywhere in their world, and she was painted on the inside of the coffin lid over the mummy, so that you might whisper with the sky at night.

Nut's body is the pathway of the Sun in the sky in the day and her dress is spangled with the stars of the night sky. Her name is a pun with the word for "container, jar." She is the *duat* which contains waking reality. Nut swallows the Sun when he sets, and she gives birth to the Sun each morning at dawn, in her form of *Meh-Urt.* Thus she is the transcendent body through which the Night Sun travels on his miraculous journey. When the Sun which travels across Nut's arched body is Re rather than Itan, Nut represents the psychic waters of the daily journey of consciousness and she contains the twelve hours of the night that comprise the journey through the *Duat.*

Her name, Nut, is the feminine form of *nu*, for "water." The sea on which Nut rests is *Mu*, the primeval ether, the eternal space/time continuum. Nut is painted on the inside of the coffin lid and is the sky above the soul in the next life.

Nut's sacred tree was the sycamore, and she is sometimes depicted as a woman stepping forth from the tree. The association of the tree and sky spirits hearkens back to prehistoric philosophies, demonstrating the ancient continuity of Nut's place in their pantheon. In this world dominated by the surrounding desert, the gentle comfort of the sycamore's shade was a daily metaphor of the comfort of the next life within Nut's heavenly realm, the *duat.*

GEB:
COMMON GROUND OF WAKING REALITY

GEB, (sometimes as ZEB,) is the *Urpat,* which means That Oldest One, of the *Natur,* and the original father of the Greater *Pot Natur.* Geb is the father of everything because he is the round Earth, flat and solid beneath our feet. Geb is the common ground of reality upon which living souls are met.

Geb, the Earth, and Nut, the Sky, are the original lovers, and are shown in intimate embrace, but they were separated by Shu, who is the atmosphere and the breath in the nostrils. Shu, who represents the movement of the passing moment of now, forever separates the past, Geb, from the future, Nut. This separation is the movement of life and time.

Geb is represented by the hieroglyph and figure of the Geb-goose, and he is often drawn as a *Natur* with a goose's head. He is known as the "Great Cackler," whose voice awoke the world into being, and the primeval goose who laid the egg out of which the universe was born. Geese and ducks were the barnyard fowl of the Nile, and the Great Cackler's first cry at the dawn of time awoke the Sun just as the rooster's cry is the call of dawn in European culture. This cry of nature that wakens the day is the inner value of Geb's archetype. He is the reality of the waking day, and the impulse of consciousness to wake out of inert sleep. Geb is the latent power of inanimate matter to waken consciousness out of itself by the light of the soul.

SHU:
EVERY BREATH YOU TAKE IN THE MAGIC MOMENT NOW

SHU's name is a synonym for light and comes down to us in the word "shine," the verb of light. Shu is the movement of light in the air because light, like the breath of life, travels as part of the moment now, and disappears into the past in a moment. Ultimately, the movement of light defines the now.

Shu is the fire of breath in the nostrils. His very name is an exhalation of breath, "Shu!" He is represented by the feather of *ma'at,* symbol of reality, because the passing of the moment from future to past is the immediacy of reality. Now is passing with each breath. Now is past and gone every time you exhale and, indeed, the separation between living and dead is in a single breath.

Shu is the atmosphere that separates Earth and Sky, Geb and Nut. Shu is visible in the columns of sunlight through clouds on the horizon, and Shu is called the Support of the Sky. Shu is the link between Re, the light of consciousness in the mind, and Itan, the light of the Sun in the sky.

Itan shines the light of Shu into the living eyes of Osiris-Re in order that the soul might perceive reality on top of the Earth. Shu is called upon in funeral texts, because the reality of the moment of death comes to slave and pharaoh alike.

Now passes in "the millions of years," as it does in life, in the perception of Re.

Tafnut: Twin Sister Of Shu, The Wetness Of Life

Tafnut is the twin sister of Shu, and her unusual birth gave Victorian Egyptologists fits of embarrassment. Tafnut has been politely labeled the "moisture of the air," and the verb associated with her powers is modestly translated as "exuding moisture." The meaning of her symbol, like much of ancient Egyptian life, was earthier than Victorian scholars liked.

The hieroglyph for Tafnut is a mouth spitting out liquid. Her name is a classic example of the visual-verbal puns of which the ancients were so fond. Humidity is a vital issue in Africa and the ability to sweat enough is, literally, a life and death matter. To this day there is in use the Swahili greeting, "How do you sweat?" For ten thousand years, water has been collected in the desert from morning dew condensing and dripping off the outside of special pottery vessels. Tafnut is the personification of a verb, of a process, and "sweating" is only one of the politer translations.

Tafnut is every kind of sweating, the ability of the air to sweat water. Tafnut is moisture, condensation, humidity, osmosis, ejaculation, orgasm, and all bodily processes which produce wetness. She is the motion of water flowing. She is the mystery of chemical action. These are measures of the moment now, with the immediacy of the moment, thus that Tafnut is the physical twin of Shu.

Her sexual connotations gave early Egyptologists some difficulty, but sexuality was more openly and casually dealt with in the ancient Egyptian civilization than in our own.

Too Many Creation Myths: Which Came First, The Cackle Or The Egg?

The many wonderful images of animal-headed figures in fantastical array have established the impression of ancient Egypt as a dark place obsessed with death, magic, miracles and mummification. The arcane rituals of multiple gods display a bewildering inner world of caves, crowns, serpents, aspects, faces and syntheses. Their philosophies seem a chaos of rival priesthoods and temple organizations, a mad, millennia-long jumble of forms, rituals and quasi-realism cloaked in the mysticism of archaic design.

The chaos begins at the very beginning. There are too many creation myths. Each great complex for the House Of The *Natur* had its own variation on the story. The priests of Memphis, *Innu* and *Khemmenu* (Heliopolis and Hermopolis) claimed to have within their complexes the primordial mound from which Egypt arose.

Central to the variations on the creation story is this primordial mound, the "Island Of Creation" which appeared out of the primeval abyss in the "First Occasion." This metaphor is drawn from the Nile's inundation as it subsides, revealing mounds or muddy islands. Also central is the bird who either alights upon this mound and awakens the world with its cry, or else lays the egg from which Re is born. The first cry of this bird is the awakening of the world, the divine vibration which initiates the light and divides the darkness. This is variously Geb, in his goose form as "the Great Cackler;" the *bennu*-phoenix of Re alighting upon the first obelisk, known as "*benben*;" the hawk form of Re Horus or the ibis form of Thoth. Each priesthood was devoted to the *Natur* which inspired them, and they studied the role of the *Natur* from creation onward. Each House Of The *Natur* was consecrated to be this primordial mound, a manifestation of that instant of creation.

The Heliopolitan creation myth relates to the calendar. The oldest written form comes from the *Pyramid Texts* and was preserved by the priestly schools of Re in the royal city of *Innu* (Heliopolis.) Despite the antiquity of the texts, the Heliopolitan story can be compared to the modern theories of the creation. The Cosmos before creation was seen as the primeval abyss known as Nun, and within Nun stirred the principle of the field of time, personified in Atum. As in the Big Bang theory, there came an instant of awakening, represented by Khepry, the scarab *Natur*, "The Becoming One," the spirit of evolution and enlightenment. Atum creates the primordial mound, revealing the solid ground of reality for the first time. The world has been born.

> "Lord To The Limits spoke these words after his evolution:
> "I am what evolved in evolution.
> I have evolved the evolution of evolutions,
> evolved the evolutions of everything.
> Following my evolution, multitudes evolved
> as they emerged from my mouth.
> No heaven evolved, no earth evolved,
> no sons of the earth were created,
> nor creeping things in that place.
> I raised them up in Nu, in their inertness.
> I did not find a place where I could stand.
> I had my soul centered in my heart.
> I laid a foundation in *Ma'at.*
> I made all the visible forms. I was alone.
> I had not spit out as Shu.
> I had not dripped out as Tafnut.
> He did not make the evolution of another with me,
> evolving the many evolutions contained in being born,
> and in the evolutions contained in their being born.
> It was I who ejaculated in my fist.
> I ejaculated in my shadow.
> I ejaculated in my own mouth.
> I spat out as Shu. I dripped out as Tafnut."

Shu and Tefnut, along with Osiris and Re, were universal *Natur* in ancient Egypt, present in every House Of *Natur* and private shrine. Shu and Tafnut created Geb, the Earth, and Nut the Sky.

The stage has been set for the arrival of humankind and the rise of consciousness into the field of time. Once again, the ideas encapsulated in this mythological scene have analogs in the scientific evidence of the evolution of life on Earth. The earliest biological activity of the Earth, through the billions of years, created both the soil and the atmosphere which sustain us today.

The Heliopolitan story leaps ahead now to the establishment of the round of the calendar, symbolized in the Yearly Five Days and the birth of the *Natur* of the human soul. (*See above*, Calendar Introduction.) Earth and Sky, Geb and Nut, have five children who represent the primary structures of each living human being. These children are Osiris, The Original Horus, Sut, Isis and Lady Of The House. Humanity has entered the sphere of time, and begun to measure it.

There is no well-known story of the birth of Thoth, but the priests of Thoth at *Khemmenu*, "The Town Of The Eight," (Hermopolis) had an ancient creation story based on the concept of the union and division of opposites. Four primeval pairs of *Natur* rose up, *Nu* and *Nunet*, *Iman* and *Imaunut*, *Heh* and *Hehut*, *Ke* and *Kekut*. These pairs represent the archetypes of the primeval abyss, the hidden pattern, eternity, and the darkness. The males are frog-headed and the females snake-headed, and these divine forces created the first mound of Earth that rose out of the abyss. This is the survivor of a pre-dynastic creation myth. These primeval figures, frog-headed and snake-headed, are present in tomb art everywhere and in every era. The new life which springs from the muddy deposits of the inundation inspired them, representing the immediacy of creation happening in regular cycles, not as a singularity.

Re is the primary creator of humankind, formed from his tears. "The evolution of humanity is in the tears emerging from my eye." Atum's eye weeps because of the separation of the inner and outer vision of the divine being. In the *Sais* creation story, Lady Net creates a lotus bud which opens to reveal the child Re. Re weeps at his separation from her, forming humankind from his tears. Consciousness is the separation of human from animal and, as many will attest, conscious awareness brings pains and sorrows animals do not suffer. "All life is sorrowful" is a *human* expression.

As their civilization evolved, so did their contemplation of these ideas. In Memphis, Ptah the Craftsman, as part of the Ptah-Sekhmet-Nofertum trinity, shapes human beings upon his potter's wheel; although in later years, Khnumn, the *Natur* of the human form, is given this task. Ultimately however, each human being is responsible for self-creation. In this act of creation, Re is the supreme being. Consciousness is king.

Osiris and his extended family represented the complete human being, from soul outward to life-role in society. Every stage of the soul's divine existence while "on top of the Earth" was elaborately explored, described, defined, celebrated, and ritualized. From this joyous celebration of self comes the exotic, beautiful, puzzling imagery of their art and literature. The delight in metaphor, word play, visual puns and poetry that abounds in their world is evidence of the fluid creativity of the ancient imagination.

The many creation myths actually resolve into a dynamic survey of the evolving stages of human maturing, each so profound and unique an experience as to require metaphors as broad and deep as the creation of an entire world. Indeed, with each stage, the change in the individual's perception of reality is so great that the world is a new and different place.

The birth of Osiris is the creation of soul stuff from nonexistence, the most profoundly human creation. The birth of Re is the birth of self-awareness, the rise of consciousness from the dark, subliminal perceptions of existence, the awakening of the Divine Eye Within. The birth of Re each morning from the flanks of *Meh Urt* is the moment of awakening from sleep, a mystery as profound as that of life itself. The birth of Khepri is the achievement of enlightenment, a greater light than mere seeing. The birth of the world from the sky, Nut, herself born from the cosmic waters of Mu, the space/time continuum, is the birth of the solid Earth beneath our feet, and the primordial mound upon which the world is born rises out of the marsh of reeds, frogs and snakes, a process which continues around us at every moment.

And so on...

The continual unfolding of existence was a deeply abiding mystery for the ancient mind, and the exotic display of creation stories are metaphors for the discovery of the mystery of life, one soul at a time. The many priesthoods were rivals only for political attention, not for the minds and hearts of the people. Each House Of The *Natur* and its complex of priests, attendants and teachers were there for the changing needs of the individual throughout an entire lifetime, throughout generations of lifetimes.

Mythology And Relgion

Most readers' discomfort with the "creation myth" of Atum, using as it does such open masturbation images, is the same discomfort Egyptologists have suffered since they first came across it, but you must put the image into context. For one thing, the prohibition against masturbation is from the Levant, the desert-grown cultures that overwhelmed Egypt and went on to create Judaism, Christianity, and Islam. These cultures were more male-oriented than the Egyptian, and as unable to deal with sexuality then as now. Ancient Egyptian sexuality was celebrated in a way that has forced Egyptologists to hide things in back rooms and to refuse to show certain bits to the public.

Here is where the concept of "Egyptian superstition" entered into the view of them which we have inherited from Egyptologists. We, in our modern enlightenment, certainly would never have fallen in with the kind of superstitious behavior we see in Egypt, yet the same people who labeled Egypt as "superstitious" carried lucky rabbit feet, wore gold crosses on chains, believed that a big fat man in a red suit could fit down every chimney in the world, and that a virgin could get pregnant yet remain virgin. Anything that is not understood about the religion of Egypt is labeled superstition, and dismissed on that grounds.

Their so-called superstitions were truly no different from our own. Amulets were images used to focus meditation and contemplation, even as they are to our modern mind, with our own kinds of amulets, lucky pieces, and meditations. Inscriptions were the crystallization of meditation and mnemonics for psychological training. Ancient Egyptians feared the same things we do—boredom, depression, grief, rage, loneliness, despair, delusion, madness. They had very sophisticated techniques by which an individual could maintain self-control over personal mood and maintain focused attention. The success of their nation and the quality of their work is proof that their techniques were most effective. Yet we are now calling these techniques superstition. If you look at our modern world, we could use a few more such "superstitious" techniques for gaining self-control. Lack of self-control, frankly, is the biggest problem we face in America, perhaps in the entire Western world. The Western God is placed outside of the world, and the notion has evolved that He is not watching. By ancient Egyptian standards, each and every one of us are the eyes of Divinity looking out on reality, and the Divine Eye misses nothing.

If there is only the one God, removed from the world, you are, indeed, utterly dependent upon the good will of the few individuals capable of communicating with that deity. However, if you believe that you are equally divine with every other person, then *your* personal judgment and *your own* soul are your guide. *No one* can own and control you. Therefore, the notion of individual divinity has been stamped out in our world. "I'll save your soul if I have to kill you to do it," is a decidedly modern concept, obscene by ancient Egyptian standards—not just obscene, but psychotic.

The other factor in the masturbation myth is the "layering" of concepts that took place over the many millennia of Egypt's lifetime. The earliest strata were from the World Mother mythological domain, in which creation spills forth from, and returns to, the eternal womb of the World Mother, with the physical world as her body. Atum is the field of time, the fourth diemension. The image that is represented by the masturbation is that, through the course of time, life brought itself forth from itself. Modern science, in the search for the "first cell" that began all life searches for signs of that first ejaculation, as it were. The point of the image is the self-created aspect of life. It requires a concrete image for discussion. Masturbation, in a world view in which that is not a "sin," is a useful concept.

Spitting: The body's ability to produce moisture is a vital aspect of survival. "How do you sweat?" is a standard greeting in Africa. In that climate, if you are not sweating right, you are on your way to dying.

In the ancient world view, the body itself was a sacred vessel, and spittle is bodily fluid produced by a *conscious decision.* Spittle is not the automatic fluid of sweat nor of menses. It is not the deadly fluid of spilled blood, but rather the deliberate, conscious contribution of your bodily essence to the outer world. In this ancient view, there is nothing disgusting about spittle or spitting. We believe that our reaction is a normal response because there is an element of hygiene we have learned that was unknown in ancient times.

In ancient Egypt, as in the Orient today, every person is both true man *and* truly divine. The soul is the divine essence present in space/time, garmented in flesh. The stirrings of our very real souls demand a greater recognition today. People desperately need the more sophisticated "soul training" that the Egyptians offer, but when ancient Egypt speaks "over their heads" they call it superstition, and shove it away.

It is time to look at Egypt with the eyes of the new millennium, so that we might see the path ahead of us more clearly.

"He Strings The Secret Forms Like Beads
is the name of the tomb."

Slavery And The Pyramids

Hollywood did indeed invent much of the image which we have today of ancient Egypt. Of course, at the time, Hollywood was basing its information on the writings of pre-1890 Victorian scholars—people who thought that the Egyptians must have been primitive people. After all, they did not wear pants.

The Victorians created their own images of ancient Egypt, based on what was known of Rome and Greece, since these were the conquerors of Egypt. The Egyptian language was not fully translated until the 1980s, so they had none of the Egyptian literature as information about Egypt. They assumed Egypt must have been just another version of Rome. Slavery in ancient Egypt was different from the kind of slavery we have come to recognize, certainly different from slavery in Mesopotamia or Rome at the same time. Slaves were treated more like the indentured servants of colonial America. They were able to buy or work their way to freedom, and were most often well cared for. They could hold important advisory positions in government. There were several well known slaves who became high officials in the Pharaoh's court. In those ancient times, you were better off as a slave in Egypt than as a free but poor person anywhere else.

Prisoners and criminals were sent to work in the various mines which Egypt owned.

Dr. Zahi Hawass has directed the recent discoveries of the actual tombs and villages of the workers who built the Pyramids. These people were not slaves. They were workers who were very proud of their work. They put their names and the names of their work teams on the insides of the blocks of stones, names like "Perfection," and "Golden." They were allowed to build their own tombs within sight of the Pyramid, which was quite an honor.

Gold in ancient Egypt was considered to be the flesh of the Sun, and was used in the temple as the substance of immortality, since it is so incorruptible, does not tarnish, and shines like the Sun in the light. It was used to make funeral masks of the Pharaohs, and to make the inner walls of the temple sanctum, so that the reflected sunlight would light up the interiors. It was used for ornaments and for jewelry, and some of the most beautiful gold jewelry ever made is Egyptian.

The most spectacular use was as the capstone of the Great Pyramid of Giza–it was originally covered in polished white marble, with a gold cap. It must have been a dazzling sight at full noon, and probably lit up in the morning before the Sun had risen, and no doubt glowed in the twilight after sunset.

Gold was not used as currency until the Ptolemaic era–that is after Alexander the Great destroyed Egypt and replaced the priesthood and court with Greeks. After that, Egypt was no longer truly Egyptian. Until then, copper was the main metal used for currency, although again, not as coins. Coins were invented by the Greeks. The only Egyptian coins appeared during the Ptolemaic era.

From earliest times, copper was exchanged in unit weights, called *deben*, but shape and markings were less important than the weight, and the official government die-stamp that is the mark of the true coin was not yet in use..

Akhenaton
Ancient Egypt's *Titanic*

Missing: Isis. Nut. Hathor. Sekhmet. Mut. Bastet. And the rest. Where are the Egyptian *female* divinties in Akhenaton's theology?

Akhenaton created a new religion based upon the disk of the Sun in the sky, Aton, (Also spelled Itan) with the credo that this beneficent Father in Heaven was shining down equally upon his people. Akhenaton was the first monotheist, in that he declared that worship of this Sun Disk God Aton was to be the one and only acceptable official religion. All others were false idols. He took his faithful followers out into the desert and built a magnificent new city for this new religion and his new One God.

Does this scenario sound familiar? The suggestion that Akhenaton or someone in his court might be the historical Moses was first brought up by Sigmund Freud in the 1920s. Freud was actually writing about rejection of the Mother principle. This rejection appears in the religions that are based on the attempt to empower the masculine principle with both male and female functions, but without properly integrating them. A lot of our modern confusions about sex are based on the consequences, millennia later, of that rejection taken as a spiritual and biological reality.

The Sun disk, Aton, was seen as democratically available to all the populace, pharaoh and commoner alike, but so was the majesty and splendor of the night sky, who was the goddess Nut. Where is Aton at night? He is buried within the dark mystery of the universal Mother's star-spangled body, born from her each morning.

Akhenaton rejected the feminine principle, and along with her all the spiritual potential she represents. The female *Naturtu* were much loved by the people, and their dethronement never sat well. Once Akhenaton was buried, the Aton cult in Egypt died, too. There was national outrage over Akhenaton's attempt to impose a single, male deity upon them and separate them from divine nature. There was in Egyptian philosophy no single God Over All who must be addressed. Each of the *Pot Natur*, the Great Egyptian Pantheon, gets a turn at being the supreme image of meditation as needed by each individual over the course of a lifetime of emotional and spiritual needs, rather than as a Master Over His Created Servants.

There is a reason that Akhenaton chose Itan, the Sun disk, rather than Re, whom we have in modern times confused with the Sun in the sky. Faulkner's dictionary says Itan is "specifically the sun's disk." Itan is *not* the one who is joined to Horus, Amun, etc., in quite the same way. Itan is not placed on top of the heads of other figures. Re is. Re is not the Sun in the sky but the Sun of conscious light in our minds. Akhenaton was a true Sun-worshipper, not a worshipper of consciousness.

Realistic—or Just Ugly? Another issue of hot debate is the changes in the style of art depicting Akhenaton's odd physical conditions (*morfan* disease has been suggested, among others) and how "unusual" it is that he is depicted this way. Looking closer suggests that there was nothing unusual about this. Egyptian portraiture of the pharaohs has always been astonishingly lifelike. It was long ago acknowledge in art-history circles that Egyptians did, in fact, create the oldest known portraits. We mistake the smooth regularity of stone, without lifelike color, for "idealization." Look at the troubled face of the Sesostris portraits, the serene determination of the tiny, single surviving face of Khufu, and the fierce determination of the women from *Deir El Medina*. Their portraits are movingly alive. Artists in Egypt were the best in the world.

Nowhere is it indicated that the pharaoh himself had much to do with the actual artwork itself. He may have commissioned it, but his lack of involvement with affairs of state suggests that he turned this over to the artisans themselves.

Egypt is in the interesting position of being the first government whose primary communication between government and people was controlled and created entirely by artists. Artists had their own communities, and were better educated than farmers and tradesmen. Whatever it was the politicians/priests wanted declared, it was brought to the people through the eyes and hands of the artists. Artists made the final decisions about everything that was seen by the populace. There is evidence that those unflattering portraits of Akhenaton were the idea of the artists living in Amarna, and not the pharaoh. "Lifelike" is not the same as "unflattering." That is a choice of the artist and his craft. Possibly, by their lifelike painting of his deformity, these artists were telling us something about their own personal distaste for the man they had to honor.

Bad Husbandry: After a decade in Amarna, most of Akhenaton's wives were dead. It has been suggested by archeological studies that it is most likely that parasites in the water killed them.

This is one thing about the Amarna episode that gets lost in the shuffle of "his followers going with him into the desert to build his brave new city." The architects and masons—and commoners—of Egypt knew that the water supply to a city in that region would become a home for a dreadful parasite carried by water snails, and a bane to village life throughout Africa. By letting the Pharaoh build his city out there, the builders, the workmen, the commoners, all knew that he was moving into a disease zone. They let him. Did Akhenaton's contemporaries hope that he would die out there?

The modern world has become impatient for details of the Amarna period, and there is a growing body of reliable archeological data available, from DNA evidence and x-rays of mummies to reinterpretations of inscriptions, letters and historical references. The life and times of this heretical Pharaoh were more dramatic, and perhaps more tragic, than others of the long line of Pharaohs, male and female, who led Egypt. This drama will continue to draw attention to Akhenaton and his court, but it is worth noting that the drama is about a man. Egypt herself is not well represented in the images of this man's life, and the details of his life should not be applied to the rest of the nation's history or culture.

On the other hand, it is a story about identity, and self-control, and a very Egyptian story because of that. Akhenaton lost his self-identity in the glowing light, and all the power of Egypt's throne , all of Egypt's horses and all of Egypt's men could not restore him to himself.

Each of us fights a day to day struggle to stay true to whom and what we are. The Egyptian horoscope is devoted to the daily organization of that continuing effort.

IN THEIR OWN WRITE: SELECTED TRANSLATIONS

Translations by Ramona Louise Wheeler, from the papyri transcribed in E.A.Wallis Budge's 1903–1911 editions of *The Book of The Dead, Tutankhamen, The Gods of Egypt, and The Egyptian Heaven and Hell.* Dover Editions.

"If this book is learned on top of the earth, in the writings upon the coffin that is my mouthpiece, he will emerge into the day in all the metamorphoses he desired, together with going in to his place. He is not refused: he would be given cakes and the original beer which will be upon the altar which is Osiris. He will go in peace to the marsh of yarrow, to know this command of the one inside the centerpoint of courage. He would be given wheat and barley to grow in there. There would be green things around him as had been on top of the earth. He will do his desire even as those *Natur* who are in the *duat* in the circuit of immortality, millions of times, millions of times.

Now [the deceased] is Osiris!"

Table Of Contents For The Translations

Introduction To The Translation 257

The Book Of The Evolution Contained In Re, And Of Overthrowing Apep 260
The Awakening Of Re When He Shines Out Of The Eastern Horizon Which Is Heaven. 261
The Awakening Of Re, (by the soldier *Nekht*) 262
The Awakening Of Osiris, The Beautiful Being 263
The Awakening Of Osiris 264
The Awakening Of Osiris Who Is Lord Of The Mouth Of The Horizon, and Great *Pot Natur* within The *Natur* Under The Horizon 264
Words For The Divine Person Entering Immortalized In The House Of Osiris........ 265
The Beginning OfThe Emerging Awake, Praised And Immortalized, Emerging And Entering As *Natur* Under The Horizon, A Soul Distilled Within The Beautiful Western Horizon 265
You Who Make The *Ba* To Enter Perfected Into The House Of Osiris 267
The First Part Of The Glorification, The Distillation of The Emerging Soul, Going In To The Next World. 267
The Awakening Of Osiris, Lord Of Eternity, Divine Precincts Of The Lords Of The Mouth Of The Far Horizon 277
Words On How To Open The Mouth For Osiris 281
Words On How To Bring Magical Spells To Osiris 282
Words On How To Grant Memory Of His Name As The *Natur* Under The Horizon 282
Words On How To Grant A Heart To Him, For Osiris, As The *Natur* Under The Horizon 282
Words On How To Prevent Opposition To The *Ib*-heart Of Osiris *Ani*, Immortalized Through The *Natur* Under The Horizon 283
Words Of How To Prevent The *Ka* Of A Man To Be Withdrawn From By The *Natur* Under The Horizon 284
Words Of How To Receive Breaths As The *Natur* Under The Horizon 284
Words For A Drinking Supply As The *Natur* Under The Horizon 284
Words Of How Not To Be Scalded By The Water 284
The Twenty One Portals Of The Double Coiled Serpent 285
Words Upon Arriving At The Innermost Chamber Of Dual Reality 288
Above The Head Of *Inpu* 290

Introduction To The Translations

These translations are incomplete. There are many variations and elaborations of the translations of the chapters, or "Words," of the *Per Em Hru.* There are many variations of the *Books of The Hours of the Day and the Night.* I have included selected samples, purely as a study aid for the text in this volume.

These are also imperfect translations. *All* translations are imperfect. That is an inevitable result of the nature of language and of translation. Even our modern languages cannot be perfectly transformed from one to the other, which makes the task of understanding the ancient Egyptian intention even more challenging. (Out of sight and out of mind? Or is it blind and crazy? Was the spirit willing but the flesh weak? Or was it just that the meat was spoiled but the wine was good?) Every translator brings his or her own intentions to the translation, and the reader needs to be aware of this. The best way to grasp the ancient meaning is to read the original or else a variety of translations, keeping in mind the differences.

The most inspiring, fitting and poetic modern translations are those of **John L. Foster,** (*see below,* Bibliography). If you are interested in memorizing text from the Egyptian, I recommend his works above all others. The most scholarly and most complete of the modern translations are those of **Raymond O. Faulkner.** Both authors have books available in libraries and via the Internet.

Faulkner and Budge do bring to their work, however, the unspoken belief that the ancients were theologically primitive and that the metaphors of Re and Osiris are only those of the material and physical resurrection of the individual in the Next Life. They miss, thereby, the most poetic, profound and moving dimension of the ancient literature.

For example, when the hieroglyph for "soul," the crowned stork, is written with the determinative for a verb form, Faulkner hesitates at the concept of a "verb form of the soul." He translates this as "power," or "might," and "equipped," reinforcing a militaristic interpretation. I have translated this as "immortalized." The emphasis in my translation is on the relationship of immortal conscious perception, represented by Re, and on the immortal substance of the soul, represented by Osiris.

The E.A. Wallis Budge texts (Dover editions) are the easiest to find. These books have considerable hieroglyphic material available. Although Budge's translation is the most inflected, his books do provide a wealth of native material. Budge presents the hieroglyphic texts line by line with transliterations as well as his English translation, making it possible to study the material in depth. Modern texts usually present only the transliteration, losing the visual element of the hieroglyhps themselves. (As, alas, with this book. Hieroglyphic fonts are expensive and awkward to typeset, although an improvement over most handwritten attempts.)

Every ornamented tomb in Egypt which has funeral texts and prayers adorning it is slightly different from every other. These differing versions of similar texts reflect more than the difference of wealth, time, and generation. The artwork of each tomb is as unique as the individual who died, no matter how universal the beliefs which inspired them, and the private nature of these prayers reveals the differing personalities of the persons who used them as meditations for their journey on "the great pathway of radiance," in other words, for death.

For example, in "The Awakening of Re" of the *Per Em Hru*, there are two variations of the prayer which greets awakened consciousness to the eternal life which Osiris has made in the next world. It is a statement of whom you wish to find yourself as when you awake from dying. The temple accountant, *Ani*, prays to awake as a purely enlightened soul, as Khepry, shining as light, designer of the *Natur* as the powers and experiences of eternity. *Ani* lived his life surrounded by the images and education of the temple environs, so his prayer is carefully detailed.

The soldier, *Nekht*, prays to awake as Atum Horus Of The Two Horizons, in the full peak of his adult life, his stride uninterrupted by the transition of realities, his continuity insured. As Re Horus Of The Two Horizons he can go on with the exciting life which he enjoyed "on top of the Earth."

In the text of *Ani*, an expression of delight at the successful journey is written, "The heights should awaken! The depths should awaken!" because he sees the next life from the point of view of one who is "Geedy To Attain Knowledge Of Wisdom," trained in the finer levels of religious discipline represented by the Serpentine-Embraced. The soldier *Nekht*, more involved in a life of action than meditation, gives the same expression in more general terms: "Re exists as the truth of beauty." It is equally poetic, but clearly showing a differing need from eternity.

These kinds of personal revelations are everywhere in the funeral art and writings, phrases and imagery that give intimate glimpses into the hearts and thoughts of individual lives. What is clearest, however, is their joy in life and their pride in the lives they made for themselves. It is this ability to love life that they wanted most to communicate, which lends considerable irony to fact that they are today most often perceived as a nation obsessed with death.

There is a wealth of material available now for exploring the literature of the ancient Egyptians. The following sample provides only a taste. The educational opportunities for serious studies in reading and writing in this ancient language have expanded considerably with the rise of the Internet. There are websites and discussion groups for sharing in translation work. This is an exciting time to be involved in the rediscovery of ancient Egypt, and the authors encourage everyone to join in. Even a minimal understanding of the hieroglyphic alphabet will open a wonderfully new glimpse into this ancient world.

(Note: the deceased is referred to as Osiris. *The name of the person for whom the prayer is made is added to that of* Osiris, *as if it were a final title in life.)*

The Book Of The Evolution Contained In Re And Of Overthrowing Apep.

Lord To The Limits spoke these words after his evolution:
"I am what evolved in evolution.
I have evolved the evolution of evolutions,
evolved the evolutions of everything.
Following my evolution, multitudes evolved
as they emerged from my mouth.
No heaven evolved, no earth evolved,
no sons of the earth were created,
nor creeping things in that place.
I raised them up in Nu, in their inertness.
I did not find a place where I could stand.
I had my soul centered in my heart.
I laid a foundation in *Ma'at.*
I made all the visible forms. I was alone.
I had not spit out as Shu.
I had not dripped out as Tafnut.
He did not make the evolution of another with me,
evolving the many evolutions contained in being born,
and in the evolutions contained in their being born.
It was I who ejaculated in my fist. I ejaculated in my shadow.
I ejaculated in my own mouth.
I spat out as Shu. I dripped out as Tafnut."

Now my father Nu:

"They threaten my eye behind them because for a long, long time they had traveled about for me. After my evolution as the *Natur,* the one *Natur* of three, it is for myself that I evolved in the Earth, raising up therefore Shu and Tafnut in the inert Nu where they were. They brought to me my eye in their following. When I had rejoined my organs, I wept over them. The evolution of humanity is in the tears emerging from my eye. My eye, she raged at me after she had arrived, for she found that I had made another in her place. She is initiated by the *sekhem*-spirit I have made, and I stood her in the front which is her place in my face, and, afterwards, she rules this Earth to his limits. The plants will fall down in their season; I have initiated the process inside her. I emerged as the plants and all creeping things, and all the evolution inside them. Now are born Shu and Tafnut together with Nut. Now are born Geb, and Nut, and Osiris, and Horus Without Eyes, and Sut, and Isis, and Lady Of The House in the flesh. Each one is behind the one inside them. They are born. They multiply in this Earth."

The Awakening Of Re When He Shines Out Of The Eastern Horizon Which Is Heaven.

Now: The Scribe Of Holy Offerings Of All The *Natur,* Osiris-Ani. He says:

"Orient your face: Come forth as Khepry, Khepry as the designer of the *Naturu.* You rise. You shine the radiance of your mother, the resurrection as the King of the *Naturu.* By her two hands, Mother Nut works for you by doing worship. Mount Manu should receive you in peace. *Ma'at* should embrace you at both moments. He gives the *akh,* the soul, out of immortality, coming through as a living *ba,* to see Horus Of The Two Horizons of the *Ka* of the Scribe Osiris-*Ani,* immortalized before Osiris."

He says:

"O! All you *Naturu,* contained in the House Of The *Ba,* weighing heaven and Earth in the balance, feeding the *Ka* with cosmic-food, the *Jaffau. Natur* Under The Horizon, One, Maker of mankind and the *Pot Natur,* south, north, east and west! Accordingly, give praise of Re, Lord of Heaven, The Prince Life! Strength! Health! Worker of the *Natur.* You all awaken him in his beautiful form as he rises out of the *mendet*-boat.

The heights should awaken! The depths should awaken!

Thoth and *Ma'at* record your moments every day. Your enemy-serpent, *Sebiu,* agent of fire, is fallen; both his arms tied up, his legs weakened by Re. The dreadful results of anxiety, they were not!

The house of the Prince is partying, the voice of rejoicing in the Old Place. The *Natur,* while partying, are seen by Re as he rises. The Face beams out the light of the worlds. This ancient *Natur* advances in majesty. He enters the world at Mt. *Manu,* illuminating the world at his birth each day. He departs from his position of yesterday.

"You calm me. I see your beauties.
I advance on top of the earth.
I kick the mighty Ass. I crush *Sebiu.*
I have destroyed Apep in his moment.
I have seen the *ibtu*-fish of his time,
who guides the evolving of the *int*-fish,
and of the *int*-boat, out of its watery way.
I have seen Horus while holding the rudder of Thoth and *Ma'at.*
The Face seizes the bow in the *siktet*-boat with his two hands,
the stern in *mendet*-boat.
The sun's globe gives sight of the Moon every day without fail.
My *ba* comes through to imagine
it can walk about any place it desires.

My name is proclaimed;
it is found upon the board of things sacrificed.
I am given the offerings out of the embodiment
just like the followers of Horus.
I shall have made a seat out of the boat
the day the boat of the *Natur* sets out.
I receive the embodiment of Osiris in
the land of the immortality of the *ka* of Osiris-Ani."

THE AWAKENING OF RE

[The above prayer, as recited by *Nekht*, a soldier of the temple.]

Now: the royal scribe and captain of soldiers, *Nekht*. He says:

Orient your face, endowed with the power of the soul. Atum Horus Of The Two Horizons, You will rise out of the horizon which is Heaven. 0h! To you in the mouth of the face of all peoples, beautified, seasoned, in the globe in the palm of the hand of your mother Hathor rising. You are risen. You hold each in place, each heart opened forever. Both *iterti*-halls come to you in homage; they give out an "O!" for your shining. Both rise out of the horizon which is Heaven. You shoot the two worlds with emerald light. It is Re Horus Of Both Horizons, that boy of the twin *Natur*, heir of the millions of years, conceived him, born him himself, king of this world, prince of the *duat*, face of the head of the mountains of *Yugert*, coming through in the now, drawing him out of Nu, nursing him, arranging his incarnations; *Natur* of life, Lord Of Love, life of the face of all people, you glow, crowned as king of the *Natur*. The maker of Nut and the shaper of your face should embrace *ma'at* at each moment. You are praised by your followers. They bow the face to the Earth as you meet them, Lord Of Heaven, King Of The Earth, King Of *Ma'at*, Lord Of The Millions Of Years, designer of heaven, he is established out of her centerpoint. The *Pot Natur* in ecstasy while you shine. The Earth out of the relief of seeing beams of light. The ancestors come through out of joy to see you beautify every day. You navigate Heaven and Earth every day supported by your mother Nut. You journey through the heights, your heart opened, the Pool Of Flame evolving in peace. *Sebiu* is fallen, both his hands cut off, his joints chopped through by the knife.

Re exists as the truth of beauty.

The *siktet*-boat is drawn on; it departs. You lead on, south, north, west, east: You awaken the Face, *Pot Natur* of the Earth, evolving himself. Lady Isis and Lady Of The House salute you. They should sing songs for you while in the boat, while their hands protect your back. The *ba* of the east should follow you. You have excited the *ba* of the west. You rule all the *Natur.* You receive the opened heart out of the centerpoint of your *ka*-shrine.

The serpent Nik sentenced to the Fire, your *ib*-heart opened for forever, your Mother Nut is declared to you by your Father Nu.

THE AWAKENING OF OSIRIS, THE BEAUTIFUL BEING

Mighty *Natur,* face of the *ib*-heart in heart's-centerpoint, King Of The Millions Of Years, Lord Of Forever, journeying millions of years while he endures, first son of the flesh of Nut, sired by Geb, the great father, lord of the Uraeus-crown, the noble, white crown, leader of *Natur* and of people, he is received of the crook, the flail, the sovereignty of his Fathers.

Open your *ib*-heart which is in the western mountains.
Your son Horus establishes the face of your throne.
You will rise as Lord Of *Jadjadu,*
as prince inside Heart's Centerpoint.

You are made living and green by the dual-worlds out of my immortality, embodied in the hand of the Lord To The Limits. He is led about by that which is not evolving in his name Earth Is Led About By The Face. He draws the dual-worlds together in his name that is Sokar. His power opens up much mightiness in his name that is Osiris. He has been on the two-fold path millions of years out of his name, Beautiful Being.

Orient your face! King Of Kings! Lord Of Lords! Prince Of Princes! wanderer of the earth out of the flesh of Nut, who is ruled by the worlds of *Yugert.* Gold of limbs, blue of head, emerald of face and both hands, *Innu* of the millions, broad of body, beautiful face inside the land under, you give the soul in heaven, courage on Earth, immortality in the Next World. Sailing down to *Jadjadu* as a living *ba,* sailing up to Heart's Centerpoint out of the *bennu*-phoenix, going in, emerging, the face should be unchallenged by any of the pylons of the *duat.*

Loaves of bread will be given to me in the House Of Cool Waters, offspring in *Innu,* offspring established out of the Marsh Of Yarrow, wheat and barley in it for the scribe Osiris-Ani.

THE AWAKENING OF OSIRIS

Now Osiris speaks:

"I am immortalized Osiris without any opposition.
I have immortalized Osiris without any opposition,
just as I have immortalized the embodiment of
The divine precincts which are within Re
who is within Osiris, who is in the Heart's Centerpoint.

The night of the things of darkness is that night of the arm struggling to make the Guardians Of Special Occasions. It is the moment of the perishing of the opposition of Lord To The Limits."

Now, Thoth:

"I have immortalized Osiris without any opposition.
I have immortalized Osiris without any opposition,
just as I have always immortalized Osiris without any opposition,
because of the divine precincts who are within Re,
who is within Osiris, who is within Heart's Centerpoint.

The night of the things of darkness is that night of struggling to make the Guardians Of Special Occasions. That is the moment when the opposition of The Lord To The Limits perish."

THE AWAKENING OF OSIRIS
who is Lord Of The Mouth Of The Horizon, and Great *Pot Natur* within the *Natur* Under The Horizon.

Now Osiris speaks:

"Orient your face, Facade Of The Hidden World,
Beautiful Being Of The Face And Heart!
Coming to Heart's Centerpoint has been because of you,
and my heart is possessed of reality.
There is nothing wrong with my body.
I refuse to lie while knowing it!
I will not do that! I will not do that!"

Now the speech of his beloved son. He says:

"Lords Of *Ma'aty*, you have granted holy breads to me in order to emerge embodied in the face of the altar, to come and go as the *Natur* Under The Horizon. One does not curse a divine person, a socket of the solar globe, one who views the full Moon forever and ever. Osiris, you have been brought because of all your divine precincts within the Mouth Of The Far Horizon, breads, water, breaths, and an estate in Tranquil Meadows, just like those in the Company of Horus."

WORDS FOR THE DIVINE PERSON TO ENTER IMMORTALIZED IN THE HOUSE OF OSIRIS

They cause the divine person to enter, trustworthy to Osiris Immortalized together with those at the House of Osiris. He hears as you hear. He sees as you see. He stands as you stand. He sits as you sit.

"Oh! You givers of breads and beer to the deserving persons in the House of Osiris, you give breads and beer at the dual cycling of my person as Osiris immortalized, carrying all the *Natur* of the Heart's Centerpoint, immortalized together with all of you.

Oh! Clearers of the way and messengers of the pathways for deserving persons in the House Of Osiris! If they have cleared a way to it, then are the messengers of the pathways of my person, as Osiris and his titles, immortalized together with you.

He goes in as the sacrifice.
He emerges peacefully in the House of Osiris.
He will not be turned away. He will not be turned back.
He enters my pleasure. He emerges from my love.
He will immortalize the forms of his command
in the House Of Osiris.
He walks about. He speaks together with you all.
He did not find in there
that the scales have been wasted by his turn."

THE BEGINNING OF THE EMERGING AWAKE, Praised And Immortalized, Emerging And Entering As *Natur* Under The Horizon, A Soul Distilled Within The Beautiful Western Horizon

Words for the day of burial and for after emerging awake:

Now, the soul of the deceased speaks:
"Orient your face! Bull Of The Western Horizon!
Now! Thoth, ruler of the millions of years, is within me.
I am the great *Natur* inside the *Mendet*-boat.
I have struggled for your face.
I am one of those existing *Natur* who are in charge.
I immortalize Osiris without any opposition,
that day of weighing words.
I am your humanity, Osiris.
I am as one of those *Natur* born of Nut,
cutting off the opposition to Osiris,

restraining that which rebels against his face.
I am your humanity, Horus. I have struggled for your face.
I have carried the face of your name.
I am Thoth immortalizing Osiris without any opposition
that day of weighing words in the House
of the Original Old Man dwelling in *Innu* centerpoint.
I am *Jadjady*, son of the *Jadjad* conceived within me,
in the *Jadjad* centerpoint.
I am delivered in the *Jadjad* centerpoint.
I was together with the weepers and wailers,
Osiris as the extent of the human duality,
immortalized without any opposition.

Re makes Thoth calm.

I immortalized Osiris without any opposition.
I have been made calm by Thoth.
I will be together with Horus,
the day of wrapping the crushed *Natur*,
opening holes in order to cleanse the still heart,
unlocking the voice of secret things
in the Mouth Of The Dual Horizon.
I will be together with Horus while being oriented.
It is the left shoulder of Osiris within the centerpoint of spirit.
I enter and I emerge as one of those within the *Natur*,
the day of driving away those who resist
in the centerpoint of the spirit.
I was together with Horus the day of the festivals of Osiris,
making offerings on the *Sixth Day*
which is the festival of sharing in *Innu* centerpoint.
I am the purifier in *Jadjad* centerpoint, voice of the divine Lion
of the two within the House Of Osiris, holding up the world.
I am the two eyes of the secret things
in this Mouth Of The Horizon.
I am my chapter of the service
of the divine person within *Jadjad* center.
I am the caretaker of his possessions.
I am the original spirit of the balance,
the day of placing Sokar upon the sleigh
in which he draws you along.

I am the receiver of the plowing of love
the Day Of Plowing The Earth in childhood."

YOU WHO MAKE THE BA TO ENTER PERFECTED INTO THE HOUSE OF OSIRIS

You make the *ba* to enter into Osiris, perfect, the scribe Osiris Ani. immortalized with you in the House of Osiris. He hears them. He sees as they see. He does as they do. He rests as they rest.

Oh! Givers of cakes and beer to the *ba*, perfected in the House Of Osiris, They give you cakes and beer at the second birth of the *ba* of Osiris, immortalized before all the *Natur* of Heart's Centerpoint, immortalized together with them. Oh! Activators Of The Way! Runners of the roads of the *ba* perfected in the House Of Osiris, keep the way activated for him. You keep open the roads of the scribe Osiris-Ani, accountant of the offerings of all the *Natur.* Together with you, he goes forth in confidence. He emerges in peace from the House of Osiris. He should not be challenged. He should not be refused. He goes in as he wishes. He emerges as he desires. He is immortalized. His commands are done in the House Of Osiris. He sends his words together with you, and his soul together with you. He should not have found in there that the scales would be empty this time.

THE FIRST PART OF THE GLORIFICATION, THE DISTILLATION OF THE EMERGING SOUL, GOING IN TO THE NEXT WORLD.

The soul is distilled in the beautiful Hidden Land, emerging in time in all the evolutions he desires, playing at the *sunnit*-game, relaxing in the hall, coming through as a living *ba.*

Speaks now: The Scribe Osiris-Ani, after his arrival in port.
Now his soul is distilled by his deeds on top of the Earth, evolving words.

"Lord Atum, I am Atum in the beginning.
I am one. I am evolved in Nu.
I am Re in his rising in the beginning, this prince of his.

Who then is this? It is Re in the beginning.

He rose in the next world as king. In the past, the Pillars of Shu were unevolved. The face will be the peak of the one who is inside the Eight Ones' Town.

"I am the mighty *Natur* evolving himself.
That is Nu, designer of his name *Pot Natur,* as the *Natur.*"

Who then is this?

It is Re, the designer of the name of his flesh. Existence is evolved by the *Natur* in the Company of Re.

"I am without denial in the *Natur*."

Who then is this? It is Atum inside his globe.

In other words:

It is Re, while he rises in the eastern horizon which is of heaven.

"I am yesterday. I have known morning."

Who then is this:

If yesterday is Osiris, then morning, it is Re, which is the time of destroying his opposition contained in the Lord To The Limits inside him. His son Horus should be crowned.

In other words:

It is that day which will establish the festival which should assemble the corpse which is Osiris. Now his father Re should do battle with the *Natur* when ordered by Osiris to the Hidden Land.

Who then is this?

It is the Hidden Land which should be made for the *ba* of the *Natur*, as ordered by Osiris to the mountains of the Hidden Land.

In other words:

It is the Hidden Land. It is the existence I have given Re, each *Natur* preceding to it. He has risen to fight for its face. I will have recognized that it is the *Natur* who is inside it.

In other words: His name is Re.

It is the penis of Re when he makes love within himself.

"I am the *bennu*-phoenix that is of those in *Innu*.
I am the Keeper of the Book Of What Is And What Was."

Who then is this? It is Osiris.

In other words:

If he shits, then the *khat*-flesh is of what is and what was.

In other words: it is for Time together with Forever.

If the Day is Time, then Forever is the Night.

"It is that I am *Imsu* in his emerging.
I will be given his *shuty*-plumes in my head."

Who then is this?

If *Imsu* is Horus, he orients the face of his father. If he has emerged what is his spiritual rebirth, then his *shuty*-plumes in his head guide Lady Isis, together with Lady Of The House. They have given him his skull. They have been as protectresses. They guarantee the face the stability of his head.

In other words:

Both mighty, original serpents are inside the head of their Father Atum.

In other words:

The *shuty*-plumes in his head are of his two eyes. It was Osiris Ani, scribe of the offerings of all the *Natur,* emerging in immortality in his land. He has come out of his town.

Who then is this? It is the horizon which is of his Father Atum.

"I erase my mistakes. I forget my bad-images."

What then is this:

It should be the cutting away of that which decays of the scribe Osiris Ani, immortalized before all the *Natur.* All the bad images belonging to him should be driven away.

What then is this?

It is purification on the day he should have been born. I am purified in my original, mighty, double nest which is in the next world. It is the day of the people sacrificing. It is the might of the *Natur* who is in there.

Who then is this?

Millions Of Years is the name of the one. Green Pool is the name of the other. The pool it is of natron, together with the pool that is of nitre.

In other words:

Pilot For The Millions Of Years is the name of the one.
Green Pool is the name of the other.

In other words:

Lover For The Millions of Years is the name of the one. Green Pool is the name of the other, therefore, the mighty *Natur* who is in it is Re himself.

"I have carried the face along the way.
I have known the heads of the Pool Of *Ma'at.*"

Who then is this?

If the Mouth Of The Far Horizon is in the *duat,* it is the south of that place of his rooting, the door north of the tomb. Therefore the Pool Of *Ma'at* is in Heart's Centerpoint.

In other words:

The pathway that is the journey of his father Atum, the face when he goes to the Tranquil Meadows. It is the birth of the *jaffau* of the *Natur* behind the *ka* shrine. If the *duat* is the circuit and the *duat* is of the Pillars of Shu, then the northern House of stars is of the *duat.*

In other words:

It is the two leaves of the doorway Atum crossed over when he crossed the eastern horizon which is of heaven. "Those inside the embodiment, I have internalized our two arms. I am the *Natur* whom I have evolved within us."

Who then is this?

It is the drops of blood emerging from the penis of Re after he set out to do the cutting away within himself, starting the evolution of the *Natur* who are inside the Company Of Re. Intelligence together with Sense, they were in the company of Atum, through the course of the day which is everyday."

(I was filled in by the scribe Osiris Ani.)

You Are The *Wadjet* Eye, following its failure on that day of the struggle between the Two Companions. It is the moment of Horus struggling there together with Sut, while desecrating the face of Horus, and Horus knotting up the testicles of Sut.

"Either Thoth has written this with his own fingers,
or I will raise up hair at the cycle of doom!"

Then who is he? In other words:

It is the right eye of Re, because it raged at him after he sent for it. Now Thoth will raise up hair at this, because he had delivered it to his master alive, healthy, and vigorous, without weariness! Because the eye must be in pain, then the face must weep for its second.

Thereupon, Thoth spat in it.

"I who have seen Re born thus yesterday from the loins of *Meh Urt,*
he prospers and I prosper, and the other way around."

Then who is he? This watery pool of heaven.

In other words:

The image is the eye of Re which one awakens, when he is born each day. If *Meh Urt* is the *Wadjet* Eye of Re upon that which is, then Osiris Immortalized is an original one of those *Natur* who are among the Company of Horus.

Words of the face of his head: Then who is he?
I am beloved of his lord.
Been Born,
Hapy,
Star Of His Mother,
and
He Keeps Them Cool.

Orient your faces, Lords of Reality! Holy Precincts behind Osiris, accepting sacrifices for the wrongs of those who are among the company of the calm of strong nerves.

"It is I who will have come here because of you.
You have driven away all the sadness belonging to me,
just like that which had been done
by the seven divine states of the soul,
those who are among the companions of their lord."

The divine beasts made a position for *Inpu* that day of the dual boy who has come to you there.

Then who is he?

If these Lords of *Ma'at* are Thoth, with The Holy Knife Of The Heart, Lord Of The West, then they are the Divine precincts behind Osiris:

Been Born,
Hapy,
Star Of His Mother,
and
He Keep Them Cool.

They are those in back of The Thigh in the northern sky. (Constellation Orion) If accepting the dual sacrifice of the wrongs of those among the company of the calm of strong nerves, (and Sobak is within the waters!) then the calm of strong nerves is the eye which is Re.

In other words:

The face will be flaming after Osiris, burning up the persons of his opponents. If it concerns all the wrongs which belong to Osiris Immortalized since he was sent forth from the flesh of his divine mother, then it concerns those Seven States Of The Soul:

Been Born,
Hapy,
Star Of His Mother,
He Keeps Them Cool,

Eyes Of His Mother,
Beneath His *Moringa* Tree,
and
Horus Facade For The Two Eyes.

Inpu places them as amulets on the corpse which is Osiris.
In other words: The back of the place of purifying which is Osiris.
In other words: Then these seven states of the soul are:

Tooth Tooth,
Mutilation And Slaughter,
His Fire Is Not Allowed To Blast The Dual Facade,
The Face Enters Into Its Past,
The Two Red Eyes,
That Torch Which Is Inside The House Of Bright Red-linen,
and
The Face Emerges As The Two Eyes Assume Their Station
When The Night Has Brought On The Day.

Then Horus is upon the head of the divine precincts of that hall of his, orienting the face of his father. If it concerns that day that you must come here, it is Osiris saying to Re: "You must come here."

One sees the beauty of it at the western horizon.
"I am his person, face and heart of Those Two.
He has been immortalized as a *Natur* Under The Horizon.

I speak now:

"I have radiated out of the egg from within the world of secrets. I have been given my voice. I will speak words with it, embodied as the Great *Natur*, Lord Of The *Duat*. My hand is not turned away by any of those who are in charge of the *Natur*. I am Osiris, Lord Of The Mouth of the Horizon, a portion of Osiris immortalized as that being on top of the steps. I have entered at the desire of my *ib*-heart through the Pool Of Dual Flames.

I am quenched! Orient your face, Lord Of Radiance!
facade of the original home, and face of my head,
darkness and twilight, I have gone carrying you, my soul.
I purify you. My two hands are around you.
Your portion of the head is the gift of your ancestors.
I have been given my voice. I will speak with it.
I pilot my heart in its hour of fire and dark."

Then it concerns the divine duality of Horus orienting the face of his father, together with Horus As Facade Of The Two Eyes.

In other words: then who is he?

If his dual person, face and heart of the divine duality, is the person of Re, the person is of Osiris, the person is of those inside Shu, and the person is of those inside Tafnut, so his dual person is of those inside *Jad* centerpoint. I am the Cat who is splitting the *erika* tree open at its side in *Innu* centerpoint. It is that night of destroying the opponents of his Lord To The Limits in here. The cat is a child, and is Re himself. One calls him "Cat" because of the story of the sage about him: "Just like him," and because of what he has done while evolving his name, which is Cat.

In other words:

Shu will be the face making the last will and testament of Geb for Osiris. If it concerns the splitting of the *erika* tree open at its side in *Innu* centerpoint, and the results of weakness, and it is the real face, the face they have made, then it concerns the night of the struggling arm. They have entered the eastern sky, and the arm is consciously struggling for Heaven and for Earth to its limits. Now, inside his egg, radiating within his globe, rising and shining from his horizon, making golden the face of good character, without his second among the *Natur*, the face sailing through the Pillars Of Shu, causing windstorms with the fire-blasts from his mouth.

"Brightening the dual worlds with its divine soul,
you withdraw to a new position, Lord of the Extent of Time,
in charge of the *Natur* who is of mysterious forms.
His two eyebrows will be as the two arms of the scale
on that night of reckoning with strong nerves."

Then who is he? In other words:

It is Brought By His Arm. If it concerns this night of reckoning with the nerves, and it is the night of raging against failures, then one must collect wrongs on his offering block, and butcher rams. It is *Namu*. It is the castrating of Osiris. It is Apep. He will be in the head of the one possessed of reality.

In other words:

It is Horus. He will be in the dual head, and will be the one possessed of *ma'at*, the other possessed of wrongs. He must give wrongs for the wrong-doer, and things of reality for the company of my possessions.

In other words:

> It is the mighty Horus Facade Of The Holy Place Of Spirit. It is Thoth. The provider is the calm of Atum, halting the things of opposition contained in the Lord To The Limits. You assume your role.

Then who is he?

> In charge of those shapes kindling auroras. Honored Ones, provided with cruel fingers, choppers following after Osiris, their spirits are not within me. I do not grasp their meaning even a little. It is *Inpu.* It is Horus Facade Of The Two Eyes.

In other words:

> It is the divine precincts avoiding the business of their buttocks.

In other words:

> "My original circuit of the workplace of the spiritual energy of their knives, for I am not brought down to their pettiness. That face which is mine, my name for it will be known. I will be taught what is their discipline by that which is inside the House Of Osiris and glitters in the eye when he is seen going around heaven with the flame of his mouth. I am just like the Hapy River, when he was seen. I am healthy on top of the Earth, possessing Re, and I am calmly moored in death possessing Osiris. Your sacrifices inside of me are for the faces of their lifetimes, the face which is what I am when in the company of the Lord To The Limits."

"In the writings that concern enlightenment,
I swoop down as a falcon. I cackle as the *semen*-goose.
I rule the millions of years just like Re in his lotus."

Then who is he?

> It is those who are of the faces of Heaven in their lifetimes. It is the image of the Eye Of Re, together with the Eye Of Horus. Oh! Re Atum! Lord of the Great House! Prince of Life, Energy, and Health for all the *Natur.* It is the divine power of that dual one whose face is as a dog, and his eyebrows from his life in that state relating to the enfolding of the Pool Of Flame, and to eating flesh, clasping hands at the mood of the heart, accepting the sting of smell in order to be seen.

Then who is he?

Eater Of The Millions will be his name within the pool of burial. If it concerns the burial Pool Of Flame, it is that which is for you two, and which is contained by that stone-hard door at the working place. If it is the mending of every weakness of the face, he will descend to the sacrifice.

In other words: Who Is The Knife is his name.

He is the keeper of the gateway of the western horizon.

In other words:

The Divine Crown is the name by which he keeps in control of the enfolding that is in the western horizon.

In other words: He Is Two Faced is his name.

"Oh! Lord Of Terror! Head and face of the dual worlds, Lord Of Redness, ordered to the slaughter house and living upon entrails."

Then who is he?

Keeper of the enfolding that is in the western horizon.

Then who is he?

The attitude which was from Osiris has devoured everything of the sacrifice belonging to him: the Serpent Crown, and the backbone and heart, through the facade of childhood. If he has received the Serpent Crown of the backbone and heart from the facade of childhood, it is Osiris. He was commanded to rule by the *Natur* that day of the union of the dual worlds, embodied in the hand of the Lord To The Limits.

Then who is he?

If he was commanded to rule by the *Natur*, it is the son of the lady Isis, ruling from the position of his father, Osiris. If it is that day of the union of the dual worlds, it is the joining of the dual worlds at the coffin of Osiris, the living flesh of a person, that dual one within childhood who is receiver of the *ka*, subduing wrongdoers. He has been shown the way of the road to eternity.

Then who is he?

It is Re himself, and your struggle over the great *Natur* who is the maleness of the living, physical person, lapping up corruption and living in stink, keeper of the darkness inside the night. He fears those who dwell in weariness.

Then who is he?

If it concerns divine persons, face and heart of that dual boy, it is the power of the *Natur* who is the maleness of the person, lapping up attitudes, and living in the entrails, relating to the night. Those who fear the dual one inside the Sokar Sleigh, they dwell in depression.

Then who is he? In other words:

It is Sut. The original wild-calf is the divine person of Geb.

"Oh, Khepry! The face and heart are his sacred sunboat.
The Dual *Pot Natur* is his flesh.
You deliver Osiris immortalized into the power
of those who are the keepers of judgment.
They have accepted the Lord To The Limit
because his soul was distilled in order
to ward off the evil of his opposition.
those accepting sacrifice in the slaughterhouse,
and those beings emerging have warded off evil...
Their knives are not thrust into me.
I do not enter into their slaughterhouses.
I have not grown fat in the interior of their slaughterhouses.
I have not done the things
of those who are the evil of the *Natur.*
The face which I am is clean."

He has brought the face of the Milky Way. It is the starlight celebration in the gleaming, within the *Pot Natur* of childhood.

Then who is he?

Khepry is face and heart of his sacred sunboat and is Re himself. It is the baboons greeting dawn. It is Lady Isis. It is Lady Of The House. If that shit which the *Natur* hate is deceit, then the face and heart of the Milky Way galaxy are hurrying to the beautiful house of embalming. It is *Inpu.* He will be behind the wooden chest carrying the inner flesh of Osiris. If he has received the Starlight Celebration Of That Within The Gleaming, it is Osiris.

In other words:

If the Starlight Celebration In The Gleaming is of that Lesser *Pot Natur* of childhood, it is Heaven and it is Earth. The grinding down of Shu of the dual worlds starts in childhood. If the Starlight Celebration In The Gleaming is the eye of Horus, then the Lesser *Pot Natur* of Childhood is the union of the seat and throne of Osiris. Having built your house, Atum measures out the foundation of your House Of The Twin Lions *Naturu* (Yesterday and

Tomorrow) accomplished by mortaring the reeds of Horus, dual *Natur* who is Sut, and the other way around. He has come into this world. He has tread upon it with his two feet, Osiris [deceased and his titles]. Possessing Osiris, he was Atum. He will be your centerpoint. Behind you is the Divine Companion, brightening the mouth and the box of the head, held back by his leonine strength.

In other words:

Keeping on guard keeps him restrained and he is not seen. Lady Isis is his dual guardian, that of Osiris. In order to be found by that, he shaves the hair of his face, and curls it at his forehead. He initiates conception because of lady Isis. He becomes erect because of Lady Of The House. They replace his crew.

The fears that follow after you are of that awe and majesty of the head, and his two hands and of your shoulders. You are encircled by the support of humanity for the millions of years. The associates of your opposition raise up the hindquarters of wisdom. You have given their support to the sisters of your delight.

Your forms are of the Duality Within, concerning the struggle for the centerpoint, and the Duality Within *Innu*. You are feared by every original great *Natur*, and you respect every *Natur*.

Who curses him on the grounds of the House Of The *Natur*?
"You are alive when you are making love.
You are *Wadjet*, Lady Within the Heat.
Few among them come near to you with evil."

Then who is he? In other words:
He Strings The Secret Forms Like Beads is the name of the tomb.
The Face And Hands Are Seen By Him
is the name of the storm clouds.

THE AWAKENING OF OSIRIS, LORD OF ETERNITY, DIVINE PRECINCTS OF THE LORDS OF THE MOUTH OF THE FAR HORIZON.

Now Osiris speaks:

"Orient your face, King Of The Next World! The prince inside *Yugert* has arrived because of you and according to your plans. You have been equipped with your forms in the *duat*. You have given me a station as The *Natur* Under The Horizon among the Lords of *Ma'at*. My estate is established in Tranquil Meadows, receiving the offerings of your embodiment."

If the divine precincts of the great thing within Heart's Centerpoint are Atum, Shu, and Tafnut, then the Guardians Of Special Occasions have provided for the minions of Sut, or one will offend him.

Now Thoth:
"I immortalize Osiris without any opposition by means of the divine precincts of the great thing within *Jadjad* enterpoint. It is the night for spiritualizing the *Jad* within *Jadjad* enterpoint."

If the divine precincts of the great thing within *jadjad* centerpoint are Osiris, and Isis, and Lady Of The House, and Horus Who Orients His Face, then the spiritualization of the *jad* is through *jadjad* centerpoint. It is the shoulder of Horus, facade of the centerpoint of the House Of Spirit. They are around Osiris with the woven wrappings of linen.

Now Thoth:
"I immortalized Osiris without any opposition by means of the divine precincts of the great thing within the centerpoint of the House Of The *Natur* of the spirit, on the night of the things of night time, in the centerpoint of the House Of Spirit."

As to the divine precincts of the great thing within the centerpoint of the House Of Life Of The Spirit, belonging to Horus The Facade Without The Two Eyes, and Thoth, they are from the divine precincts of this house of his stiffening.

As to the night, it is for the things of night time.

Now Thoth:
"I immortalized Osiris without any opposition. I immortalized Osiris without any opposition by means of the divine precincts of the great thing within the *Pot Natur* at the centerpoint of *Dopp* City.
It is the night of standing up the Pillars Of Horus. He has been established as the heir of his father, Osiris."

If the divine precincts of the great thing within the *Pot Natur* of the Centerpoint of *Dopp* City are Horus, and Isis, and Been-Born and Hapy, then the Pillars Of Horus have been spiritualized. The pillars have been spiritualized by this!

Now Thoth:
"I immortalized Osiris without any opposition. I immortalized Osiris, immortalized without his opposition by means of the divine precincts of the great thing within *Khemmet* at the Centerpoint of humanity. It is the night Isis lies down, and one supports the face who is making lamentations for the face of her brother, Osiris."

As to the divine precincts of the great thing wthin *Khemmet* at the centerpoint of humanity, they are Isis, and Horus, who has been born.

Now Thoth:
"I immortalized Osiris without his opposition, Osiris immortalized without his opposition by means of the divine precincts of the great thing within the Heart's Centerpoint."

It is the night of the *Haker* Festival, when the dead are counted by the Judge Of Souls, when the ritual dances are evolved out of this centerpoint. As to the divine precincts of the great thing within the heart's centerpoint, they are Osiris, and Isis, and Opener Of The Ways.

Now Thoth:
"I immortalized Osiris without his opposition, Osiris immortalized without his opposition by means of the divine precincts within the dead."

It is the night for making judgments of their deaths. If The divine precincts of the great thing within the judge of the dead are Thoth, and Osiris, and *Inpu*, and Heaviness Of The Heart, then the judge of the deaths they have died has been restrained by those things which are of the face and the results of his weakness.

Now Thoth:
"I immortalized Osiris without his opposition. I immortalized Osiris without his opposition by means of the divine precincts of the great thing within reducing the world into *Jadjad* Centerpoint. It is the night of her reducing the world within their blood. I immortalized Osiris without his opposition."

As to the divine precincts within the great thing which is within her reduction of the world into *jadjad*-centerpoint, that is the arrival of the minions of Sut. They have completed their evolutions as animals. They have been spiritualized by making the sacrifice of the embodiment and hand of those *Natur*, when strongly pressed and blood rises within them, having been given by the judges of that within *Jadjad*-Centerpoint.

Now Thoth:
"I immortalized Osiris without his opposition. I immortalized Osiris without his opposition by means of the divine precincts of the great thing within this House Of His Stiffening. That is the night for the mysteries of forms."

If the divine precincts of the great thing within this house of his stiffening are Re, and Osiris, and Shu, and *Baby*, then it is the night of the mysteries of forms, and will be the face of the burial of the stellar Haunch Of Osiris and the stellar Side Flank, and the stellar Thigh Of Osiris, Beautiful Being.

Now Thoth:
"I immortalized Osiris without any opposition. I immortalized Osiris, immortalized because of Osiris without any opposition, by means of the divine precincts of the great thing within The Mouth Of The Far Horizon. That is the night of *Inpu* lying down, and his two hands and face are the things around Osiris.

"I immortalize Horus without any opposition."

If the divine precincts of the great thing within The Mouth Of The Far Horizon are Horus, Osiris, and Isis, the Osiris of his heart will be sweet, and the Horus of his heart will be expanded. The dual passageways will be calmed by her face.

Now Thoth:
"I immortalized Osiris without his opposition. I immortalized Osiris and his titles, immortalized without his opposition by means of the divine precincts of the great thing of The Ten within Re, who is within Osiris, who is within every *Natur* and *naturt* embodied in the hand of The Lord To The Limits."
This removes his opposition. He removes every evil of his belongings. This instruction will be said to purify the emerging awake following after the mooring of death. The divine image has accepted

his heart. If even a portion of all this instruction is preserved, his face will be healthy. He will have made the head of the dual worlds. He will emerge from all the fire. Nothing evil will be around him, (but rather) all his belongings, circling reality millions of times.

If this book is learned on top of the Earth, in the writings upon the coffin that is my mouthpiece, he will emerge into the day in all the metamorphoses he desired, together with going in to his place. He is not refused: he would be given cakes and the original beer which will be upon the altar which is Osiris. He will go in peace to the marsh of yarrow, to know this command of the one inside the centerpoint of courage. He would be given wheat and barley to grow in there. There would be green things around him as had been on top of the earth. He will do his desire even as those *Natur* who are in the *duat* in the circuit of immortality, millions of times, millions of times.

Now [the deceased] is Osiris!

WORDS ON HOW TO OPEN THE MOUTH FOR OSIRIS.

The speech while my mouth is opened by Ptah:

"Loosen the bond! Loosen the bond!
The needs of my mother are for the *Natur* of my centerpoint.
Welcome Thoth, completed and equipped with magical spells.
Loosen the bonds!
Loosen the bonds of Sut, who is guardian of my mouth.
You have opposed the guardians of Sut
whom Atum had appointed."

Shu opens my mouth with his tool which is that bronze of Heaven, that by which he has spread open the mouth of the *Natur* who is inside. I am Sekhmet. I have stationed the face properly at the side of that which is inside the importance of breath, and the great thing within Heaven. I am the territory of the *duat* of the Serpent, the importance of the face and heart of the persons of *Innu* Centerpoint. As to all the magical spells and all the words spoken to me, Sut has raised the *Natur* up for it, for the *Pot Natur* of the Reassembled *Natur.* He has been immortalized as a *Natur* Under The Horizon.

Words On How To Bring Magical Spells To Osiris

I am Atum Khepry evolving himself, from the quarter of the sky of his mother to the ends of the jackals, by means of the duality within Nu. Animal nature is driven off by those within the divine precincts.

Behold now the assembling through magical spells of this thing which he will be because of the person he is, because of him, he who is more dangerous than the dogs who are swifter than shadow. Now I have brought the morning boat which is Re.

You go straight forward steadily. With the North Wind, you sail southward to the Pool Of Dual Flame of the Centerpoint, inside the *Natur* Under The Horizon. Now you have assembled the magical spells for this, from every place there is, because the person he is, because of he who is more dangerous than the dogs who are swifter than shadow.

In order to make these transformations since outside mother until those *Natur* of silence have been designed, and the warmth of the Mother was given by the *Natur.* I will have received these magical spells from the dual one who is more dangerous than those dogs who are swifter than shadow.

In other words:

Swifter than shadow.

Words On How To Grant Memory Of His Name As The *Natur* Under The Horizon

"I have been given my name in the Register Shrine of the House Of The *Natur,* and I remember my name in the Common House. It is the night of counting years, not adding up months.

I am that which is within the dual *Natur.* I have stationed the face properly upon the eastern horizon of Heaven. The totality of every *Natur* is behind me, and I say his name."

Words On How To Grant A Heart To Him, For Osiris, As The Natur Under The Horizon

"My *ib*-heart was in the shrine of *ib*-hearts.
My *haty*-heart was in the shrine of *haty*-hearts.

My heart will have been granted all the offerings
on the board of offerings.
I will not have been within that which is sacrificed,
but in the journey-boat while you sail downstream,
and you sail upstream.
I do not just go under, but sail downstream within you.

I have my mouth and I will speak with it,
my two legs to walk around with,
and my two arms to throw down my enemy.
I have opened the doors of Heaven.

I have woven unto me the two jaws of Geb, Chief of the *Natur*,
and he opens my two eyes that were closed.
He stretches out my two legs that were contracted.
Strengthened by *Inpu*, my two knees are knotted to me,
and I stretch out.
I will be the serpent *Natur*, Sekhmet, inside Heaven,
doing what I have commanded, inside the centerpoint
of the House Of The Re Of Ptah.

My knowledge is in my heart, and my spirit is in my attitude.
My spirit is inside my two arms. My spirit is inside my two legs.
My spirit is inside my *ka* when making love.
My person will not be imprisoned.

The stargates contained in the Hidden World are my flesh,
through which I enter in peace and emerge in peace."

WORDS ON HOW TO PREVENT OPPOSITION To The Ib-heart Of Osiris Ani, Immortalized Through The Natur Under The Horizon.

He says:

"My *ib*-heart from my mother! My *ib*-heart from my mother! My *haty*-heart from evolving in spirit, from testimony about me, from opposition against me from the divine precincts, from making you incline toward the embodiment of the Keeper Of The Scales.

You are my *ka* within my flesh, and Khnoum making healthy my body. You have emerged at the Beautiful Place, having gone there speedily. My name is not made to stink by the head-sheriffs who make humanity from the shrines of the spirit."

Words Of How To Prevent The Ka Of A Man To Be Withdrawn From By The *Natur* Under The Horizon

"I am what I am.
Emerging from the viscous water should have been granted.
I have abundance of divine spirit while the river flows."

Words Of How To Receive Breaths As The Natur Under The Horizon.

A speech by Osiris:

"I am the egg within the Great Cackler. I will have guarded the seat of that Great Thing, the mission of Geb to the world. I live and the egg lives, living as I live. I breathe breaths, having come around from behind into his egg.

Awakening is the chief moment of Sut. Now the sweetness of the dual world is with the abundance, and within the blue stones.

My child has gone forth to you.

Words For A Drinking Supply As The Natur Under The Horizon

"I am what I am."

In order to emerge from Geb, he has been granted a flood of abundance of his spirit in there through Hapy.

"I am The Dual Son. I have opened the two doors of Heaven. I have woven the two doors of the purification through Thoth and through Hapy. You have given my spirit through the waters just like Sut when stealing his voice, the early morning that is the storm of the dual worlds."

Words Of How Not To Be Scalded By The Water

"I am the canal and the oar that is the equipment of rowing, and, because Re is the Old Man in it, he does not row across. He is boatless but he is not burned. I did seat the face of divine radiance, Khnoumu, in front of the cats, surely cutting himself out by means of the journey, and being in charge of the pathway, and emerging through it."

THE TWENTY ONE PORTALS OF THE DOUBLE COILED SERPENT

Words concerning arrival at the First Portal,
to be spoken by Osirisn immortalized.

"Lady of the weakness of the height, of the ramparts of the face and head! Lady distorting the name of words! Hold back disastrous rage to be safe from falling away from welcome!

The name of its doorkeeper is: Dreadful Protector."

Words concerning arrival at the Second Serpent Portal,
to be spoken by Osiris immortalized, Lord Of Heaven!

"Mistress of the dual worlds, she licks up each one of the totality of humanity, everyone everywhere.

The name of its doorkeeper is: Born Of Ptah."

Words concerning arrival at the Third Serpent Portal,
which is the house of Osiris,
spoken by Osiris, immortalized, immortalized.

"Lady of the flowery altar! The great importance of attachments is to cause pain for each *Natur* who is sailing up to Heart's Centerpoint.

The name of the doorkeeper is: Clean Character."

Words concerning arrival at the Fourth Serpent Portal,
spoken by Osiris:

"Spirit energy of the knives of the Mistress Of The Dual Worlds will destroy the oppositions contained in the weariness of the divine heart and make wisdom that had been lacking at conception.

The name of its doorkeeper is Long-Horned Bull."

Words concerning arrival at the Fifth Serpent Portal,
Spoken by Osiris:

"Fiery lady of excess joy! His head will not fall to her demands and he will not go to her.

The name of its doorkeeper is:
Greedy To Attain Knowledge Of Wisdom."

Words concerning arrival at the Sixth Serpent Portal,
Spoken by Osiris

"Lady of obscuring darkness and mighty war cries! Her length and her breadth are not known. Character is not to be found through wandering. The serpent is her face. No experience of those

who have been born is superior to the weariness of the divine face.
The name of its doorkeeper is: Union Of The Dual *Ma'aty.*"

Words concerning arrival at the Seventh Serpent Portal,
Spoken by Osiris:
"The linen wrappings that cloak the nakedness of the Wearied One, She Who Is Mourned, she loves the wrappings.
The name of its doorkeeper is: His Dual Evening Boat."

Words concerning arrival at the Eighth Serpent Portal,
Spoken by Osiris:
"Heat of the inner flame must absorb the fire in order to heat the triangle of the Pot of Flames. Cast down the hand of the killer! Unless oriented, her face will never cross over for fear of her escape.
The name of its doorkeeper is: To Protect Himself."

Words concerning arrival at the Ninth Serpent Portal,
Spoken by Osiris:
"All her children dwelling in the forehead are strong and contented."
(The wood of the coffin is 350 units in circumference and sealed with a command of stone.) Wreathe wheat stalks about the secret form and cloak the Wearied One. The Lady eats every face.
The name of its doorkeeper is: To Form Himself."

Words concerning arrival at the Tenth Serpent Portal,
Spoken by Osiris:
"Raise the voice and lift up laughter to awaken dreadful awe of her awesome dreadfulness! She is not frightened by what is inside her.
The name of its doorkeeper is:
Might Of The Spirit Energy Of The Serpentine Embraced."

(The source text switches from Ani to Next at this point.)

To complete Portal Eleven, Repeat:
"Command fire from rebellious flints! She has made ready the portals, Lady of the eyes rejoicing for the moment of nightfall.
She is subject to the destiny that cloaks the Wearied One."

To complete Portal Twelve, Repeat:
"Invoke her dual worlds and erase having to welcome in morn-

ings and noon. Lady of the soul, listen to her master, Lord Re!
She is subject to the destiny that cloaks the Wearied One."

To complete Portal Thirteen:
"Her two arms are stretched over it by Isis, brightening Hapy in his hidden corner.
She is subject to the destiny that cloaks the Wearied One."

To complete Portal Fourteen:
"Lady of the flint, she has worked to reduce the wrathful face, on the festival of hearing wrongdoing.
She is subject to the destiny that cloaks the Wearied One."

To complete Portal Fifteen:
"Wrathful lady persons, coming to slaughter with plaited hair and dimmed eyes, emerging by night to end their rebellion against the face who does the double-coil, and to give their help to the Wearied Heart in his day. The eye sets out to emerge.
She is subject to the destiny that cloaks the Wearied One."

To complete Portal Sixteen:
The speech of Osiris when he arrives at this portal:
"Awesome One, Lady of the dew, casting off the thousandsto the ploughlands of the dead of humanity through this person of humanity, revealing the emergence of the design.
She is subject to the destiny that cloaks the Wearied One."

To complete Portal Seventeen:
"Distorting the bloody face, sistrum dancer, lady taking counsel of the flowers.
She is subject to the destiny that cloaks the Wearied One."

To complete Portal Eighteen:
"Smoldering love that purifies the left-handed knife, she loves the sacrifice of the heads. Revered lady of the House Of The *Naturu*, cutting away the rebellious ones of nightfall.
She is subject to the destiny that cloaks the Wearied One."

To complete Portal Nineteen:
"To reveal the dawning of her lifetime, spend time with the passion of the lady strengthened by the writings of Thoth himself.
She is subject to the destiny cloaked by the procession of emergence."

To complete portal Twenty:

"Within the interior of the depths of her Lord, Cloak is her name, is the hidden corner of her form. To change attitudes, she gulps water.

She is subject to the destiny cloaked by the procession of emergence."

To complete portal Twenty-one:

"She is sharpened by the blade at my command, doing well to grasp the meaning of her flames.

She is subject to hidden plans."

A speech by The priest presiding over the funeral ceremony.
He says:

"You divine precincts of the great thing which is inside Heaven and Earth, you must welcome The *Natur* Ruling Underground. He has done no wrong to any of the *Natur*! Grant that he will be together with you every day."

Words Upon Arriving At The Innermost Chamber Of Dual Reality

"Awaken Osiris, Dweller In The West! "

Now speaks Osiris Immortalized:

"I have followed the Great Pathway to see your beauties. My two hands have truthfully glorified your name. I have followed the Great Pathway where no *ash* tree was growing, where no *shendit* tree was seeded to create ground for *tuzur* plants."

Now, I have arrived at the control seat of secret things.
There, I spoke together with Sut.

"I have seen the spirit-bodies of ancient *Khemmet.*
I have been as a *jaddu.* I have been silenced.
I have received the spirit from the *Natur* on these two legs.
I have been in the place atop his horizons.
I have seen the dweller of the *Natur's* house.
I must have arrived at the place of Osiris.
I have been wrapped in the wrappings of he who is in there.
I have arrived at the Mouth Of The Horizon.
I have seen the secrets which I had hidden inside there.
I found a passage.

I will have come to his place of
No Longer Must He Walk Through Halls.
I will have put the coverings which were there on the naked face.
I gave the finest cream of women from the dirt of mankind.
I am Sut. I must speak from his face.
I will speak while you are weighing out the face of your hearts."

Now his majesty *Inpu* speaks:

"You must know the name of this door in order to speak more to me."

Now Osiris answers:

Immortalized through the offerings of this immortalization. "Blocker Of Light is the name of this door."

Now his majesty *Inpu* speaks:

"You must know the name of the upper lobe and of the lower lobe."

"Lord Of Dual *Ma'aty* And A Face Atop Its Two Legs must be the name above the face. "

"Lord Of The Hindparts Driving Cattle, you must pass through the cattle. You will recognize Osiris deceased who was offered to the *Pot Natur* of the Lords of Thebes, Osiris immortalized, Lord Of The Celebrations."

To be spoken after attaining the innermost chamber which is dual *ma'aty*, and sorting through all the mistakes he has made while seeing the faces of each *Natur.*

"Orient yourself, great *Natur,* Lord of Dual *Ma'aty*!
I have come before you, my lord. I have brought myself.
I see your beauties. I must know you.

I must know my name for The *Natur,* and the Forty-two who will be together with you in this Innermost Chamber of Dual *Ma'aty,* of living through the *Natur* who punish sins as punishment for sinners who were trapped by their blood, that day of adding up debts before Beautiful Being.

I am the Dual Humanity Beloved Of His Two Eyes,
which is what I name the Dual *Ma'aty.*
I am as I have come before you. I have brought reality to you.
I have driven away evil for you. I have not done evil to humanity."

Above The Head Of Inpu:

Speaks now: The Dweller In The Tomb:
"Allow the face, weighed *ma'at*, to stand upright in the balance."

Speaks now: Thoth,
truthful judge of the mighty *Pot Natur* who embody Osiris.
"Listen to these decisions. Be truthful now, judged by the *ib*-heart of Osiris."

Now, his *ib*-heart stands up as witness for him.
"He declares truthfully before the mighty balance.
None of his mistakes have been written down therein.
He has not wasted sacrificial food in the temples.
He has not done wicked deeds.
He has not let evil go forth out of his mouth
while he was on top of the Earth."

Speak now: The mighty *Pot Natur* to Thoth, dwelling in Thoth's Centerpoint.

"It is guaranteed that which comes forth from your mouth is real and powerful. The scribe Osiris-Ani immortalized, he has not done evil. He does not stink before us. It is not decreed that *Immomet* should take power inside of him. Concerning the giving of holy bread to him: come forth in the presence of Osiris. A field stands ready in the Marsh Of Peace for the Company of Horus."

Speaks Now: Horus Son Of Isis
"I have come before you, Beautiful Being, I have brought to you Osiris Ani. His *ib*-heart truly comes forth immortalized. He has not done evil against any *Natur*, nor any *Naturu*."

The weigher of him, Thoth, out of the word written
by the *Pot Natur* to him, "Measured genuine *ma'at*."

Accordingly, he should be given cakes and beer.
He comes through embodied in Osiris.
He is as one in the Company of Horus forever!"

Speaks now: Osiris-Ani. He says:
"From you, from your embodiment,
Lord Of The Hidden Land,
no sins out of my *khat*-flesh,

I have not spoken lies while knowing it,
No! No!
Accordingly, I was just like the friends who are your Company,
Osiris, mighty friend of the beautiful *Natur.*"

"Beloved of the Lord Of The Two Lands, he loves the trusty, royal scribe, Ani, immortalized before Osiris."

BIBLIOGRAPHY

Aristophanes (1962) *The Complete Plays Of Aristophanes*, edited by Moses Hadas. Bantam Books, New York.

Baines, John, and Malek, Jaromir (1980). *Atlas of Ancient Egypt.* Equinox Books. New York.

Bakir, Adb EL-Mohsen. (1966) *The Cairo Calendar,* Cairo: general Organization for Government Printing Offices. Cairo, Egypt.

Betro, Maria Carmela (1995). *Hieroglyphics–The Writing of Ancient Egypt.* Abbeville Press Publishers.

Bhaktivedanta Swami, A.C. ((1970) *KRSNA, The Supreme Personality Of Godhead,* Iskon Press, Boston.

Bonaparte, Napoleon (1789) *Description De L'Egypte.* 1994 edition. Benedikt Taschen. Germany.

Brier, Bob (1981) *Ancient Egyptian Magic.* Quill Books. New York.

Budge, E.A.Wallis

(1905) *The Ancient Egyptian Book of The Dead.* 1960 edition, Dover Publications

(1905) *The Egyptian Heaven and Hell,* Vol.i.,ii.,iii. 1994 edition, Dover Publications.

(1911) *An Egyptian Hieroglyphic Dictionary in Two Volumes.* 1978 edition, Dover Publications.

(1905) *Legends of The Egyptian Gods–Hieroglyphic Texts and Translations.* 1994 edition Dover Publications.

(1905) *The Liturgy of Funerary Offerings–The Egyptian Texts With English Translations.* 1994 edition, Dover Publications.

(1911) *Osiris and The Egyptian Resurrection.* Vol.i.,ii. 1973 edition, Dover Publications.

Campbell, Joseph

(1951) *The Flight of The Wild Gander: Explorations in the Mythological Dimension.* Pantheon Books. New York.

(1949) *The Hero With A Thousand Faces.* Pantheon Books. New York.

(1986) *Inner Reaches of Outer Space: Metaphor as Myth and as Religion.* HarperCollins. New York.

(1959-1968) *The Masks of God.* Four Volumes. Viking Press.
Vol.i, *Primitive Mythology.* (1959)
Vol.ii., *Oriental Mythology.* (1962)
Vol.iii., *Occidental Mythology.* (1964)
Vol.iv., *Creative Mythology.* (1968) New York.

(1959-1987) *The Mythic Dimension: Selected Essays–1959-1987.* Edited by Anthony Van Couvering. Harper Collins. San Francisco.

(1974) *The Mythic Image–Bollingen Series C.* Princeton University Press. New Jersey.

(1972) *Myths To Live By: How We Recreate Ancient Legends In Our Daily Lives To Release Human Potential.* Penguin Books. New York.

(1988) *Historical Atlas of World Mythology, Vol.i., The Way of The Animal Powers,* Part 1: *Mythologies of The Primitive Hunters and Gatherers.* Harper and Row. The Netherlands. Part 2: *Mythologies of The Great Hunt* Harper and Row. The Netherlands.

(1988) *The Power of Myth.* With Bill Moyers. Doubleday. New York.

Joseph Campbell Audio Taped Lectures:

(1969, 1972) The World Mythology Series, Big Sur Tapes: *World Mythology and The Individual Adventure* Volumes I, II, recorded at Esalen Institute

(1990) *The World of Joseph Campbell: Transformations of Myth Through Time,*
Volume I, *Transformations of Myth Through Time*
Volume II, *The Wisdom of The East*
Volume III, *The Western Way*
The Highbridge Company

(1995) *Wings of Art: Joseph Campbell on James Joyce* The Joseph Campbell Foundation, and The Highbridge Company

(1997) *The Wisdom of Joseph Campbell, In Conversation with Michael Toms*, New Dimensions, Hay House

(1997) *The Way of Art: The Writing of James Joyce,* Theater of the Open Eye, NYC, Mystic Fire Audio

(1998) *Myth and Metaphor in Society, A Conversation with Joseph Campbell and Jamake Highwater,* The Joseph Campbell Foundation and the Native Land Foundation

Clark, Rosemary (2000) *The Sacred Tradition in Ancient Egypt,* Llewellyn Publications, St. Paul, Minnesota.

Coulson, David and Alec Campbell (2001) *African Rock Art, Paintings And Engravings On Stone,* Harry N. Abrams, Inc., New York. Printed in Japan.

Conman, Joann (2000) *The Cenotaph Of Seti I*, Internet
David, Rosalie (1988) *Handbook to Life in Ancient Egypt.* Facts on File Library. New York.
Davies, Vivian and Friedman, Renee (1998) *Egypt Uncovered.* Stewart, Tabori & Chang. New York.
Eliade, Mircea (1957) *The Sacred & The Profane: The Nature of Religion.* Translated from the French by Willard. R. Trask. Harvest/HJB Books. New York.
Eliot, Alexander (1993) *The Global Myths: Exploring Primitive, Pagan, Sacred, And Scientific Mythologies.* Penguin Group.
Erman, Adolf (1923) *Ancient Egyptian Poetry and Prose.* Translated from the German edition by Aylward M. Blackman, 1995. Dover Editions.
Faulkner, Raymond O. (translations)
(1972) *The Ancient Egyptian Book Of The Dead.* University of Texas Press, in cooperation with the British Museum Press. Texas.
(1994) *The Ancient Egyptian Book of The Dead.* Chronicle Press. San Francisco.
(1994) *The Ancient Egyptian Coffin Texts.* Aris & Phillilps. Warminster, England.
(1986) *A Concise Dictionary of Middle Egyptian* Griffith Institute.
Fletcher, Joann (2000) *Chronicle Of A Pharaoh, The Intimate Life Of Amenhotep III,* Oxford University Press, New York.
Foster, John. L. (translations)
(1992) *Echoes Of Egyptian Voices: An Anthology Of Ancient Egyptian Poetry.* University of Oklahoma Press, Norman, Publishing Division of the University.
(1974) *Love Songs of the new Kingdom: Translations from the Ancient Egyptian.* University of Austin Press.
Freud, Sigmund, Ph.d., (1953) *The Basic Writing Of Sigmund Freud,* Edited by James Strachey. Modern Library Series. New York.
Gimbutas, Marija (1989) *The Language of The Goddess, Unearthing The Hidden Symbols Of Western Civilization.* Harper Press. San Francisco..
Hart, George (1990) *The Legendary Past: Egyptian Myths.* Texas. British Museum Publication.
Ions, Veronica (1988) *Library Of The World's Myths and Legends: Egyptian Mythology.* New York. Peter Bedrick Books.
Hornung, Eric (1982) *Conceptions Of God In Ancient Egypt,* translated from the German by John Bates. Cornell University Press.

Jung, Carl. G., Ph.d.,
(1959) *The Archetypes And The Collective Unconscious.* Translated from German by R.F.C. Hull.
Princeton University Press. New Jersey.
(1974) *Dreams*–Bollingen Series XX. Translated from German by R.F.C. Hull.
Princeton University Press. New Jersey.
(1960) *On The Nature Of The Psyche*–Bollingen Series XX, Vol. viii. Translated from the German by R.F.C. Hull. New Jersey. Princeton University Press.
(1953) *Psychology And Alchemy.* New Jersey. Translated from German by R.F.C. Hull.
Princeton University Press. New Jersey.
(1956) *Symbols of Transformation.* Translated from the German by R.F.C. Hull.
Princeton University Press. New Jersey.

Lamy, Lucie (1981) *Egyptian Mysteries: New Light On Ancient Knowledge.* Thames and Hudson.

Lichtheim, Miriam (1980) *Ancient Egyptian Literature.*
Vol.i. *The Old And Middle Kingdoms.* University of California Press.
Vol.ii. *The New Kingdom.* University of California Press.
Vol.iii. *The Late Period.* University of California Press.

Malek, Jaromir (1993) *The Cat In Ancient Egypt.* University of Pennsylvania Press. Philadelphia.

Marshack, Alexander (1970) *The Roots Of Civilization.* University of Texas Press.

Mellaart, James (1967) *Catal Huyuk: A Neolithic Town In Anatolia.* McGraw-Hill. New York.

Mohen, Jean-Pierre (1989) *The World Of Megaliths,* Facts On File, Inc., New York. Printed in Portugal.

Morenz, Siegfried (1973) *Egyptian Religion,* Cornell University Press, Ithaca, NY.

Ockinga, Boyo (1979) *An Outline Of Middle Egyptian Grammar.* Austria. Akademische Druk.

Plato (c. 425 b.c.) *Timaeus And Critias.* Translated from the ancient Greek by Desmond Lee. (1965) Penguin Classics.

Puhvel, Jaan (1989) *Comparative Mythology.* The Johns Hokins University Press.

Quirke, Stephen
(1997) *Ancient Egyptian Religion,* Dover Publications, NY.
(2001) *The Cult Of Ra, Sun-Worship In Ancient Egypt,* Thames and Hudson, New York

Romer, John
(1984) *Ancient Lives–Daily Life In Egypt Of The Pharaohs.* Henry Holt & Co. New York.
(1989) *People of The Nile–A New Light On The Civilization of Ancient Egypt.* Penguin Books. London.

Ruspoli, Mario (1987) *The Cave Of Lascaux, The Final Photographs,* Harry N. Abrams, Inc., New York.

Schulz, Regine, and Seidel, Matthias, editors ((1998) *Egypt, The World Of The Pharaohs,* Konemann Verlagsgesellschaft, Koln. Printed in France.

Shafer, Byron E. (1991) *Religion In Ancient Egypt; Gods, Myths, And Personal Practice,* Cornell University Press. London.

Seton-Williams, M.V. (1988) *Egyptian Legends and Stories.* Rubicon Press. London.

Simpson, William Kelly, editor (1972) *The Literature of Ancient Egypt – An Anthology of Stories, Instructions and Poetry.* Yale University Press. London.

Spence, Lewis (1990) *Ancient Egyptian Myths and Gods,* Dover Publications, Inc. New York.

Sullivan, Lawrence E. (1988) *Icanchu's Drum: An Orientation to Meaning in South American Religions.* McMillan Publishing Company. New York.

Tiradritti, Francesco, editor (1998, 2000) *Egyptian Treasures From The Egyptian Museum In Cairo,* White Star S.r.k, Vercelli, Italy.

von Zabern, Philipp
(1980) *Tutanchamun*, Hamburg Museum Fur Kunst Und Gewerbe, Hamburg, Germany.
(1987) *Official Catalog of The Egyptian Museum In Cairo.* Translated by Peter Der Manuelian. Prestel-Verlag.

The Tibetan Book of the Dead, or, The After-Death Experiences on the Bardo Plane: according to Lama Kazi Dawa-Samdup's English rendering. (1960) Compiled and edited by W. Y. Evans-Wentz. Oxford University Press. New York

Boston Museum Of Science (1988) *Ramesses The Great, An Exhibition At The Boston Museum Of Scienc*e, National Endowment For The Humanities, Boston.

Insight Guides (1988) *Egypt.* Directed by Hans Johannes Hoefer. Prentice-Hall. Singapore.

The Editors of Time-Life Books (1999) *Egypt: Land of The Pharaohs.* Time-Life Books. Virginia.

Great Museums of The World:
(1967) *Louvre, Paris.* Paul Hamlyn. London.
(1972) *Egyptian Museum, Cairo.* Paul Hamlyn. London.

www.ingramcontent.com/pod-product-compliance
Lightning Source LLC
Chambersburg PA
CBHW030414100426
42812CB00028B/2953/J

* 9 7 8 1 5 9 2 2 4 6 0 1 4 *